Memory and
Instruction

Memory and Instruction

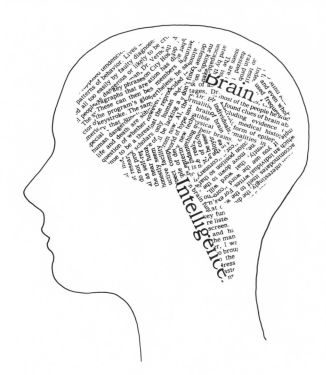

David Baine

Educational Psychology
University of Alberta
Edmonton, Alberta, Canada

Educational Technology Publications
Englewood Cliffs, New Jersey 07632

Library of Congress Cataloging-in-Publication Data

Baine, David.
  Memory and instruction.

  Bibliography: p.
  Includes index.
  1. Memory. 2. Memory in children. 3. Learning.
4. Recollection (Psychology) 5. Mnemonics. I. Title.
LB1063.B34   1986   370.15'22   85-16216
ISBN 0-87778-192-3

Printed in the United States of America.

Library of Congress Catalog Card Number:
85-16216.

International Standard Book Number:
0-87778-192-3.

First Printing: January, 1986.

Acknowledgments

Preparation of this book was assisted by a grant awarded by the University of Alberta, Faculty of Education, Support for the Advancement of Scholarship Fund. Considerable essential support was also received from Karen. I cherish the support of my colleagues and my wife—thank you!

Table of Contents

Memory and Instruction

Chapter One

Memory Models and Research

This chapter provides a review of several aspects of memory models and research. First, an examination is made of the rationale, structures, benefits and limitations of some of the recent and contemporary models of memory. Second, the nature of human memory and its measurement is discussed. Third, methods are described of experimental, laboratory research used to develop models and theories of human memory. Finally, the discussion reviews problems of ecological validity affecting application of the results of laboratory memory research in the natural environment.

The discussion is designed to provide the reader with an appreciation of both the nature and purpose of experimental, laboratory research of memory, and the limitations involved in generalizing the results of this research to practical, instructional applications. The discussion also introduces the basic terminology and concepts referred to throughout the remainder of the book. Essentially, the chapter provides an understanding of the nature of the currently available information about memory on which the remainder of the book is based.

In the past, most of the research on memory was conducted in highly controlled, experimental laboratory settings. Subjects within these experiments were observed to perform in certain characteristic ways under specified conditions. On the basis of

these observations, models of memory functioning were constructed. These models were comprised of hypothetical structures and
processes developed to explain the orderly nature of the observations, and to permit predictions to be made about the manner in
which subjects were expected to perform under various conditions. When a model failed to fulfill either one or both of the
explanatory or predictive functions, the model was either revised
or rejected, and new models were developed to fit the evidence.
The construction, revision and rejection of various models of
memory are described in the discussion that follows.

Waugh and Norman: Multistore Model

Waugh and Norman (1965) proposed a *multistore model* of
memory, and adopted the terms *primary* and *secondary* memory,
originally used by William James in 1890. In this model, each
verbal stimulus to which a subject attended was perceived in
primary memory. The primary memory had a very *limited
capacity*. As new stimuli were regarded, and as the capacity of the
primary memory was reached, stimuli previously perceived in the
primary memory were displaced and forgotten. However, when
information was *rehearsed*, it was either retained in short-term
storage in the primary memory, or it was transferred to long-term
storage in the secondary memory. The more often an item in
primary memory was rehearsed, the more likely it was to be
transferred to secondary memory. Waugh and Norman's model
may be conceptualized in the manner illustrated in Figure 1.1.

Atkinson and Shiffrin: Multistore Model

Atkinson and Shiffrin (1968) extended the Waugh and Norman
multistore model by proposing three, fixed *structural features*: a
sensory register, a *short-term store*, and a *long-term store*. The
model is illustrated in Figure 1.2.

Sensory register. External input transmitted via the sense organs
stimulated the sensory register regardless of whether or not the
subject was consciously attending, and registered a literal copy of
the stimulus. The image that registered was maintained for only a
short period of time, and either decayed and was lost from the
register in two seconds or less, or was transferred to the short-term

Figure 1.1. Waugh and Norman's Multistore Model.

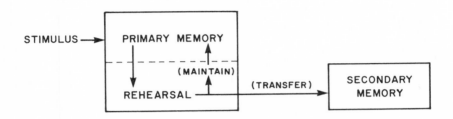

store, when the subject consciously attended to the image. Atkinson and Shiffrin initially described only a visual (*iconic*) sensory register; insufficient evidence existed at the time to justify postulating memories for other sense modalities (Adams, 1980). Subsequent evidence, however, supported the notion of an auditory (*echoic*) memory. Memories for other sense modalities such as motor and tactile may also be represented.

Short-term store. In the model, new information was passed from the sensory register to the short-term store, when the subject attended to the sensory image. Previously stored information could also be transferred from the long-term store (LTS) to the short-term store (STS), for example, either during recall, during the formation of associations, while coding an item or during the comparison of one event with the memory of another. Information entered the STS directly from the LTS, but only indirectly

Figure 1.2. Atkinson and Shiffrin's Multistore Model.
(Atkinson and Shiffrin, 1968, p. 88-195)

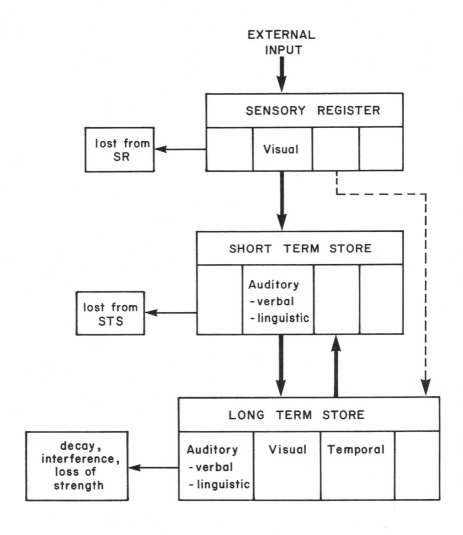

from the sensory register. A word, for example, could not enter the STS as a verbal unit until it had been identified in the LTS. This identification was fast and automatic for familiar stimuli (Atkinson and Shiffrin, 1968). The dash line in Figure 1.2 shows the contact that verbal inputs had to make with their learned representations in LTS so that they would be recognized and named; it was this information that entered the STS.

The short-term memory was viewed as a temporary store of limited capacity, and unless information that entered the store was rehearsed, it would decay in 10-15 seconds. As long as rehearsal continued, the information was retained (Atkinson and Wickens, 1971). Considering both the decay and rehearsal rates, only a limited number of items could be processed. This number of seven (+ or -) two items was referred to as the capacity or *memory span*. Atkinson and Shiffrin believed that transfer of these items from the STS to the LTS was determined by the amount of time the items had been retained in STS. Decay and rehearsal as well as interference with incoming items determined the amount of time items spent in STS (Adams, 1980).

Atkinson and Shiffrin (1968) also believed that rehearsal of information in the STS would automatically lead to transfer of the information to LTS. Two independent processes were considered to be responsible for LTS. Rehearsal was thought to be sufficient for establishing a weak memory trace in LTS; however, *coding* was believed to establish a more durable, readily retrievable memory trace (Atkinson and Shiffrin, 1968). Coding involved a *reductive* or *elaborative* transformation of a stimulus into a more memorable form. Verbal items were thought to be *coded phonemically* in STS and *semantically* in the LTS.

Long-term store. Information in LTS was thought to be stored indefinitely. The information, however, was not always available for immediate recall, as the recall strategy employed by the subject may have been inadequate, or because information similar to that originally stored may have interfered with recall (Atkinson and Wickens, 1971).

Control processes. Atkinson and Shiffrin (1968), in addition to describing *structural features* of memory, also referred to *control processes* that determined the operation of the memory system.

Whereas the structural features were fixed, the control processes that a subject used to operate upon the information in the memory structures were variable. The processes in operation at any one time were considered to be a function of the instructional set, and/or the perceived purpose of working with particular material, the nature of the material under study and the history of the subject. In the model, the control processes operating at the sensory register were concerned primarily with the selection or filtering of materials for transfer to the short-term store. Irrelevant material was discarded as soon as possible. Control processes associated with the short-term store involved either (a) rehearsal to prevent decay of information, (b) transfer of information to the long-term store, or (c) search and retrieval of information in the short-term store. According to Atkinson and Wickens (1971), transfer from the STS to the LTS was achieved by a control process selected by the subject, and could be quite different in nature from one task to the next. The two control processes postulated were *rehearsal* and *coding*. In one task, a subject might use the STS to rehearse several items simultaneously to maintain them over a short retention interval. In another task, each item may be independently studied and coded to form separate mental images for long-term storage. The control processes associated with LTS were assumed to be concerned with storage and the determination of appropriate memory search and retrieval routines (Atkinson and Wickens, 1971).

Limitations of the Atkinson and Shiffrin model. Evidence has been established that not all rehearsal leads to improvement in retention. In fact, there appears to be two types of rehearsal, maintenance and elaborative. *Maintenance rehearsal* involves continuous attention, repetition or review of information in the original form in which it was perceived, and is usually associated with maintenance of the information in short-term storage; no long-term storage is usually derived. *Elaborative rehearsal* or *coding* involves a transformation of the information through associations, meanings and images into a memorable form leading to long-term storage. According to Adams (1980), Atkinson and Shiffrin's assumption that all rehearsal improves retention is probably invalid (Adams, 1980). Shallice and Warrington (1970) have presented evidence contrary to the notion that information must necessarily "pass through" STS to enter LTS.

Craik and Lockhart (1972) indicated that the exact nature of the limited capacity of the STS was somewhat obscure. It was unclear whether the capacity limitation was one of processing, storage or an interaction between the two. Attempts to measure the STS capacity have produced quite a range of values from two to twenty words. The most widely accepted explanation of this variation is that STS capacity is limited in terms of *chunks* of information, and that a few or many items can be recoded (reorganized) into a single chunk (Craik and Lockhart, 1972). The process of chunking information as a mnemonic strategy is discussed in Chapter Two.

The notion that information is coded acoustically in the STS and semantically in the LTS has been blurred by the evidence from further research. It has been shown that STS coding can be either acoustic or articulatory, and that even with verbal material, STS coding can sometimes be visual. While differences in the type of coding might originally have seemed to be an acceptable basis for the distinction between short- and long-term stores, the distinction no longer appears to be satisfactory (Craik and Lockhart, 1972).

For Shiffrin (1975), the original Atkinson and Shiffrin model underwent substantial change. In his revised description of the model, the three memory stores became more unified. Shiffrin suggested that stimulation from the sensory register passed directly to LTS where it activated a permanent trace. Also, in Shiffrin's revision, the STS was not separated from the LTS. Instead, the LTS was thought of as being similar to a collection of electrical wires where the STS was represented by those wires that were currently carrying an electric charge. In the revised model, rehearsal and coding were still considered to be involved in maintanance and transfer of information from STS to LTS.

Klapp, Marshburn and Lester (1983) have provided a review of short-term memory and memory span. Their conclusion, after conducting a series of experiments, was that there must be a *working memory* that is distinct from the span memory. "Short-term memory does not measure the limited working space of mental processing (consciousness)" (p. 262). Information located in long-term memory storage must be gathered together, translated into an appropriate form, organized, verified and then retained briefly in a more readily available store until the required response can be programmed and emitted. Further, missing or vague information must be noted and, where necessary, substitute information created to complete a reasonable memory. Working memory is the component of the retrieval process where these necessary operations are performed (Ellis, Bennett, Daniel and Rickert, 1979).

Craik and Lockhart: Levels of Processing Model

Craik and Lockhart (1972) proposed a levels of processing model. In this model, memory was not viewed as a series of independent stores, but as a continuum of various levels of perceptual processing or *encoding* operations. Encoding was believed to proceed from one end of the continuum where processing was *shallow*, and a stimulus was analyzed in terms of its physical features such as lines, angles, brightness, pitch and loudness, to the other end of the continuum where processing was *deep*. Deep processing was considered to be conceptual, semantic and associative, and concerned with matching input with stored abstractions from past history. After a stimulus had been recognized, it could undergo enrichment or elaboration; it could also trigger associations and images. According to the authors, the deeper the processing, the greater the degree of semantic or cognitive analysis, and the stronger, more elaborate and durable the memory trace. Seamon (1980) has provided the following illustration of the levels of processing model depicted in Table 1.1.

In the case of verbal material, the progression would be from a shallow analysis of acoustic-articulatory features to an analysis of deeper semantic features. Craik and Lockhart suggested that coding followed a certain sequence and that it was the depth of coding reached that determined the strength of the *memory trace*. One factor that appeared to affect the level of processing achieved was the time available for the task. Conceptual or semantic coding was believed to require relatively more time to perform than shallower types of coding. Note that in Table 1.1 each level of

Table 1.1

Craik and Lockhart's Levels of Processing Model

GIVEN THE STIMULUS: an apple:

Perceptual Classification		Type of Analysis		Level of Processing Continuum
Is it red? Is it small?	-------►	visual	------►	shallow
Does it rhyme with chapel?	-------►	auditory	------►	moderate
Is it edible? Is it good?	-------►	conceptual	------►	deep

perceptual classification is represented by a different type of *question*. It was inferred that, if a subject responded to questions of the type shown, she/he would be making the corresponding type and level of analysis indicated. Craik and Tulving (1975) have described three typical questions that they used in a series of experiments on levels of processing. According to these authors, an analysis of the physical structure of a word was achieved by directly asking about its physical structure, for example, "Is the word printed in capital letters?" A phonemic level of analysis was induced by asking about the word's rhyming characteristics, for example, "Does the word rhyme with *train*?" A semantic analysis was activated by asking either categorical questions, such as "Is the word an animal name?" or sentence questions like "Would the word fit the following sentence: "The girl played the . . . on the table?" The results of a series of experiments conducted by Craik and Lockhart indicated that responses to semantic or affective questions led to better retention than did responses to questions about structural or syntactic aspects. It seemed clear to the authors that attention to word meaning was a necessary prerequisite to good retention.

Craik and Lockhart also suggested that the *primary memory* was superimposed on the levels of processing model. The primary memory was viewed as a limited-capacity central processor that recirculated information at one level of processing, producing the phenomenon of short-term memory. According to the authors, the primary memory that they had conceptualized was unlike that proposed by Atkinson and Shiffrin. Craik and Lockhart's notion of the primary memory was not limited in terms of the type of coding it could employ, the level of processing at which it could function or the number of items it could process, all of which, according to the authors, depended upon the level at which the processor was operating. In the model, primary memory processing required continuous processing. When attention was diverted from an item, the information was lost at a rate appropriate to the level of processing. This processing, referred to by the authors as *type 1*, prolonged an item's high accessibility without leading to the establishment of more permanent memory traces. The notion was parallel to Atkinson and Shiffrin's concept of *rehearsal*. In contrast, *type 2* processing was believed to involve deeper analysis leading to improved memory performance. This type of processing was similar to Atkinson and Shiffrin's notion of *coding*. Brown (1974) suggested that the status of short-term memory was the main difference between an information processing model like that described by Atkinson and Shiffrin, and a levels of processing approach. Within an information processing model, short-term storage was viewed as a structural feature of the memory system. In a levels of analysis approach, the processes used in the STS for information processing were seen as deliberate strategies employed by an individual to maintain and prolong perceptual experience by continuing to attend to some salient aspect of the stimulation. Whether an item was maintained at the STS level was thought to be an optional strategy rather than a structural feature (Craik, 1973).

Limitations of Craik and Lockhart's model. According to Kolers (1975) and Kolers and Ostry (1974), a physical analysis of stimuli need not always produce only brief memory traces. Research results have indicated that physical aspects of stimulation can be retained for appreciable periods of time, and in some instances, for up to a month. Bransford, Franks, Morris and Stein (1979) suggested that goodness of encoding could not be understood adequately in terms of the type of encoding alone (e.g., semantic or orthographic), because the value of encoding must also be judged in terms of how well the encoding matched the subsequent retrieval demands.

Craik and Tulving (1975) in a series of studies observed that words about which questions were asked were recalled more often, if the subjects in the experiments responded "yes" rather than "no" to the question. The authors contended that the observed differences in retention should be attributed to degrees of stimulus *elaboration* rather than to differences in depth of processing. For example, when the question, "Is it *(the bear)* a four footed animal? was posed, and the subject responds with, "yes," the stimulus word "bear" was elaborated by attachment of the information in the sentence to the stimulus word to become "the bear is a four footed animal." The authors believed that this elaboration of the stimulus word does not happen in the case of a question to which the subject responds negatively, because the information in the sentence does not belong with the stimulus word. For example, the authors suggested, in the sentence, "Is it *(the cloud)* a four footed animal?," to which a subject replies, "no," the same level of processing is required to answer this and the previous question; however, the stimulus word is elaborated only in the affirmative case. Thus, according to Craik and Tulving, the levels of processing model does not hold, as different levels of retention are achieved with the same stimulus material at the same level of processing. Craik and Tulving concluded that the notions that memory performance depends upon the depth to which a stimulus is analyzed, and that a stimulus is processed through a fixed series of analyzers, were unsatisfactory. Further, in the opinion of Craik and Tulving, the postulated series of analyzers could not lie on a continuum, since structural analyses do not shade into semantic analyses. According to Craik and Tulving, many of the ideas suggested by Craik and Lockhart in 1972 were in need of considerable modification, if the processing model was to remain useful.

According to Adams (1980), another difficulty associated with the levels of processing model was that of obtaining an independent measure of depth of processing. To avoid the hazards of intuition, some investigators have considered the time span between the posing of a question and the response made to the question as an index of the depth of processing. For example, if a subject took longer to respond to a question about a word's meaning then about its typography, it was inferred that meaning was processed at a greater depth than were typographical features. However, Adams suggested, if a shallow, nonsemantic task were made difficult to perform, the level of processing would presumably be shallow; however, a relatively long processing time would be required. Moreover, Adams argued, it should be possible to find a semantic task that is easy to perform and that requires a relatively brief processing time.

In the opinion of Wickelgren (1981), "the levels of processing fad is over in the field of learning and memory" (p. 40). Wickelgren suggested that one of the criticisms of the model is that it failed to add to the precise theoretical specification of the levels concept in either coding or processing domains. Semantic processing by itself is no guarantee of a high level of learning. An example provided by Schulman (1971) states that deciding that an ostrich is not a geographical location results in very little memory for having processed "ostrich" compared to deciding that ostrich is a living thing. Furthermore, as Nelson (1977) suggested, since substantial learning takes place at lower structural levels of coding, and since repetition of processing at lower structural levels further increases the degree of learning, it is not necessary to process at semantic levels to achieve further increases in the degree of learning.

Wickelgren also described limitations to the notion that elaboration enhances memory. "Certain kinds of elaboration increase memorability more than other kinds. Elaboration that merely adds to what must be learned does not increase the memorability of the other material and often decreases it. Elaboration that increases the amount of the other material that can be encoded using already learned *schemata* is beneficial to learning. This means that elaboration of the stimulus input may be benefitting memory because it is requiring a less elaborate addition to memory than nominally simpler stimulus input" (Wickelgren, 1981, p. 42).

Schemas and Scripts

Other currently popular models of memory are schemas and scripts (Hall, 1982; Nelson, Fivush, Hudson and Lucariello, 1983; Norman, 1982). Bartlett (1932) introduced the concept of a schema. A schema is a model representing one's knowledge of the world. Thorndyke and Hayes-Roth (1979) have described some of the properties that they believe characterize a schema. According to them, a schema represents a basic abstraction of a concept. For example, the schema for a *face* would undoubtedly contain all of the essential elements: two eyes, a nose, a mouth and two ears. A schema is derived from past experience which usually provides numerous examples of the concept it represents. Presumably, the concept of face is abstracted after many faces have been seen. A schema can guide the organization of incoming information into clusters of knowledge that are examples of the schema. When one of the constituent parts of a schema is missing in the input, its features are usually inferred. For example, if a face is in shadow, and one cannot see the mouth, one may still infer that it has two lips (Thorndyke and Hayes-Roth, 1979). Nelson, Fivush, Hudson and Lucariello (1983) describe schemas as spatially-temporally organized sets of expectations about what things, people, places and events will look like, or the order in which events will occur.

A schema may also function as a *script*. Scripts are derived from the experience of episodes in the real world. They provide a form of general rather than specific knowledge (Nelson *et al.*, 1983). The basic idea is that some sequences follow relatively fixed patterns as if they were written in a script that guides behavior. Such scripts allow the observer of an event to predict what will happen next. In the case of a new instance of an common event, the script provides guidance on how to proceed. The proposal is that human memory structures contain script-like knowledge units that allow the interpretation and prediction of ongoing events, and the storage and retrieval of the remembrance of a prior event (Norman, 1982). Norman provided the following example of a restaurant script. One enters a restaurant and finds an empty table, sometimes by himself, sometimes by waiting for someone to direct him. He sits, then waits. A waiter arrives to give him a menu. The waiter leaves, returns, takes his order, leaves and returns with food. The food is eaten. The waiter brings the bill. Either the waiter or the cashier is paid. There are of course variations to the schema depending on the nature of the restaurant. The schema is expanded by experience with a variety of restaurants. When one enters a new restaurant, she/he examines the physical organization, other diners and the waiters, and in this manner classifies the nature of the restaurant. Once the restaurant is classified as, for example, a cafeteria, the script guides behavior (Norman, 1982).

Nelson *et al.* (1983) report research describing the use of scripts by young children. According to Norman, the concept of scripts is subject to some debate as they seem too rigid and simplistic to capture real situations with all of their multitude of variations. Norman also stated that although schemas provide useful representations of information in memory, they will not pass the test of sufficiency. How long will the concepts of schemas and scripts endure?

What Is Memory?

Human memory is a hypothetical construct referring, in various models, to covert, cognitive structures and processes such as short-term store, rehearsal and semantic processing. The notion of structures and processes has been developed to explain and predict the occurrence of particular types of behavior interpreted as evidence of *recall* or *recognition* of previously presented stimuli.

Recall may be demonstrated in many ways, for example, when an individual:

- (a) performs a previously demonstrated or verbally described sequence of steps;
- (b) draws a facsimile of a previously available object or picture;
- (c) describes the content of a previously read passage of prose;
- (d) recites a poem, or
- (e) uses a musical instrument to play a previously read sheet of music.

Recall may not result in an exact *reproduction* of the original stimulus. For example, an individual performing a previously demonstrated set of steps may resequence, eliminate or add to the steps demonstrated while imitating the *essential features* of the modeled performance. This type of edited recall in some cases is desirable and, as is discussed later in the text, is prerequisite to the *generalization* and adaptation of recalled strategies to novel applications. Also, rather than provide a verbatim recitation of a previously read passage of prose—an impossible task with a lengthy or complex passage—readers may describe the general sequence of events, the major points or the gist of the topic expressed in the text. The *form* in which the recalled information is demonstrated may be the same as that of the original stimulus, or various degrees of transformation may be involved. For example, an individual may exhibit recall of a sheet of music by later writing each of the previously presented notes onto an empty staff, or by transforming each musical symbol into its corresponding musical tone. Obviously, a transformation of this nature involves more than simple recall. Thus, it is apparent that there are different types of recall requiring different skills to learn and perform. When teaching or evaluating recall, one must be aware of the type of recall under consideration.

As indicated in the foregoing discussion, it is difficult to obtain a *pure* measure of recall. Frequently, measures of recall are confounded by other types of cognitive, affective or motor behavior. For example, if an individual is asked to recall a series of pictures, objects and/or labels of objects or numbers, the skills required—in addition to recall—depend upon (a) whether the performer is familiar with the stimuli presented, and with the response required, (b) whether the labels used by the examiner to describe the stimuli are consistent with those commonly used by the subject and (c) whether the task-related instructions are understood.

Recognition memory is usually demonstrated by having an individual select a previously presented *target* stimulus that has been redisplayed among an array of *distractor* stimuli. The difficulty of the recognition task may be influenced by the number, type and degree of similarities between the target and the distractor stimuli. Also, the performer's history of experience with the distractor stimuli may be an influence. For example, if the performer's amount and recency of experience with the target and distractor stimuli are similar, the task may be more difficult than otherwise. Hall (1983) has provided a review of a variety of factors influencing the measurement of recognition. These factors make it difficult to compare the results obtained by recall and recognition. Hall points out that as a result of these often ignored difficulties, some of the theoretical formulations based on these comparisons are suspect.

It is apparent that the task of teaching and assessing both recall and recognition is not simple. When designing instruction to teach recall and recognition, one must be careful to teach skills that correspond to those commonly required in the natural environment. In this manner, instruction becomes *ecologically valid*. Also, when evaluating a learner's acquisition, generalization and maintenance of recall and recognition skills, one must develop tests that are congruent with the skills taught in the instructional program.

Memory Research

Over the past one hundred years, the vast majority of memory research has been concerned primarily with the study of basic rather than applied problems. *Applied research*, such as the evaluation of the effectiveness of a particular mnemonic strategy, is practical and has direct application to the understanding and improvement of problems of memory occurring in the natural environment. In contrast, *basic memory research* is more concerned with theoretical issues, such as the development and validation of a levels of processing model of memory (Craik and Lockhart, 1972) designed to explain and predict how the human memory functions. *Basic research* is usually conducted in a laboratory-type setting, and may involve the study of relatively contrived tasks, such as, *paired-associate learning* of nonsense syllables presented on a memory drum. Typically, memory research has involved the study of college students, each of whom is presented with a highly controlled, standardized set of conditions and materials. For example, experimental control is achieved by giving each subject an identical list of pairs of familiar words each having the same numerical index of their *imagery value* (representing the ease with which the words may be visualized). The pairs of words are presented individually, in the same order, for the same interval of time. The *experimental subjects* may be asked to imagine the nouns in each pair interacting with each other, for example, a *dog* may be visualized driving a *car*. The *control subjects*, who are identical to the experimental subjects in terms of potentially influential characteristics such as age, IQ and experience, are presented with a set of conditions and materials the same as those presented to the experimental subjects except in a specified and controlled way. For example, the control subjects may receive the same list of pairs of words, but these subjects may be instructed to rehearse the words to themselves. An experiment of this nature is designed to determine if the difference in instructions given to the experimental and control subjects (presumably leading to different types of mnemonic behavior) will produce a difference in the amount and/or type of recall between subjects in the two groups. Thus, by observing if and how the two groups differ in their recall, inferences may be made about various hypothetical memory processes and structures to explain why the observed difference in recall occurred.

Alternatively, rather than instruct experimental subjects to employ a particularly mnemonic strategy, the experimenter might have instructed them simply to use any method they wished so as to remember the items in a later recall test. This experimental approach provides an assessment of the results of *intentional memory*. In an assessment of *incidental memory*, experimental subjects are instructed simply to look at or manipulate the stimulus items that are presented; no indication is given that the subjects should attempt to remember the items. Later, a recall test is given to assess the amount of incidental recall.

Variations may be introduced in the duration of the interval between presentation of the last item presented and the later recall test, to assess either *immediate* or *delayed recall*. In experiments employing delayed recall, the period before the recall test may be unstructured, and experimental subjects may be given the opportunity to become involved in any activity that happens to occur during the interval. Alternatively, to control for the amount and type of cognitive activity in which subjects may become involved, for example, rehearsal of the items previously presented, a researcher may instruct the subjects to count backwards so as to prevent rehearsal.

Several experimental strategies have characterized memory research. In *serial learning*, subjects are usually given a list of words, letters, or numbers, one item at a time, at a fixed rate of presentation of perhaps two seconds per word. Following the presentation, each subject is instructed to recall the words in the order in which they were originally presented. Alternatively, given a second sequential presentation of the words in the list, subjects may be instructed to *anticipate* the next item in the list. The items used in this task are familiar to the learner so that the learner is required to recall familiar items rather than both learn and recall previously unfamiliar material.

In the *paired-associates* experimental paradigm, subjects are presented with a list of pairs of items, typically pairs of nonsense syllables, words, pictures, pictures and words or actual objects. The first item of each pair is designated the *stimulus*, the second, the *response*. The items in each pair may be shown simultaneously, side-by-side or as *interacting* items, such as a *bird* in a *shoe*. Alternatively, the stimulus item may be presented for two seconds, followed by presentation for two seconds of both members of the pair. In most of the research, the paired items have been nouns such as *dog-gate* and *chain-bowl*, and recall is tested by observing, if upon subsequent presentation of the stimulus words *dog* and *chain*, a subject provides the respective response words *gate* and *bowl*.

In *free recall* experiments, subjects are presented with a list of words, one item at a time, at a fixed rate. Several trials may take place in which the order of presentation is randomized. Later, the subject is requested to recall the items in the list in any order she/he wishes. The order in which the items are recalled is thought to provide clues about the manner in which the words were stored in memory and/or the manner in which they were retrieved. For example, some subjects may recall a randomly presented list of words of animals in terms of *conceptual categories* such as mammals, reptiles, and amphibians. Sometimes *cued recall* is employed. Subjects may be assisted to recall words in a list when they are given the name of the first item in the series, the serial order of a particular item (e.g., the sixth word), or the name of a category of which one or more of the items is a member. By altering the information provided in the cue, it is often possible to deduce something of the nature of the storage and recall processes.

Ecological Validity

As was mentioned earlier, most of the memory research conducted in the past has been basic research where the concern has been with *internal validity* and the control of *independent* (experimental) and *incidental* sources of influence upon the performance of the experimental subjects. This research has been concerned with theoretical issues rather than with *external (ecological) validity* and the application of the experimental results to the understanding and improvement of everyday memory functioning in the natural environment.

Brooks and Baumeister (1977 a,b) have discussed the problems associated with the lack of ecological validity of laboratory research. These authors have suggested that when an investigator observes a subject's performance on a highly contrived task, administered by unfamiliar adults, in an atypical environment, she/he must insure that the measurements obtained under these conditions relate in some meaningful and direct way to the natural circumstances of those individuals. If what researchers observe in the laboratory is to be generalized to problems of daily living, then it is absolutely essential to show that these laboratory tasks possess validity in an ecological sense. Gillis (1971) stated that it has become apparent that the laboratory settings and experimental paradigms that guide a substantial portion of the research do not allow generalization of results to real-life situations. Further, it is often not possible to confirm in real-life situations what the results of laboratory experiments would lead one to expect. Gillis suggested that the form of the natural environment must be accurately represented in laboratory models, if results are to be ecologically meaningful.

Brooks and Baumeister stated that they emphatically did not

recommend discarding the experimental method, but that experimenters should be forced to leave the security of their laboratories, tolerate greater ambiguity, and go where people actually live. According to the authors, every behavioral act has meaning only in the context in which the behavior occurs.

A study by Istomina (1982) demonstrated the problems involved in generalizing from laboratory research to the natural environment. Two equivalent experiments were conducted, one in a kindergarten, the other in a laboratory-type setting. In the kindergarten, three- to seven-year-old children were individually given, by their teacher, a list of items to purchase at a playstore. When the children went to the store, they were asked what items they had been sent to purchase. In the laboratory-type condition, each of the kindergarten children was also required to participate in an experiment. An experimenter took each child aside and asked him/her to remember a list of words equivalent to those used in the shopping game. The words were presented at three second intervals; after a pause of 60-90 seconds, each child was asked to recall as many of the words as possible. Although the kindergarten shopping game was potentially more difficult than the laboratory task, because the length of the retention interval varied, and although there were more distractions in the kindergarten, performance in the kindergarten shopping game was markedly better than that in the laboratory environment. For example, four- to five-year-old children recalled on the average twice as many words in the kindergarten as they did in the laboratory-type setting. According to Istomina, the critical difference between the two environments was that in the "natural" kindergarten setting, the task fit into the naturally occurring sequence of events.

Cole, Hood and McDermott (1982) also conducted a study that demonstrated the difficulty of generalizing the results obtained in artifically non-distracting, laboratory environments to complex, constantly changing, natural environments. These researchers studied the memory related activities of a group of eight- to ten-year-old children involved in baking cakes and planting seeds. In their observations, Cole *et al.*, found that they could not identify how the tasks were accomplished in a way that was directly related to those intellectual tasks that are considered to be the backbone of process oriented cognitive psychology. They observed that the everyday world consisted of dynamically organized environments that were not represented in laboratory models of intellectual activity. The authors claimed that the analytical procedures brought to these environments from the laboratory did not apply. Everyday life activities were replete with both human and physical cues that facilitated recall. The fact that many natural environments such as kitchens are physically structured in a manner that lessens memory load is so ubiquitous that it is difficult to see. For example, utensils and ingredients are stored in separate places so that, if a child needed to remember where the spoons were located, she/he needs only to remember where the utensils, in general, are stored (Cole *et al.*, 1982). Another factor influencing recall in the Cole *et al.* study was the interaction of the children who facilitated the locating of required materials and the number, nature and sequence of steps taken to complete each task.

Neisser (1982) claimed that the orthodox, laboratory study of memory, although conducted by some of the best minds in psychology, has very little to show for one hundred years of effort. Neisser suggested that these researchers have not been concerned with practical problems in natural settings, because they have believed that they were working on something more important, a general theory of memory and a scientific understanding of its underlying mechanisms. The preference of these researchers for artificial tasks has a rational basis; control variables and conditions can be more easily manipulated in the laboratory than in a natural setting. What are the results of one hundred years of the psychological study of memory? According to Neisser, "we have established firm empirical generalizations, so obvious that every ten-year-old knows them anyway. We have made discoveries, but they are only marginally about memory; in many cases, we don't know what to do with them, and wear them out with endless experimental variations. We have an intellectually impressive group of theories, but history offers little confidence that they will provide any meaningful insight into natural behavior" (Neisser, 1982, p. 11).

Kramer, Nagle and Engle (1980) expressed a less pessimistic view than that voiced by Neisser. They claimed that, "during the past fifteen years, researchers working in the field of mental retardation have witnessed the accumulation of a sizeable literature concerned with improving the memory skills of retarded individuals" (p. 306). Kramer *et al.* cite numerous examples of research demonstrating that this area of study harbors "great hope for the eventual development of programs designed to improve the educational skills of retarded children" (p. 306). Winschell and Lawrence (1975) also expressed optimism when they wrote that the body of knowledge and derived strategies which have been amassed in laboratory experiments and modest classroom training programs warrants extensive implementation in classroom settings. Bower (1973) has further suggested that schools should teach memory skills just as they teach the skills of reading and writing. "By systematically applying the knowledge that we now have about learning, we should be able to improve our skills so that we spend less time memorizing facts. By the strategic use of mnemonics, we might free ourselves for those tasks we consider more important than memorization" (Bower, 1973, p. 70). Belmont (1978) also took an optimistic position: "The only limitation on the retarded child's improvement is the degree of completeness of the programs supplied" (p. 181). Thus, according to a number of authors, it is time to apply the knowledge that has been accumulated to overcome the memory difficulties experienced by intellectually normal and by retarded children as well.

However, although techniques have been developed to improve the performance of memory among various types of children, considerable caution must be exercised in interpreting and applying the results of memory research studies. Many of the studies of memory have been conducted on college students whose level and style of functioning may not be characteristic of that of either adults, in general, or children in particular. The artificial nature of many of the experimental tasks, their method of presentation and the unnatural laboratory environments may influence and delimit the nature of the responses made by experimental subjects, and make it difficult to generalize experimental results to performance on tasks that occur in the natural environment. Furthermore, the results of research studies with children of one type, for example, mentally retarded individuals, may not be applicable to children of another type, for example, persons with a learning disability. An additional factor limiting application of experimental results is that many of the studies do not provide sufficient detail of precisely what experimental procedures, instructions and materials were employed to produce the obtained results. The failure to adequately describe experimental procedures arises from the fact that the majority of the studies have been designed to evaluate the generality of models and theories of memory, rather that assess the efficacy of specific instructional methods. Consequently, many studies provide considerably more description of the premises upon which theories have been established than they do of the instructional procedures employed. Unfortunately, however, if an attempt is to be made to generalize laboratory findings to the natural environment, the exact nature of the experimental procedures must be known.

Thus, in the discussion that follows in subsequent chapters of this text, extensive review is made of research conducted in both laboratory and natural settings. The focus is primarily upon children from preschool to adolescence. Research on adults is reported only where it is suggestive of methods that may be applicable to children. The reader is cautioned not to overgeneralize the results of any study beyond the specific population, task and environment studied. Where similarities exist between these experimental variables and a memory task in the natural environment, a teacher or instructional designer may adopt an empirical, diagnostic approach in implementing and evaluating the procedures with a particular child. The research results that currently exist provide only a tentative starting point for the design of instruction. The effects of any method employed must be thoroughly and scientifically evaluated on the specific children to which they are applied.

Chapter Two

Mnemonic Strategies: One

Evidence, presented in this chapter, indicates that children and adolescents in special and regular education can be taught to successfully employ mnemonic strategies in a variety of school and nonschool domains. This chapter and the two that follow review the nature, application and efficacy of various mnemonic strategies. Methods for teaching children how and when to use each of the strategies are also discussed.

The word *mnemonic* is an adjective derived from the Greek words *mnemon* and *mnasthia*, meaning, respectively, "mindful" and "to remember" (*Webster's*, 1980). Mnemonic strategies are practical techniques used to make information more memorable and easily retrievable. Scientific studies have demonstrated that rather than being something extraordinary, as they have sometimes been considered, mnemonic strategies are simply techniques that may be used systematically by children and youth in their regular daily activities to make more effective use of their memories.

Various mnemonics strategies involve a variety of techniques that may be used individually or in combination. For example, recall of a large quantity of information (e.g., a list of food items) may be simplified by *reorganizing* the information into a few *conceptual categories*, such as vegetables, fruits, meats and dairy products. To recall sequentially ordered information that is not readily classified into categories, or where such classification may destroy the sequential ordering of the material, a prememorized mnemonic system may be employed. For example, in the *peg word mnemonic* method, an individual prelearns a number of words each of which rhymes with the ordinal numbers one, two . . . . Through a process described later in this chapter, sequentially ordered information may be memorized by associating it with these rhyming words. Where a mnemonic strategy involves the addition of information, in this manner, to enhance recall, the process is referred to as one of *elaboration*. Alternatively, some mnemonic techniques involve *reduction* rather than elaboration of the material to be memorized. For instance, the trigonometric functions involving the *S*ine, *C*osine, and *T*angent, and the *O*pposite, *A*djacent, and *H*ypotenus sides of a triangle can be quite simply recalled by remembering the word *SOH-CAH-TOA*. SOH refers to the formula in which the *S*ine of a triangle equals the *O*pposite side over the *A*djacent side. Many mnemonic strategies involve the use of visual imagery which according to evidence discussed later is associated with memory enhancement.

The following example exhibits some of the features common to a variety of mnemonic strategies. Asked how he remembered that the major river in the country of Burma is the Irrawaddy, a colleague known for his mnemonic skills replied, "The words Burma and river remind me of the word *berm* meaning a strip of ground along a *river*; berms are also used as *sound barriers* along noisy highways. "*Sound barriers* remind me of earplugs, and earplugs remind me of a *wad in the ear*, and the Irrawaddy (ear-a-wad) River." A chain of association links each part of the mnemonic, and like a chain, the mnemonic is as strong as each of its *associative links*. The mnemonic chain is examined below.

a. Presented with the *recall demand cue*, the question, "What is the major river in Burma?" the mnemonist associated the words *river*, and *Burma* with the word *berm*. The association between the recall demand cue and the first part of the chain is called the *primary associative link*. The strength or durability of this link depends upon the probability that the mnemonist will recall the word *berm*, when given the words *Burma* and *river*. If an individual characteristically associates these words, the primary link in the chain will be strong. Alternatively, if the word *berm* is unfamiliar, the association of these words is improbable. As a result of a weak primary association, the probability is decreased that the remainder of the mnemonic chain will be recalled. Thus, it is important, when building a mnemonic chain, to insure that there is a strong associative link between the recall demand cues and the first part of the chain. For these reasons, perhaps, researchers have found that it is generally better to generate one's own mnemonic rather than adopt one that has worked for other people; however, this statement is valid only if the learner is capable of generating the mnemonic himself. If the learner is too young, or if the task of discovering an appropriate mnemonic is too difficult, then providing the learner with memory aids will assist retention (Bellezza, 1981).

Building an effective mnemonic chain begins with identification of the recall demand cues. In the present example, the most likely recall demand cues are the questions: "What is the major river in Burma?" or "In what country is the Irrawaddy River?" A primary associative link must be made to each of these recall cues. The strength of association of the remaining links in the chain may be examined in the same manner. Note, also, that since one must either recall the country given the river, or recall the river given the country, each link in the chain must be reversible. Each link in a mnemonic chain should be examined for its strength and reversibility.

b. Three additional features of the Burma-Irrawaddy chain that are noteworthy are the use of *phonetic links, semantic links* and *imagery* to enhance recall. There are two phonetic links in the chain: one between the words *Burma* and *berm*, and the other between the words *ear wads* and *Irrawaddy*. The strength of the associative link, in each case, is a function of the similar sounds between the words. The semantic link in the chain is between the use of a berm and an earwad as sound barriers. The strength of this association depends upon the extent to which the different parts of the chain share a similar meaning. Finally, most parts of the chain—the river, berm, and the earwads—are easily visualized, and this feature, according to evidence discussed below, improves recall. Thus, for some people, depending upon the strength of each associative link in the chain, this mnemonic *encoding* of Burma and the Irrawaddy will be excellent; for other persons, for whom one or more of the links is weak, recall of the chain may be short-lived.

Interesting perhaps, but why bother with such a complicated procedure? Wouldn't it be easier simply to *remember* that the Irrawaddy is in Burma? In some cases, yes. If a particular piece of information can be readily, accurately and automatically recalled for as long as the information may be required, there is no need for a mnemonic strategy. The task for the individual is to identify the types of information that are memorable to him/her, and thereby decide whether or not a mnemonic stragegy is required in a given situation. A second consideration is that the mnemonic strategy discussed above appears complicated only because it has been described in detail. The average person, as a matter of common daily occurrence, quickly and automatically processes many far more complex cognitive operations without even being aware of the activity. Practice leads to automatic and efficient processing. Fortunately for many of us, we didn't reject the use of automobiles because of the complexity of their operation. Think of the thousands of complicated calculations that we unconsciously make each day as we guide tons of steel at high speeds down an ever-changing maze of highway on the way to and from work. If the thousands of complex calculations required to perform this task were described, the task might appear overwhelming, yet with practice those first inept attempts at driving are shaped into a subconscious, reflexive act. In the same manner, the use of mnemonic strategies, far less complex than driving a car, can become automatic and beneficial.

According to Brown (1975), *preschoolers* are generally able to recognize familiar places and people, and can reconstruct meaningful events without the need to employ mnemonic strategies. It is only when these children encounter information that is not inherently meaningful, or that they are required to reproduce exactly, that deliberate mnemonic strategies may be required. Smirnov and Zinchenko (1969) found that there were three general stages through which children's *memory development* evolved. In the first stage, young children are dependent upon involuntary memory and exhibit no purposeful memory behavior. During stage two, children voluntarily and actively attempt to memorize; however, they lack the appropriate means. In the final stage, children acquire the necessary methods for voluntary memory. Initially, however, these techniques amount mostly to repetition of words, and only in a few cases do the children actually group material in any meaningful way. This description of the development of memory skills is very similar to that outlined by Flavell (1970) and Brown (1974). The task for teachers and instructional designers is to design instruction to maximize both incidental and intentional recall; also, to teach the effective use of mnemonic strategies.

Norman (1976) cited research evidence showing that the simple practice of memorization does not improve memory. Memory is not like a muscle that is strengthened by *practice* alone. To improve one's memory, techniques must be learned and practiced. One study cited by Norman was conducted by Woodrow (1927). Woodrow found that a group of students who simply practiced memorizing lists for several hours did no better memorizing new lists than did a control group that did not practice. Alternatively, a group of students who had been instructed in suitable techniques of memorizing did much better after the same amount of study.

Through the use of mnemonic techniques some spectacular results in recall performance have been obtained (Bellezza, 1981). Bower and Clark (1969), for example, found 93 percent recall in a mnemonic group, compared to 13 percent recall in a control group. Ericsson, Chase and Faloon (1980), worked with a college student of average intelligence and memory ability whose *memory span* after 230 hours of practice increased from 7 to 79 digits. His performance on memory tests of digits equaled that of memory experts with life-long training. The authors concluded that, with an appropriate *mnemonic system, retrieval method* and *practice* there is seemingly no limit to memory skills.

Not only have *retarded* individuals learned to use mnemonic strategies effectively, but they have also retained the strategies for up to one year (Brown, Campione and Barclay, 1979). This level of performance may be produced by no more than two or three training sessions, each of approximately one hour in duration, spread over two days (Borkowski and Cavanaugh, 1979).

Although most people express the desire to improve their memories, it appears that few people actually adopt the highly successful mnemonic strategies that are available. Harris (1982) conducted a prompted interview of thirty university students to discover what mnemonic strategies they employed in their daily lives. Few of the cognitive techniques that Harris described to his subjects (e.g., first letter mnemonics, rhymes, loci and story method) were reported to be used on a frequent basis. The students did report that it was common to write memos to one's self, put things in a special place as a reminder, or ask someone to give them a reminder. If a mnemonic strategy is to be used, it appears necessary to teach the potential user how, and when, to use the strategy, and to provide ample opportunity for its successful application.

A variety of mnemonic strategies are grouped in Table 2.1 according to common uses or characteristics; alternate terminology is shown in parentheses. These techniques are described in the remainder of this and in the next two chapters. Each strategy is defined, various practical applications are demonstrated, techniques used to teach the strategies to children are discussed and evidence is presented as to the effectiveness of each technique in various applications.

Methods of labelling, rehearsal, chunking and categorizing are discussed in the remainder of this chapter.

Labelling

The use of labelling to improve recall has been examined with a number of different tasks. The effects of overt and covert labelling, as well as the effects of providing a label to a learner or requiring an individual to generate a label have also been studied. With tasks in which *categorization* of items into groups would facilitate recall, presentation of a category label before or during presentation of the items helps children to discover and use the categories into which the items in the list may be grouped. No such effect, however, has been demonstrated with young children (Moely, 1977). For instance, Kobasigawa and Middleton (1972)

Table 2.1

Classification of Mnemonic Strategies

Underlying Strategies

1. Labelling
2. Visual imagery
3. Maintenance rehearsal

Basic Strategies

Methods used for storing and recalling lists of words, or objects:

1. Link method (interactive imagery): linking items in a list into a series of overlapping images in a chain; retains serial order of items; numerical order may be obtained indirectly. Used as an alternative to the peg-word mnemonic described below.
2. Method of Loci: e.g., associating a list of items with a sequence of fixed and familiar physical locations; retains serial order of items; numerical order may be obtained indirectly.
3. First letter recoding (acronym encoding): e.g., *c*ar, *r*acket, and *b*ell = CRAB: retains serial order of items; numerical order may be otained indirectly.
4. Peg-word (hook) strategy: e.g., "one is a bun, two is a shoe. . .; retains numerical *and* serial order of items.
5. Syntactic encoding (natural language mediator): involves associating items in a list with a preposition or a conjunction, or linking items in a phrase, clause, sentence or story, e.g., list: *dog, bone, hill* becomes, *the dog hid the bone on the hill*; may also include rhyming, e.g., *thirty days hath September . . .*; retains serial order of items; numerical order may be obtained indirectly.
6. Conceptual categorizing (taxonomic grouping, or semantic categorizing): e.g., grouping food items in a list into categories, such as vegetables, meats, etc.
7. Semantic encoding: associating two or more words according to a common meaning, e.g., *berm* and *earplug* = *sound barriers*; substituting a single abstract word for a concrete word having the same meaning, e.g., *origin* = *egg*.
8. Phonetic encoding: associating words that have similar speech sounds, or substituting abstract words for concrete words having similar speech sounds, e.g., *Irrawaddy* = *ear wad*.

(Continued)

Table 2.1 (Continued)

9. Bridging strategy: associating two or more words with an intermediate word with which the other words are usually associated, e.g., associating the words *soup* and *letter* with the word *alphabet*.
10. Interrogative strategies: asking questions relating to the syntactic or semantic nature of words so as to establish a relationship by which to associate the words.

Methods used for storing and retrieving numbers

1. Digit-consonant encoding (analytic substitution): e.g., substituting letters for numbers to form words when 1=1; 2=n and 3=m
2. Chunking: analyzing an unbroken sequence of numbers into smaller units to assist retention, e.g., 436-7529.

found that children in the fifth grade, but not younger children, showed greater recall and organization of a list of items after categories had been labelled during presentation. Alternatively, Horowitz (1969) reported better recall but no increased organization by five- and eight-year-olds who were required to label auditory or visual stimuli during presentation compared to children who simply looked at or listened to the items. Nelson (1961) taught five- and eight-year-old children the names of the categories of items which were subsequently presented. *Prelabelling* did not improve recall. A similar lack of improvement in recall was observed by Williams and Goulet (1975), who gave category labels to four-year-old children prior to presentation or recall.

Pressley (1977) reviewed several *picture recognition studies* of young children who labelled stimuli. Ward and Legant (1971) found that with three different types of pictorial materials, four-year-old children who *overtly labelled* the pictures made fewer errors in picture recognition than children who did not label the pictures. Verbal labelling improved the recognition memory of five-year-olds and adults in a study by Nelson and Kosslyn (1976). Bacharach, Carr and Mehner (1976) found that providing labels to children in the first grade, before a picture was presented, modified the child's *attention* to elements in the picture.

Pressley (1977) also reviewed a number of studies in which the addition of labels to pictures aided *paired-associate learning* of children in kindergarten, and in the first, third and sixth grades (Rohwer, Lynch, Levin and Suzuki, 1967). In other studies, however, labelling pictorial stimuli did not aid paired-associate learning of children in the second grade (Rohwer, Kee and Guy, 1975), or children in nursery school and the first or fourth grade (Means and Rohwer, 1974). Thus, it is not generally clear that adding verbal labels will improve children's recall of pictorial paired-associates. The value of providing labels in this circumstance must be validated with particular groups of children or individuals.

Hagen and Kingsley (1968) required one group of nursery school children (approximately five years of age) to *overtly label* the names of pictures of animals. No difference in recall of the *serial position* of items in a list was found between this group and a group that did not label overtly. In a second study by the same researchers, it was found that overt verbal labelling facilitated the serial recall of six-, seven- and eight-year-old children who did not use labels spontaneously; labelling did not improve the recall of ten-year-old children who did spontaneously label. At ages five and ten, overt labelling did not facilitate memory performance. Ghatala and Levin (1976) found that for elementary school children, overt labelling produced substantially better recall than *covert* labelling. Pressley concluded after his review of the literature on the use of labelling in serial recall, that requiring young school age children to label their pictures aided their serial recall. However, by the age of ten, children do not benefit from instruction to label pictures, since children at this age *covertly rehearse* materials to be recalled and overt labelling may interfere with this process.

Gold and Barclay (1973) demonstrated an interesting benefit of the use of labels. In their study of moderately and severely mentally *retarded* individuals assembling bicycle brakes, the authors found that groups given verbal labels for various parts of the brakes learned the task more rapidly (recalled the sequence of assembly) better than groups did that were not given labels. No testing was conducted to ascertain if the learners understood the labels used.

Brown and Barclay (1976) evaluated a *label training strategy* with two groups of retarded individuals whose IQs ranged from approximately 47 to 86. The youngest group were on the average approximately 9.9 years of age, while the average of the older group was approximately 12 years. Subjects were trained to expose serially several pictures of objects, one at a time, while labelling each picture, and then repeat each list several times. Subjects were encouraged to continue using this labelling strategy until they had learned an extended list of items. On the day immediately following training, each subject was given a new set of pictures, was reminded of the labelling procedure, and was told to continue using the strategy. Training in the use of labels did not produce an improvement in retention of the new list of pictures. Any benefit that may have been derived from the use of labels was not maintained with a new list of pictures.

In *conclusion*, providing labels for pictures, objects or categories, or requiring subjects to generate their own covert or overt
labels improves recall on some tasks at some age levels, but not at
others tasks or age levels. No consistent patterns of benefit are
apparent across learners and tasks. Thus, the potential effects
upon recall of using labelling *alone* in a specific instructional
condition must be evaluated on a group or individual basis. Note,
however, that labelling is frequently not used alone, but is
included as an integral part of other effective mnemonic strategies
(e.g., categorizing, and semantic or syntactic methods). Thus,
although initially, labelling alone may not provide mnemonic
advantage, where it does not impede performance, it should be
included in the instructional process as a prerequisite to other
types of mnemonic strategies to be introduced following
mastery of the labelling response. Also, in situations with young or
developmentally delayed individuals where labelling appears neither to enhance nor hinder recall, labelling should not be
automatically eliminated, as benefits may be derived in the area of
language acquisition. With older children—ten years of age or
older—it appears that overt labelling reduces recall. At this age
level, overt labelling may actually interfere with other mnemonic
strategies that these subjects may be spontaneously using. With
younger subjects who do not spontaneously use a mnemonic
strategy, labelling may not interfere in the same manner.

Maintenance Rehearsal

Maintenance rehearsal involves the rote or cyclic repetition or
recirculation of information to maintain the information in
consciousness, short-term storage (Craik and Watkins, 1973) or a
rehearsal buffer (Craik and Lockhart, 1972) so that the information can be immediately and accurately recalled at any time during
which it is being rehearsed. The process does not affect long-term
memory. Maintenance rehearsal is also referred to as *type 1*, or
same-level processing (Craik and Lockhart, 1972), as *primary
rehearsal* (Bjork, 1975) and as *echoing* (Darley and Glass, 1975).
The process of repetition may be overt or covert. The items being
rehearsed may be words involving *acoustic/articulatory rehearsal*,
or *physical actions*, sounds or visual scenes, in which case,

rehearsal tends to mimic the nature of these events. For example, rehearsal may involve mentally going through the action of hitting a ball. For normal-hearing individuals, when the items being rehearsed are words, rehearsal appears to be vocal. For a congenitally deaf person, however, words appear to be rehearsed through sign language, and the errors made by a deaf person reflect confusions among memories for signs (Bellugi, Klima and Siple, 1975). The purpose of maintenance rehearsal is to retain information in short-term storage so that *coding*—mnemonic processing—can take place and transfer the information to long-term storage. The longer the information is maintained in short-term storage, the greater the opportunity for mnemonic processing and storage (Seamon, 1980). Unless coding takes place, an item retained in short-term storage is remembered only as long as the item is rehearsed; when maintenance rehearsal ceases, memory of the item is lost. Elaborative rehearsal leads to long-term storage.

Elaborative rehearsal is concerned not only with the number or duration of repetitions of information, but also with *coding, deeper processing* (Craik and Lockhart, 1972), forming *associations* and enriching a memory trace to produce long-term storage. Elaborative rehearsal may involve categorizing, visualizing, semantic encoding or any of the mnemonic methods discussed later in this and the next two chapters.

Another type of rehearsal, discussed more fully in Chapter Nine, on *maintenance* and generalization, is that of *distributed practice*. Distributed practice incorporates the processes of retrieval from long-term memory, and overt or covert rehearsal or practice.

After a set of verbal or motor responses has been acquired, distributed practice is employed to enhance maintenance of the learning. In this procedure, the learner is required to practice the acquired responses after successively longer retention intervals in the absence of any further instruction. Through successive increments the length of the retention interval is extended. Part of an active approach to learning should involve frequent *self-testing* or recall of learned material at various points following acquisition. There is considerable evidence indicating that the act of review improves the probability of recall in the future. A test immediately following instruction improves long-term storage (Hunter, 1979).

Since *maintenance rehearsal* may be covert and unobservable, one cannot be certain whether an individual is actually rehearsing. In an attempt to evaluate the inferred effect of rehearsal, a researcher may present a number of stimuli for later recall. Following presentation of the stimuli, a retention interval is provided in which one group of subjects may be required to count backwards to prevent rehearsal from taking place, while another group of subjects is allowed, without interruption, to covertly rehearse the stimuli during the interval. Any difference in recall between the two groups is inferred to arise from rehearsal.

A number of studies has been conducted to determine the *developmental* nature of rehearsal, to compare the effects of maintenance and elaborative rehearsal and to evaluate various methods of teaching rehearsal. For example, Glidden (1977) tested the recall of five-year-old children on five consecutive days; little evidence of spontaneous rehearsal was observed. Flavell, Beach and Chinsky (1966) found spontaneous rehearsal among 10 percent of five-year-olds, 60 percent of seven-year-olds and 85 percent of ten-year-olds. Thus, rehearsal is first seen with some regularity at approximately seven years of age.

Keeney, Cannizzo and Flavell (1967) presented color slides of common subjects to six- and seven-year-old children. The pretest separated children who *spontaneously rehearsed* from those children who did not. The serial recall of the spontaneous rehearsers was significantly better than that of the non-rehearsers. The non-rehearsers were then given *training* to induce maintenance rehearsal. The following instructions were given, "As I point to a picture, you say out loud (overt), what it is a picture of. Now, I'm going to point to two of the pictures, and you will say the name of each one as I point to it. Then I'll pull your visor down for a few seconds, and you will keep on whispering the names over and over again (maintenance rehearsal) until I pull your visor up." Two "whispering" trials were given; more trials were provided if a child required prompting to continue whispering until the visor came up. On these two training trials, the subject was not required to point to the picture when the visor came up. When this training was completed, a number of additional practice trials were given. Eventually, the children were told, "I'm not going to tell you to say the names over and over again any more. You can say them if you want to, but you don't have to." The training induced the non-rehearsers to rehearse on 75 percent of the trials, and improved their immediate recall score so that it was almost indistinguishable from those of the spontaneous rehearsers. On later trials, however, when given the option to rehearse, 10 of the 17 newly taught rehearsers abandoned the strategy. The researchers suggested that the absence of explicit feedback to the children regarding the benefits of the rehearsal may have led to the rapid cessation of rehearsal. The reader will observe repeatedly in the studies that are reported throughout this text that newly acquired skills are not generally automatically maintained *unless maintenance procedures have been incorporated into the training program.* Techniques to enhance generalization and maintenance of learning are discussed in Chapter Nine.

In a study of children in the first grade, recall of pictures of common objects was significantly improved when the *children were taught* to rehearse and recall overtly in the following manner. Rehearsal was first guided by a sequential presentation of the stimulus pictures in a horizontal, linear array. Then the rehearsal, in the absence of the pictures, was guided by a sequential presentation of cue lights in the same position as the pictures had previously been presented. This latter rehearsal also required recall. Rehearsal taught by this method produced significantly more recall than that resulting from a passive rehearsal condition in which rehearsal was guided by sequential presentation of the pictures without use of the lights, as the pictures remained in view during each rehearsal trial. This passive rehearsal training did not significantly improve recall beyond that obtained by a *labelling* procedure in which the pictures were presented and labelled by the children once. However, the labelling improved recall only in the last serial position and, therefore, cannot be considered an effective mnemonic strategy. Two additional experiments conducted by the authors confirmed that ordered *repetition and retrieval practice* is an important component of an effective rehearsal strategy for young children. However, the facilitative effects are relatively short-term and a ten second interval filled with the child reading aloud a series of randomly presented numbers was sufficient to eliminate the facilitative effect of both ordered repetition and retrieval practice. These results confirm the notion that maintenance rehearsal improves immediate recall of ordered information by children while elaboration is necessary for long-term retention (Ferguson and Bray, 1976).

A deficiency in the use of rehearsal is one of the most firmly established cognitive characteristics of *retarded children* (Brown, 1974). However, there is considerable evidence indicating that although retarded children do not spontaneously rehearse, they can be trained to do so relatively easily (Belmont and Butterfield, 1969, 1971; Brown, Campione, Bray and Wilcox, 1973; Ellis, 1970).

Moderately *retarded adolescents* (mean IQ: 61; mean CA: 16) were *taught* a *cumulative rehearsal strategy* by Brown, Campione and Murphy (1974). The experimenter sat beside the subject and demonstrated (*modeled*) the *overt* cumulative rehearsal strategy required. To make the task easier, all items in the inspection set remained visible during the viewing period so that the subject did not need to remember a previous item to rehearse it cumulatively. After observing the experimenter rehearsing for several trials, the subject was encouraged to *imitate* her, and they rehearsed together (*leading*). Finally, the experimenter stopped rehearsing (lead withdrawn), but continued to encourage (*verbal prompt*) the subject to rehearse cumulatively. An example of the *covert* cumulative rehearsal is: *cat, cat - dress; cat - dress - cake.* Pilot testing had indicated that overt cumulative rehearsal of four items was difficult for these subjects to maintain, so they were trained to cumulatively rehearse the first three items in the inspection set and "just try to remember the last item." *Six months after* the original training, eight of the twenty subjects maintained their rehearsal strategy, even in the absence of instruction to do so. The instruction procedures of modeling, imitation, prompting and leading used in this study are discussed in Chapter Ten, on instructional methods.

Brown and Barclay (1976) studied the effects of rehearsal

training on young *retarded children* (mean CA: 9.9; mean IQ: 69) and on older retarded children (mean CA: 12; mean IQ: 71). Six pictures in each trial were individually presented and removed in sequence. Subjects were trained to pass through the list once exposing and *labelling* each item. Then, the experimenter used leading and modeling (Brown referred to this procedure as shadowing) to induce a cumulative rehearsal strategy similar to that described in the previous study. On the day immediately following training, each subject was given three new sets of pictures, was reminded of the training procedure, and was told to continue using the strategy, "Say their names over and over again until you know them." The day following the first post-test, subjects were given three new sets of pictures and were told to play the game, but no specific mention of the training strategy was used. After approximately two weeks, subjects were given three new sets of pictures and were told to play the game, but no specific mention of the training strategy was made. These three post-tests provided a measure of *maintenance* and *generalization* of the newly acquired rehearsal strategy. Training in cumulative rehearsal resulted in a significant increase in immediate recall (maintenance) for both the young and older retarded children, when they were tested on new sets of pictures (generalization), and when they were reminded (prompted) to use the training strategy. The older subjects, but not the younger ones, continued to use the strategy and maintained their improvement in recall two weeks later when they were given new sets of pictures and not reminded to continue using rehearsal.

Thus, at least for the older subjects in this and the previous study, training in cumulative rehearsal produced an enduring application of the technique and a corresponding improvement in immediate recall. Cumulative rehearsal, alone, is not an effective method of establishing long-term retention (Craik and Watkins, 1973); however, rehearsal (sequential and cumulative) is prerequisite to elaborative rehearsal. For example, following the removal of a set of stimuli, the items are retained in short-term memory by the processes of sequential or cumulative rehearsal, during which time elaborative rehearsal may involve an analysis of the semantic, phonetic, or taxonomic relationships among the items; this process results in a transfer of the items to long-term memory.

Childs (1983) successfully taught a *spelling* rehearsal strategy to elementary age *educable, mentally retarded* children. The Cover-Write Method was taught to criterion in an average of three hours and 40 minutes. The procedure involved 10 steps: (a) Look at word. Say it; (b) Write word two times; (c) Cover and write one time; (d) Check work; (3) Write word two times; (f) Cover and write one time; (g) Check work; (h) Write word three times; (i) Cover and write one time; (j) Check work. All five children in the study reportedly maintained use of the strategy at 5, 10 and 15 week intervals following termination of instruction. The procedure also resulted in an improvement in spelling proficiency.

Chunking and Categorizing

Chunking. Chunking involves the organization of a number of stimuli into various groups. For example, the telephone number 4363591 may be chunked in several ways without altering the order of the numbers. With *temporal chunking*, the numbers would be regrouped with a *pause* between the groups, e.g., 436 (pause) 3591. If the numbers were *spatially chunked*, the pause would be replaced by a space, e.g., 436 (space) 3591. The subgroups of numbers may also be demarked by changes in verbal inflection or rhythm, e.g., 4363591, where the numbers 6 and 1 are given more emphasis. Usually, chunking involves numbers; however, the procedure may be used to regroup any information. For example, Furukawa (1970) studied the effect of chunking information units in *programmed instruction*. Groups of information of various sizes were divided by questions.

Chunking provides a method of coping with the limitations of short-term memory. Miller (1956) established that the *span of immediate memory* is seven (+ or -) two chunks of information. For example, most people, when asked to recall the 12 digit sequence 7 5 1 6 8 3 5 9 2 4 1 7 immediately after they have been given the opportunity to read the number, will usually recall between five and nine of the numbers where each number is a chunk of information. However, if the numbers are divided spatially or temporally, by the speaker or the listener, into four chunks of three digits each, the number of digits recalled will improve significantly.

A *chunk* may be *defined* as a subjectively perceived unit of information. For example, the sequence of eight letters 1 b n y s t w p may be perceived by a young child as eight separate chunks of information regardless of whether the letters are grouped into four chunks of two letters each, or two chunks of four letters each. Alternatively, an older child or adult presented with a continuous sequence of eight letters, or a sequence of four groups of two letters each, may perceive and rehearse the sequence as two chunks of four letters each. Regardless of the grouping of the information, the manner in which the observer subjectively chunks and rehearses the items will determine how effectively the information is recalled. On the other hand, a chunked presentation of material is usually better recalled than one that is not chunked.

Hunter (1964) established that the *span* of immediate memory actually *varies with age*. At four years of age, children could recall four chunks of information; at seven years of age, five chunks; at ten years, six chunks; at 16 years, seven; and during the mid 50s, six chunks. How many chunks are recalled at each age level is believed to be function of the manner in which an individual attends to the stimuli, the size of the chunks used to organize the material in memory and the active use of rehearsal.

A large number of studies has been conducted on the effects of chunking numbers. As most of these studies have focused on adults, and as the educational significance of the findings has been minimal, selected examples of the studies are summarized in this paragraph. In other cases, where the procedures used or the results obtained are instructionally relevant, studies are described in detail. Chunking a group of nine numbers into three chunks of three numbers each by introducing a pause during a *vocal* presentation improved recall, decreased transposition errors and made numbers within the sequence as memorable as numbers at the beginning and end of the sequence. Chunking numbers into equal size groups of 3-3-3 leads to better recall than irregular groupings, such as 2-4-3 and 1-7-1 (Ryan, 1969). In a *visual* presentation of nine digits, children in grades four and six recalled more digits when the first slide displayed three digits, the second slide displayed the same three digits, plus three more, and the third slide displayed these six digits plus three more. Recall under this condition was better than that in which the numbers were either ungrouped, or presented spatially as three groups of three each. For children in grade two, recall was better when the numbers were grouped; however, the type of grouping did not affect the nature of the recall (Harris and Burke, 1972).

A remarkable study by Ericsson, Chase and Faloon (1980) described how an undergraduate student with average intelligence and memory abilities employed chunking of digits to increase his immediate recall from seven digits to almost 80 digits. The student engaged in a memory span task for about one hour per day, three to five days a week for 18 months. During each session, random digits were read to him at the rate of one digit per second; he then recalled the sequence. During the 230 hours of testing, the subject began to employ a hierarchic series of chunks in which numbers were grouped into chunks of three, four or five numbers; these groups were then organized into groups of threes. In this manner, the subject never chunked a group larger than five, and never recalled more than seven chunks of information.

The mnemonic method by which English speaking children commonly learn the letters of the alphabet demonstrates an effective combination of chunking, rhyme and rhythm. The alphabet is divided into three chunks enclosed by brackets:

[(ab-cd) (ef-g)] [(hi-jk) (lmno-p)] [(qrs-tuv) (w-xyz)]

Each chunk is comprised of two elements containing from one to four letters. Thus, no single chunk is large enough to strain the capacity of primary memory (Norman, 1976).

As mentioned earlier, chunking may be used to group various types of information into manageable size units. Furukawa (1970), for example, evaluated chunking as a method of determining appropriateness of step-size in *programmed instruction* of subjects with either large or small short-term memory. He found that matching the number of response chunks in a question frame with the number of chunks in a subject's short-term memory improved recall performance on immediate and delayed (two-day) post-tests for subjects with either large or small short-term memories. Furukawa defined a chunk in programmed instruction as the one or more words (usually a noun or adjective-noun combination) that a subject had to learn to respond correctly to a single question. The results of the study indicated that for subjects with small short-term memories, a seven chunk step-size was optimal, while a 14 chunk step-size was most suitable for subjects with large short-term memories. An important observation made by Furukawa in a later study (1972) is that the number of words in a chunk does not affect recall. Furukawa concluded that the implications of his studies were that textbooks and classroom instruction must provide for the ready identification of the chunks that subjects must learn. These chunks can be further structured into meaningful wholes and learned in quantities that are appropriate to a subject's specific learning ability.

Categorizing or clustering. Like chunking, categorizing involves a reorganization of separate units of information into groups to facilitate encoding and retrieval of the information. Categorizing usually involves the grouping of nouns or pictures of objects into semantic categories. These categories may be *conceptual* or *taxonomic* in which items of clothing are separately grouped from items of furniture. *Associative groupings* may also be made in which *plate, table* and *chair* are grouped into one category, while *pen, desk* and *lamp* are grouped into another. *Hierarchic, superordinate* and *subordinate* relationships may also result in separate groupings. Each category is usually *labelled* to assist storage and retrieval.

Evidence of the use of categorizing as a mnemonic technique is usually obtained in one of two ways. In the first method, subjects are given a list of randomly ordered pictures or words where each item has been selected from one of a limited number of categories, such as clothing, fruit or furniture. After the items have been removed, the subject is asked to recall as many of the items as possible. The manner in which the subject recalls the items is analyzed to determine if the items were categorized to assist recall. Alternatively, subjects may be given both randomly and categorically sequenced lists of items for the purpose of determining whether a particular type of categorizing improves memory. An important point to emphasize is that just as an effective chunk is a subjectively perceived unit of information, a category designed to improve recall must be a familiar classification of the items to the particular learner involved.

There are *developmental* differences in the use of categorizing mnemonics. In one study, children in kindergarten and grades one, three and five were shown a circular array of black and white, line-drawings of objects selected from animal, furniture, vehicle and clothing categories (Moely, Olson, Halwes and Flavell, 1969). The children in grade five sorted the pictures into categories, when the experimenter left the room for two minutes, after giving the instructions that the children could move the pictures around any way they wanted to help them remember. Children in grade three required additional assistance before they began sorting the pictures. With these children, the experimenter *labelled* each category in the array and pointed out the corresponding members in the circular array. Children in kindergarten and grade one began to sort the pictures only after the experimenter actually assisted them to sort the items, labelled the categories, counted the number of pictures in each and then instructed the children that they could move the pictures around any way they wished to help them remember.

Similar results were obtained by Zinobar, Cermak, Cermak and Dickerson (1975). In their study, children in the third and fifth grades spontaneously used taxonomic categories as an encoding tool, whereas children in the second grade did not. Denney and Ziobrowski (1972) found that children in the first grade tended to cluster, if at all, according to complementary groupings, e.g., words were clustered because they shared some complementary interrelationship, such as *pipe-tobacco*, or *baby-crib*. College students, however, clustered according to conceptual similarity, such as *king-ruler*, or *crib-bed*.

Adults typically detect the categorized nature of a list at the time of its presentation. Later, during retrieval, an adult usually recalls a category name, then retrieves examples within this category before proceeding to the next category. According to Kobasigawa (1974) and Moely (1968), *younger children* may fail to exhaustively search each category unless explicitly instructed to do so. This finding suggests that part of children's failure to retrieve stored information may be insufficient memory search as well as a failure to encode information in categories. In Kobasigawa's study, six-year-old children searched for stored information only long enough to recall one item from a given category. Scribner and Cole (1972) employed a *constrained recall* procedure with seven-, nine- and eleven-year-old children. The children were reminded at presentation and at recall that there were four categories; they were also required to recall all of the items from one category before moving onto the next. For all ages, the children who used constrained recall remembered more than control group children who used *free recall*. Yussen, Kunen and Buss (1975), however, found that with *preschool children* free-recall was superior to constrained recall.

Davies and Brown (1979) also evaluated the effects of prompting recall by *labelling* the category and *blocking* items on presentation. Four- and five-year-old children were presented with an array of closed boxes which the experimenter opened one at a time while asking the children to name the objects they saw inside. For one-half of the children, all of the items in a given box were from the same category (blocked presentation). For the remaining children, each box contained a random selection of objects. After all of the items had been observed, the children were invited to recall the items. One-half of the subjects attempted free recall, while the other half were *prompted* with category labels, "Now tell me all of the flowers or fruit, etc., I showed you." The blocked presentation, and use of category labels as *retrieval prompts*, both increased recall. The authors acknowledged that these results are in contrast to those obtained by other researchers studying young children. The authors postulated that pictures or photographs of items, as used in previous studies of young children, rather than actual objects, as used in the present study, appeared to inhibit spontaneous categorization (Sigel, 1978). A study by Davies and Rushton (1979) confirmed that pictures and photographs produce much weaker effects than those obtained by the use of actual objects, especially for blocked presentations.

Moely and Jeffrey (1974) studied the *generalization* of categorizing skills taught to six- and seven-year-old children. *Training* involved telling the subjects that there was a way to help them remember the black and white line-drawings more easily. The experimenter suggested that the items could be divided into "groups of things that are alike in some way or kind of go together" (p. 137). Most children were able to sort the items with no further instruction. If a child hesitated, however, she/he was assisted in sorting. The child was then asked and/or helped to label the categories. She/he was also told that, when attempting to recall the pictures, think of a category label and then name all of the members in the category, then follow the same method with each of the other categories. This training procedure produced improved recall in the number of categories remembered, in the number of items per category and in the number of items recalled in a *transfer task* where items from different categories were presented.

Bjorklund, Ornstein and Haig (1977) reported that most of the children in the third and fifth grade that they had studied were unable to categorize items in any systematic way, when given the freedom to sort weakly related items to aid their recall. When the same children, however, were given explicit instructions to attend to possible conceptual relations among items, they showed marked improvement in both sorting and recall. Thus, type of *orienting instructions* would seem to be a critical determinant of the application of categorization.

Black and Rollins (1982) *trained children* in the first grade in the use of a *taxonomic organizational strategy*. The children were trained to categorize pictures of common objects such as furniture, clothes, animals and food, etc., represented by line-drawings in the Peabody Picture Vocabulary Test. Two methods of instruction were used: explanatory and questioning. *Explanatory methods* were designed to maximize the amount of information presented to the child, and give the trainer control over the order in which the information was presented. The *questioning approaches* were designed to lead the child by direct questioning to consider ways to remember. The child was also required to develop a verbal explanation of the strategy. Piaget (1951) believed that this method would more likely lead to successful retention and transfer since it guaranteed understanding of the strategy. Four training groups were employed; training lasted from 10.5 to 12 minutes. In all training groups, the children were taught to place the cards into categories, but the instructions varied in each group. In the *general* explanation group, the examiner manipulated the cards while explaining why organization was helpful in recall. For example, "If I put cards together that are similar, such as all the animals, it will be easier to remember." In the *specific* explanation group, the instructions were directed toward specific items and not toward an organizational strategy. For example, "I will put the dog next to the cat." In the *general* question group, the examiner asked questions, and encouraged the child to manipulate the cards. The questions emphasized the purpose for an organizational strategy, for example, "Why do we put the animals together?" Correct answers were provided, if a child did not express them. In the *specific* question group, the questions were directed to specific material, for example, "Where is the dog? What was next to the cat?"

All four types of training enhanced the childrens' use of organization in studying and recalling the pictures. The improvement in the use of organization was *maintained* for several weeks, and *generalized* to a new set of categories after a delay of several weeks. There was little or no difference between the results obtained by the four types of instruction. The minor differences that did occur were in favor of the explanation over the question training strategy. Also, the *general* explanation and questioning strategies were superior to the corresponding *specific* training techniques.

Educable mentally retarded (CA: 13-14) individuals generally perform poorly in free-recall tasks when compared to individuals with normal intelligence (Fagan, 1969: Gallagher, 1969). This memory deficit has been attributed to a failure to employ organizational strategies spontaneously, rather than an inability to organize (e.g., Campione and Brown, 1977). Although mentally retarded individuals may possess sufficient knowledge of categories, they apparently fail to realize that certain situations require deliberate application of a categorizing mnemonic.

Brown (1974) reviewed the literature on the use of categorization by *mentally retarded* subjects: a number of the studies reviewed are reported below. There is a tendency for developmentally young persons to cluster, if at all, according to idiosyncratic relations. However, various *training* procedures can be devised to increase the tendency to cluster more frequently, and to cluster according to more adult criteria. Blocked presentations have successfully increased grouping among mentally retarded adolescents (IQ: 45-70; mean IQ: 57), Bilsky and Evans (1979); (IQ: 50-75; reading grade score 1.8-5.5), Bilsky, Evans and Gilbert (1972). A study by Gerjuoy and Spitz (1966) of educable, mentally handicapped adolescents found that (a) blocked presentation and (b) random presentation with prerecall instructions, such as "Tell me all the animals you remember from the list" significantly and equally improved recall over control conditions.

Brown noted that while it appeared that young children and retarded individuals could be induced to use organizational strategies, there was a *limit on the long-term effectiveness* of such training. For example, in a study by Moely, Olson, Halwes and Flavell (1969), children in grades k, 1, 2, 3 and 5 taught to sort items manually into appropriate groups, and label the categories, failed to continue using the strategy when reminders to organize and label were no longer provided.

Although Bilsky and Evans (1970) found that experience with blocked word lists facilitated the spontaneous use of clustering by retarded adolescents on subsequently presented randomly organized word lists using the same materials, this facilitation did not *generalize* to lists containing new verbal materials (Bilsky *et al.* 1972). Some generalization to new lists by trainable, mentally retarded individuals (CA: 16-48) has been reported when *extended training* (15 days) was undertaken, but again the effect was far more pronounced for the items used in training than for new items (Nye, McManis and Haugen, 1972). Thus, a general pattern emerges: the developmentally young do not spontaneously adopt organizational strategies and, even when induced to do so, the effectiveness of such training is limited (Brown, 1974).

Hamre-Nietupski, Nietupski, Vincent and Wambold (1982) taught a categorization strategy to mildly and to moderately *mentally retarded* adolescents. The *instructional procedures* used incorporated modeling, labelling, praise, correction procedures and prompts. In the strategy training group, at the beginning of each session, the teacher *modeled* the categorization strategy. She (a) presented a horizontal array of objects familiar to the subjects, (b) indicated that she was going to show the students a way to remember, (c) *labelled* the first object and its category, (d) located the other members of that category and (e) formed the three objects into a group, while again stating the category label and corresponding objects. This modeling procedure was repeated with the two remaining categories. Subsequently, the teacher again labelled each category and the objects within, removed the objects from sight and stated each category and its corresponding objects in succession as she pointed to the place on the table where the objects had been.

In the *imitation* phase, the teacher placed a different set of objects before a student and directed him/her to use the same procedure, as had been demonstrated, to remember what was presented. Correct initial attempts to use the sorting portion of the strategy were *rewarded* with *verbal praise*. If the student erred, a hierarchy of *correction procedures* was employed, beginning with *verbal prompts*, proceeding if still incorrect, to a pairing of *gestural* and verbal *prompts*, and finally, if still incorrect, to teacher modeling. After the student had sorted the objects according to their respective categories and had restated each category name and object label, the teacher removed the objects from sight and directed the student to recall the items. Praise was provided, if the student exhibited correct initial attempts to use the "grouping for recall" portion of the strategy. If the student did not recall any object within 10-15 seconds, a hierarchy of verbal prompts was employed, beginning with "prompts of encouragement," followed by "object prompts." This strategy training procedure significantly increased the recall performance on both *near* and *intermediate transfer*. A near transfer task involves different objects from the same initial categories. An intermediate transfer task involves different objects from different categories. The training also improved maintenance; subjects still employed the strategy one week following instruction. Also, the group that received strategy training maintained the significant increase in recall performance on both near and intermediate transfer objects over the one week period following training. The instructional techniques of modeling, prompting and correcting performance are fully discussed in chapter Ten.

To what extent do intellectually *normal children* at various age levels understand the value of a categorical method of mnemonics, and how does this knowledge affect their recall? Wimmer and Tornquist (1980) attempted to answer these questions in a study of students seven, ten and seventeen years of age. The students were presented with three displays in which the same 27 items were arranged in three different ways; one according to categories and two without categorical groupings. The students were asked which one of the three displays would be easiest to remember. In a second test, the children were given a random display of nine pictures of objects from three categories. They were asked what they could do to remember as many of the pictures as possible. Fifty percent of the seven-year-olds understood the beneficial effects upon recall of grouping. Sixty percent of the ten-year-olds had a similar understanding, as did nearly all of the seventeen-year-olds. In addition, over all of the ages studied, use of the categories in a recall task was significantly related to knowledge of the benefits of categorizing.

Cermak (1975) discussed an interesting application of a *categorizing* mnemonic that also *incorporated* several *other techniques*. The example described an attempt to recall a shopping list of the following items that were not readily classified into conventional categories: *milk, carrots, peanut butter, potato chips, spinach, cider, roast beef, bread* and *fish*. The mnemonic involved two steps. The first step consisted of (a) *organizing* the items into "meal categories," (b) *linking* each successive item in the category to the previously introduced item and (c) *visualizing* construction of the category. For example one might visualize two slices of bread, each of which is spread (associative link) with peanut butter; the bread enclosing (link) slices of beef wrapped in (link) spinach. The "sandwich" is washed down (link) with cider. Similarly, one might visualize a large fish with a carrot slice over each eye and with potato chips where the scales should be. This delightful meal would be washed down with milk. The second step in the procedure involved application of a *loci* mnemonic. One would visualize the bread at the bakery counter and the fish in the freezer. Thus, when arriving at the supermarket, one had merely to recall the first loci, the bread counter, and then recall each of the food items linked in succession as they were introduced into the sandwich category. A parallel procedure would be used for the fish meal.

Shoppers able to remember large numbers of items during regular weekly supermarket shopping will probably think that such elaborate mnemonic measures are quite unnecessary. However, the person responsible for shopping is frequently also responsible for cooking, and may not perceive the items on the list as unrelated, but as ingredients in a recipe or as components of planned meals. Thus, without begin aware of it, the shopper has already categorized and linked the items on the list. This same shopper, who doesn't require the assistance of any contrived mnemonic strategy, may find it more difficult to remember a lengthy list of "unrelated" items requested by a neighbor. The discussion of mnemonic methods continues in the next chapter.

Chapter Three

Mnemonic Strategies: Two

The previous chapter discussed the general nature, purpose and classification of mnemonic strategies. Methods of labelling, chunking, and categorizing were described. Techniques of teaching these strategies to intellectually normal and to handicapped children were discussed. Supporting research on the efficacy of the application of the techniques by these children was presented. This chapter continues the same type of review of visual imagery and syntactic encoding mnemonics.

Visual Imagery

A mental image is a hypothetical, pictorial representation of objects or events. The existence and/or effects of mental imagery are inferred from observations made of relationships between independent variables (stimuli) and dependent variables (responses). For example, if a child, *instructed* (stimulus) to construct an interactive image for each of several word pairs (e.g., *dog-cigar*, reportedly visualized as "a dog smoking a cigar"), *recalls* (response) more word pairs than when the child was instructed merely to recall each pair, then one may infer that an interactive image was constructed that led to an improvement in recall.

Some *stimulus conditions* that have been observed to improve recall are: (a) presentation of *instructions* to create mental images;

(b) presentation of *concrete words*, such as *scissors and dripping*, rather than *abstract words*, such as *sincerity and allude*; and (c) presentation of *pictures* of concrete objects that may be represented as mental images in the same form as they are pictorially presented rather than offering *verbal* representations of concrete objects that must be first converted into a form that can be visualized.

Visual imagery appears to play a fundamental role in the majority of mnemonic strategies discussed in this text. The role of imagery in these mnemonic strategies may be implicit or explicit. For example, in the *loci mnemonic*, the use of imagery is obvious. A subject employing the technique first memorizes a sequential list of readily visualized, familiar, physical locations (*loci*). For instance, the subject may visualize loci sequenced along the entrance to his house: (a) the front gate, (b) the sidewalk, (c) the front steps, (d) the porch, (e) the screen door, etc. These loci, once memorized, serve as a general purpose aid to recalling lists of items. For example, given a list of grocery items, the subject would imagine an *interaction* between each item in the list and each of the loci. The subject may visualize (a) spaghetti draped over the top of the gate, (b) apples rolling down the inclined sidewalk, (c) rows of peas filling the slot between the two boards on each step, etc. Thus, when recalling the image of the previously memorized loci, the image will contain each of the grocery items on the list.

Less obvious, but perhaps equally important, is the role of imagery in the use of *sentence mnemonics*. If two words, such as *snake* and *man*, are coded into a sentence, such as the "snake *bit* the man" (verbal link), or the "snake *on* the man" (*prepositional link*), the words are generally more memorable than if the words are *conjunctively linked* in sentence form as in "the snake *and* the man." One may infer that the advantage of the verbal and prepositional link is that an interactive image may be formed between each member of the pair so that recall of the image of one member also produces the image of the other interacting member. A conjunctive link between the members of a pair, however, is not conducive to the production of an interactive image. In support of the notion that imagery plays a role in sentence mnemonics, Bower (1972) noted that the subjects in one of his studies spontaneously reported the experience of imagining the scene described by self-generated sentences. Richardson (1980) observed that the effect of stimulus imaginability upon recall performance is roughly the same under instructions either to form a mental image or to use a semantic mnemonic; with both types of mnemonic strategies, recall is enhanced more with high imagery stimuli than with abstract stimuli.

Following a review of the literature on the effects of *instructions* to use mental imagery, Richardson (1980) concluded that (a) under laboratory conditions, instructions to use mental imagery may lead to substantial improvements in memory performance; (b) the effects of instructions to use imagery mnemonics are entirely analogous to those achieved by instructions to use semantic mnemonics (e.g., sentence mnemonics); and (c) the resulting increases in recall performance are typically comparable in the two cases.

However, *instructions* to create images, when one or more of the stimuli in *paired-associate learning* is *abstract*, may interfere with performance. When one of the members of the pair is abstract, instructions to use a semantic mnemonic may be more effective than instructions to use visual imagery. Alternatively, according to Richardson, assumptions about the interaction between the effect of *stimulus imaginability* and that of imagery mnemonic instructions must also specify the role of the *rate of presentation* of the stimuli. Too rapid a rate may inhibit the use of mental imagery, even with concrete material, while a slow rate of presentation might provide sufficient time for images to be formed even for abstract materials. Thus, to determine the effect of imagery instructions, one must evaluate the imaginability of the stimuli, the rate of stimulus presentation and the degree of spontaneous use of mental imagery in the absence of specific mnemonic instructions. Richardson concluded that although such instructions do not typically lead to improved performance in the learning of abstract material, and although the spontaneous use of mental imagery with such material is relatively infrequent, the possibility remains that subjects instructed to use mental imagery might be able to do so even with abstract material—provided that the circumstances of the experiment permit it.

It is well established, Richardson reported, that stimulus imaginability is positively correlated with performance in a wide variety of learning tasks. This effect has been demonstrated with *free recall* (Janssen, 1976; Paivio, 1968; Paivio, Yuille and Rogers, 1969; Richardson, 1974, 1979), with *serial recall* (Paivio *et al*., 1969), with *paired-associate* learning (Paivio, Smythe and Yuille, 1968; Richardson, 1978) and with *recognition memory* (Oliver, described by Paivio, 1971). Stimulus imaginability has been found to affect both the accuracy with which material is retrieved from memory and the speed with which it is retrieved (Macht and Schierer, 1975).

Paivio, Yuille and Madigan (1968) rated the *imaginability* of 925 English nouns. In this study, *concrete nouns* were defined as those referring to objects, materials or persons; *abstract nouns* were defined as those referring to concepts that could not be experienced by the senses. A number of studies conducted by Richardson (1980) demonstrated that the imaginability of stimulus material rather than its concreteness is the critical attribute determining how easily the stimulus can be remembered.

In the past, it has been generally felt that to instruct subjects to produce *bizarre mental images* would enhance recall. However, studies that have attempted to separate the effects attributed to *plausible imagery* and to bizarre imagery have not found that bizarre imagery has significantly enhanced recall over that obtained from plausible imagery (Hauck, Walsh and Kroll, 1976; Senter and Hoffman, 1976; Wollen, Weber and Lowry, 1972). In fact, bizarre images actually take more time to construct, and may result in poorer performance (Nappe and Wollen, 1973). One reason why bizarre imagery may be ineffective is that some people find it difficult to make up bizarre images (Gruneberg, Monks, Sykes and Osborne, 1974).

When a task involves attempting to remember two or more items, recall is enhanced, if an image is formed in which the items interact with each other rather than merely sitting side-by-side. As described earlier, recall of the items *dog* and *cigar* is improved when an *interactive image* is created in which the "dog is smoking the cigar" rather than merely standing beside it. Bower (1969) reported on an experiment in which the experimental groups given concrete noun pairs were instructed to either (a) imagine a scene in which the two objects were interacting in some way, or (b) imagining the two objects one at a time, separated in space as on opposite walls of a room. On a *cued recall test*, the subjects who created interactive images recalled 71 percent, whereas the subjects who visualized separate images recalled only 46 percent of the items. Bower concluded that instructions to visualize the objects had little effect on associative learning, and that the important component was the *interaction* between the items visualized. Taylor, Josberger and Prentice (1970) studied children in the sixth grade who were required to construct images of sets of four concrete nouns (e.g., boy, lion, banana and cup). Children who formed a single interacting image of the four objects in each group had better recall of the objects than children who formed interacting images of pairs of objects within each set of four items, or who simply rehearsed the items in each group of four.

Similar research in which *pictures* were *presented*, rather than having subjects make up their own mental images, has shown that when the items in a picture are interacting, they are remembered better than when they are separated (Higbee, 1979). Another factor that may influence the effectiveness of visual imagery is the *vividness* of the image generated. Higbee (1979) suggested, for example, that recall may be improved, if rather than simply visualizing a *dog* sweeping with a *broom*, one was to imagine a particular variety of *dog* and a specific type of *broom*. For instance, one might visualize a *dachshund* sweeping mud off the porch with a *pushbroom*. Several studies have supported this suggestion (Bower, 1972; Delin, 1969; Ernest, 1977; Holmes and Murray, 1974). Studies by Richardson (1976, 1978) have indicated, however, that interaction is a more critical influence on recall than is vividness.

Lorayne and Lucas (1974) have suggested that recall is better when an individual creates his/her own images than when she/he is given *prepared images* in pictorial form. This advice is in accord with the findings of a number of studies that have shown that both visual and verbal mnemonics tend to be more effective, if subjects construct them themselves, than if the mnemonics are provided by the experimenter (Higbee, 1979). Other studies, however, have found that supplied pictorial images may be of benefit to young children (Reese, 1977) and mentally retarded persons (Campione and Brown, 1977). A number of these studies, reviewed by Reese (1977), have indicated that until the sixth grade, instructions to visualize often produce inferior recall compared to the results obtained when pictorial images are supplied. Reese observed that although supplied pictorial images appear to produce better recall among children under 12 years of age, the trend is certainly not strong. Reese suggested that a problem in interpreting *age differences* is that the difference in effectiveness of mental and pictorial imagery must depend in part on how effectively the *instructions* and pictorial representations induce interactive imagery. If the instructions are not sufficiently clear to induce interactive images, then pictorial presentations may be more effective. Alternatively, if the pictorial representations are poor in quality, instruction to visualize may be more effective than pictorial images.

Pressley (1982) reported that children as young as four years of age have the ability to generate their own mental images, if they are also required to make an *overt motor response* to depict their images. For instance, Bender and Levin (1976) presented four-year-olds with pairs of toys. The children who were told that they would have to manipulate the toys to depict their mental images recalled a larger number of the pairs of toys than did the children instructed merely to generate images of the toys.

Varley, Levin, Severson and Wolff (1974) studied the effect of *motor involvement* and imagery with children in kindergarten and grade one. The task involved paired-associate learning in which the children were given pairs of toys. Children were trained either to: (a) imagine an interaction between the toys in each pair, (b) generate interactions for each pair by playing with the toys or (c) draw a picture of the toys interacting. Within kindergarten, motoric involvement in the form of either drawing or playing with the toys produced significantly more recall than did imagery alone. However, within grade one, there was no significant difference in recall between subjects who used imagery and those who made overt motor responses. No significant difference in recall was observed between children in either grade who drew the toys and those who made overt motor responses.

Research has revealed that four-year-old children can generate *semantic mnemonics* before they can produce internal interactive images (Levin, McCabe and Bender, 1975). Children in a study by Levin *et al.* (1975) were unable to benefit from instruction to form a mental image even when they performed concurrent motor activity. A study by Bender and Levin (1976) indicated that the recall of kindergarten subjects improved, if they planned an interaction, even though they did not carry it out. By five to six years of age, children benefit from simple imagery generation instructions when learning picture object pairings (Pressley, 1982).

The research literature generally indicates that for *children five years of age and younger*, recall is not improved by instructing the children to generate their own mental images. However, recall is improved through the provision of interactive, pictorial representations (Paivio, 1980; Rohwer, Ammon and Levin, 1971). By *eight years* of age, children can successfully employ visual imagery to increase recall (Lesgold, McCormick and Golinkoff, 1975; Pressley, 1976). For college students, self-generated images are even more effective than pictorial representations (Bobrow and Bower, 1969; Bower and Winzenz, 1970).

The period from *six to seven years* of age appears to be one of transition during which children acquire the ability to generate visual imagery. Research conducted on children between ages six to seven has produced conflicting results, which may indicate that for some children, under some conditions, the ability to generate visual imagery is acquired earlier than it is for other children. Danner and Taylor (1973) and Levin and Pressley (1978) found, for example, that children five to six years of age benefited from instructions to generate visual images, when learning pairs of pictures and objects. Alternatively, Levin (1976) stated that children six or seven years old were typically unsuccessful when asked to generate their own mental images. Thus, it appears that for children six to seven years of age, decisions as to the effectiveness of imagery instructions should be made on an individual basis and in terms of specific tasks. Pressley (1977) reported that imagery effects have been shown to be more pronounced in some subjects than in others for a variety of different memory tasks.

Several studies have been conducted to assess the effectiveness of *training children to use visual imagery*. In a study by Danner and Taylor (1973) children in grades one, three and six were trained to use interactive imagery in the recall of sets of three concrete nouns. The children were assigned to three experimental conditions. In condition one, they were trained to generate their own interactive images. These children were required to draw three integrated pictures while viewing separated pictures of nouns. They had to incorporate three pictures at a time into an active and/or spatially contiguous scene. For the first practice set of stimuli, an integrated picture served as a *model* for each child's drawing. The experimenter asked each subject to describe the relations between the three items in the child's drawing, and then *cued* the child's recall of two of the items with a picture of the third. On practice sets two and three, the children received as much encouragement and correction as was necessary to produce an integrated scene.

Children assigned to condition two were shown three pictures depicting in each the integration of three concrete nouns. The experimenter showed each child the first integrated picture, named the items and asked the child to remember them. The picture was presented for 20 seconds. Recall of two of the items was cued by the presentation of a picture of the third. Practice sets two and three were presented in the same manner.

Children in the third condition were not given any training and were simply presented with pictures each of which depicted three nouns combined into an integrated scene. The results of this study indicated that children in the sixth grade recalled more items when they generated their own interactive images, than when pictures of integrated objects were supplied. These finding are consistent with the observations reported in previous paragraphs. Danner and Taylor suggested that because only 15-20 seconds had been allowed to generate each interactive image, greater benefits from self-generated imagery might have resulted, if more *time* had been available. The results also indicated that for the children in grades one and three, there was no significant difference in recall between children shown integrated pictures and those asked to generate their own images. As mentioned in previous discussion, usually children in grade one, and occasionally children in grade three, benefit more from pictures than from visual imagery. Thus, the results obtained, particularly with the children in grade one, reflect the benefits of training the children to generate their own interactive, visual imagery.

Ross and Ross (1978) used stories and related table games to *teach imagery* strategies to *educable mentally handicapped* students of approximately IQ: 66; CA: nine years. The stories all had the following characteristics: the child in the story *modeled* the use of imagery to remember sets of objects or events. The child was highly motivated to remember two or more objects or events that went together. The child thought about the way a picture suddenly appears on a television screen when the set is turned on. He pretended that he was turning the set on, and the instant the picture appeared, he saw the objects to be remembered in the picture. He then told his friend (sibling or parent) what was happening in the television picture. Later, he told his mother or some other adult how thinking of a picture with the objects in it had helped him to remember. The adult who was told the story then praised the child. Each story was followed by questions, discussion of the imagery strategy and a game designed to provide further practice in the use of imagery. The following story, which also employs modeling, was one of those used in the imagery training.

> Sandra's class was playing *Take a Picture*. In this game the teacher gave each child three pictures to look at and remember. She gave Sandra pictures of a cake, a mouse and a chair, and she gave Anne pictures of a boat, a seagull and a boy. As soon as the children had looked at their pictures, the teacher took them away. When she held up one of Sandra's pictures, like *mouse*, then Sandra had to say the other pictures that went with *mouse*, which were *chair* and *cake*. If Sandra could remember the pictures, she got a token and some new pictures to remember. The first child to get three tokens won the game.
>
> Sandra tried hard to think of a way to remember that *cake, mouse* and *chair* went together. Then she said to herself, "I think I'll put them all in a picture like on television. I'll pretend I'm turning on the TV and the minute the picture comes on, it will have the cake and the mouse and the chair in it." Sandra

pretended to turn on the TV, and there was a picture with a mouse hiding under a chair eating a piece of cake. Sandra thought about the picture; she could imagine how hungry that mouse was! Just then the teacher looked at Sandra and held up a picture of a chair, and quick as anything Sandra said, "cake and mouse."

"Good work, Sandra!" said her teacher, "You didn't have to stop for a minute to think of the pictures that went with chair. Can you tell us how you remembered so quickly?"

Questions

1. What did Sandra tell her teacher about how she remembered?

2. Anne's pictures were of a boat, seagull and boy. How could she remember them?

3. Sandra's new pictures were of a woodpecker, tree and candy. How could she remember to say tree and candy when her teacher showed her a picture of a woodpecker"

Game

Play *Take a Picture* using some high-level associates including cake, candle and birthday presents, as well as some pictures that do not elicit immediate association, such as tree, elastic and bottle. Emphasize putting the individual pictures into a television picture, the immediacy of the picture and having the objects to be remembered in some kind of interaction. (Ross and Ross, 1978, p. 463)

The training program lasted for two weeks. In a multiple associate learning task in which pictures of common objects were presented, children trained in the imagery technique recalled significantly more than children who used rote repetition. The use of modeling to train children in the use of mnemonics is discussed in Chapter Ten.

In *summary*, most memory aids rely on some form of imagery (Roediger, 1980). Simply instructing children (age eight plus) to use imagery as a mnemonic technique can enhance recall in free recall, serial learning and paired associates (Paivio, 1971) as well as prose (Richardson, 1980). Visual imagery is also useful in recall of vocabulary, acquisition of foreign languages (Atkinson, 1975) and recall of concepts (Higbee, 1979). Visual imagery may have implications for school instruction in at least two general ways.

First, visual imagery may influence the manner in which instruction and instructional material can best present information to students to assist acquisition and retention of information (e.g., concrete vs. abstract [concrete stories, examples, analogies, etc.], pictorial vs. verbal [pictures, diagrams, demonstrations, etc.] and interacting vs. separate images). Second, visual imagery may influence the kinds of activities students can be taught to increase their learning power (e.g., integrated visual imagery, vividness of imagery and drawing pictures) (Higbee, 1979). The use of imagery in the recall of prose is discussed in Chapters Seven and Eight.

While images can serve as memory aids, they may also be created to prepare for *future experiences*. Mental images may be used to visualize future situations as a form of advance rehearsal or practice. The process may involve visualizing future events to foresee outcomes, anticipate problems, find solutions and avoid difficulties. In this regard, visualizing future events may assist *prospective memory*, remembering to execute actions planned for the future. By using visual imagery, one may visualize predictable parts of the future environment, and imagine an interactive image between that part of the environment and the planned action. In this manner, a *primary associative link* may be established. Thus, when the future environment comes into view, its physical characteristics through association with the planned activity may elicit recall of that activity.

Syntactic Encoding

Syntax refers to the manner in which words are combined to form phrases, clause or sentences. In the present context, syntactic encoding refers to joining words with conjunctions or prepositions, or putting words together into stories or rhyming sequences to increase their memorability. Syntactic encoding is also referred to as *natural language mediation*.

A study of syntactic encoding using *prepositions* was conducted by Wanschura and Borkowski (1975). In the study, *moderately retarded* children (mean IQ: 44; mean CA: 12.3) were *taught syntactic encoding* in a paired-associates learning task using Peabody Picture Vocabulary Test pictures of animals (horse, dog, cat and duck), and clothing (shirt, shoe, coat, dress and pants).

The study was designed to examine the effects on recall of joining two nouns by a preposition, for example, the *cow in* the *shoe*. The study also examined the effects of variations in (a) the number of experimenter-provided examples of prepositional syntactic encoding: 9/9, 6/9 or 0 (control); (b) the number of prepositions used in the prepositional syntactic examples: 1 or 3 prepositions selected from *in, on* or *under*; and (c) the frequency of instruction: once per week for three weeks, or once per day for three days. The study is noteworthy for its instructional procedures. The brief description of the instructional procedures reported in the article is described in the following paragraphs.

The first step of *instruction* involved object recognition training. The authors did not describe the training procedures used. However, it may be assumed that because paired-associate learning is concerned with an individual's ability to recall which two *familiar* objects have been paired, object recognition training is designed to insure that, given the label of any of the objects used in the study, and a choice of these objects from which to choose, the subject will consistently pick the correct object.

The second step of instruction involved a *practice trial* designed to focus the learner's attention on the prepositional relationship between the objects that were to be presented throughout the study. Because the study was designed to evaluate the effects of prepositional syntactic encoding, the focusing of learner attention on these relationships was crucial. The experimenter, reportedly, placed the practice pair on the table with instructions to, "Put the fish *in, on or under* the pitcher." As the child was performing the action, he was told, "That will help you learn." Other studies have shown that advising a learner of the potential beneficial effects of a particular strategy will increase the likelihood that the techniques will continue to be used following the termination of instruction.

If a child failed to put the fish *in, on or under* the pitcher, as requested, she/he was *physically prompted* to complete the task in the appropriate manner. This procedure was repeated for each of the pairs of objects.

After a child had been sensitized to attend to the prepositional relationship between pairs of objects, step three of instruction was undertaken. On succeeding trials, pairs of objects were presented in appropriate prepositional relationships, e.g., soap *in* glass, along with the corresponding description e.g., "Soap in glass." Study trials were alternated with recognition trials.

The next instructional procedure in the sequence involved placing each pair of objects on the table with the instructions, "Show me how they go together." If the objects were placed in the appropriate prepositional relationship, the child was praised, "Very good, that helped you learn." (additional feedback regarding the beneficial effects of the strategy). If the objects were incorrectly related, the child was told, "No." and was instructed or physically guided to "Put the ... (in, on or under) the ...." During this period, the child was also told, "That helped you to learn." Following this phase of instruction, *each* child received *M and Ms* or *Fruit Loops*. Sweets were not dispensed according to the nature of a child's performance, and the *rewards* appear to be for participation in the study regardless of the nature of performance. The children were also reportedly "encouraged" to learn what goes together so they could play the game again. With the exception of a minor modification, these instructional procedures were repeated over the remaining two days of training following the request, "Show me how they go together"; no knowledge of results or corrections were given.

Two weeks after the final training task, the *transfer list* of objects was presented to evaluate the effects of the prepositional syntactic encoding training. During training, there was no significant difference with respect to the *percentage of errors*, or the *trials to criterion* between groups that had been shown the 9/9 or 6/9 examples of prepositional syntactic encoding. Subjects in both of these groups made significantly fewer errors than did subjects in the control group. The number of prepositions used in training (in, on or under), did not affect overall learning although transfer of learning was somewhat slower for the one-preposition group. On the transfer task, there was no significant difference between the percentage of errors made by children who had received 9/9 or 6/9 examples of prepositional, syntactic encoding. Both groups of subjects made significantly fewer errors (49 percent less) than children in the control group did. The distribution of training, every day for three days, or once per week for three weeks made no difference on transfer. The relative merits of *massed and distributed practice* are discussed in Chapter Nine. Wanschura and Borkowski (1975) attributed the success of this study to the requirement that subjects physically produce the relationships *in, on* or *under* with the sets of objects.

Thus, syntactic encoding may involve joining pairs of objects with prepositions such as *in, on* or *under* to improve recall of the objects. That is, when given one object, an individual will be able to recall the other object more readily, if the objects have been joined by a preposition or conjunction. Similar benefits may be derived in the recall of two or more objects joined into phrases, clauses or sentences. For example, in a study by Atwood (1969), experimental subjects were presented with a series of twelve *phrases* each linking three concrete nouns and describing an imaginary scene. The subjects were instructed to visualize each scene. In half the phrases, the objects were represented in "spatial proximity, but with a minimum of interdependence" (e.g., *mouse* walked by *soap* toward a *chain*). The other six phrases described imaginary scenes in which the objects were "arranged into unified wholes" (e.g., *dog* wearing a *helmet* and chewing a *watch*). Following presentation of a complete list, each subject was given the first noun in each phrase and was asked to supply the other two noun s, e.g., given *mouse*, the subject was expected to supply *soap* and *chain*. The results of the study showed that an average of 4.8 out of 6 unified images were recalled compared to only 3.2 out of 6 of the images in which the parts were merely juxtaposed (Paivio, 1971).

Rohmer (1973) described a number of considerations in the development of effective syntactic (sentence) encoding. One aspect is the extent to which the *sentence mnemonic* integrally incorporates both of the items into the sentence. If a sentence mnemonic involves one of a pair of objects in terms of a central property of the object, and involves the other object only in terms of one of its *peripheral* or *incidental characteristics*, then given one object as a cue, an individual is relatively unlikely to recall the other object. For example, a pair of items such as *man* and *book* encoded into a sentence in the form "The *man* sat on the *book*" would be less effective for retrieval than an encoding like "The *man* read the *book*." It is only an incidental property of a book that one can sit upon it, whereas the readability of a book is its central property.

An additional consideration in the development of effective sentence encoding is the extent to which the sentence describes an event for which the *objects* in the sentence *are essential*. The more essential the particular objects are to the identity of the event described, the less likely it is that the objects in the sentence will be replaced by other objects that could as easily be associated with the event. For example, an event like "shattering" could as easily be associated with a *rock*, a *vase*, a *hammer* or a *mirror*. Thus, a sentence such as "The rock shattered the vase" may be subject to *substitution* where either the rock and/or the vase is replaced by a hammer and/or a mirror.

In a study conducted by Levin and Rohwer (1968), children in the fourth and fifth grade were given a sentence mnemonic to facilitate recall of fourteen nouns. As in the example that follows, the words were presented in three or four word *phrases* that when read in sequence formed one continuous meaningful *sentence*.

> the grey *cat*
> jumped over the *log*
> and crossed the *street*
> to find the *bowl*
> of cold *milk*
> under the *chair*
> in the new *house*
> by the blue *lake*
> where the young *boy*
> lost his left *shoe*
> while eating the *fish*
> on the wooden *boat*
> during the *storm*
> that came last *year*.
> (Levin and Rohwer, 1968, p. 188)

Immediately following brief instruction, subjects in the control group were presented with 14 successive nouns at a rate of four seconds each. At the same time and rate, experimental subjects were presented with the 14 phrases. Following study of this material, each child had four seconds to recall the first noun, then four seconds to recall each of the successive nouns. According to the authors, the results of the study clearly favored the use of the sentences to enhance recall.

Negin (1978) evaluated a novel application of *sentence mnemonics* used to reduce *spelling* errors made by children in grade six. For each child, ten misspelled words were selected from the child's written assignments. The students were given two hours of instruction on the use of sentence mnemonics in spelling. They were given examples, such as "She screamed EEE as she passed the cEmEtEry"; "StationERy is for a lettER"; and "My skin shows resisTANce to a TAN." If two sections of a word proved difficult and could not be linked in one sentence, the children were told to construct two sentences. Spelling activities were conducted every Monday morning. Students were instructed to compare their misspellings with the proper form, locate the discrepancy, create a sentence associating the word with the correct spelling and rehearse the sentence in the remaining time. Students in the control group, who had not received mnemonic training, were required to compare their misspellings with the correct form, write each of the list words in a meaningful sentence, underline the difficult section and rehearse the word in the remaining time. Following each practice session, students formed pairs and dictated spelling words to each other. After six weeks, there was no significant difference between the mnemonic and the control groups; however, after ten weeks, students in the mnemonic group were significantly superior to students in the control group.

Each of the following examples of sentence mnemonics, adapted from Shaw (1965), shows a word that is difficult to spell joined together with another word that provides a cue to spelling the difficult word.

believe—	I bel*ie*ve it is a l*ie*.
capitol—	The capit*o*l has an *o* in the dome.
hear—	I h*ear* with my *ear*.
meat—	We *eat* m*eat*.
piece—	A p*ie*ce of p*ie*.
principal—	The princi*pal* is a *pal*.
there—	The*re* tells wh*ere*.

After reviewing the literature, Pressley (1982) concluded that even *nursery school* children improved in their learning, when they are instructed to *generate verbal elaborations* (mnemonics) (Levin, McCabe and Bender, 1975; Milgram, 1968). Indeed, instructions to produce syntactic encoding have been shown to facilitate the associative recall of children of all ages through adolescence to adulthood (Milgram, 1967, 1968; Pressley, Levin and McCormick, 1980; Rohwer and Beam, 1973).

Bloom and Lahey (1978) reported that even children as young as *three years of age* could successfully construct syntactic encoding. It would take most children several trials to recall a 14 item list of words, such as *cat, log, street, etc.*, in their correct serial order. However, this task is markedly simplified, when the items are presented, as in the previously mentioned study by Levin and Rohwer, in the form: "The gray *cat* jumped over the *log* and crossed the *street* to find the *bowl.* . . ." Sentence mnemonics using *verbs* (e.g., the *dog closes* the *gate*) aid children's retention more than do sentences with *prepositions* (e.g., the *dog* on the *gate*), or *conjunctions* (e.g., the *dog* and the *gate*) (Rohwer, 1966, 1970). A number of studies have found better recall of objects embedded in sentences, if the subjects generate their own linking sentences (Bobrow and Bower, 1969; Pelton, 1969). These benefits are of course dependent upon the subjects ability to generate appropriate sentences. As discussed in the next paragraphs, some mentally retarded individuals have difficulty with this task.

Several studies have also demonstrated that when *syntactic encoding is supplied to retarded subjects* in the form of sentences, paired-associate learning is improved (Jensen and Rohwer, 1963; Milgram, 1967; Turnure and Walsh, 1971). However, relatively little *transfer* has been observed of trained syntactic encoding techniques to new paired-associate tasks (Jensen and Rohwer, 1963; Milgram, 1967). Alternatively, when more than one set of stimuli have been used, Turnure and Thurlow (1973) have demonstrated transfer to new lists. Subjects receiving a single elaboration experience showed little evidence of transfer, while individuals receiving two elaboration experiences revealed clear transfer patterns. As is discussed in Chapter Nine, on generalization and maintenance, training with multiple examples facilitates generalization.

A study by Milgram and Riedel (1969) *compared* the ability of *normal and mentally retarded children* to encode pictures of events in sentence form. Normal functioning children in kindergarten (CA: 5) and in grades two (CA: 7), three and four (CA: 9) were matched with *trainable*, mentally retarded (CA: 14; MA: 5.5), and two groups of *educable* mentally retarded children (CA: 15.8; MA: 7.2) and (CA: 17.6; MA: 9.3). They were given pictures showing objects interacting, and were instructed to tell what was going on in each picture. As the experimenter presented each picture, he named each of the objects in the picture. Compared to the retarded children, the normal subjects gave more complete sentences rather than phrases; they were more likely to mention both objects in their sentences, and to add additional elements to develop better contextual relationships between the objects. They also produced slightly longer sentences. Thus, when given pictorial depictions of objects to recall, children of normal intellectual functioning (grades k-4) appeared to be better able than mentally retarded children (matched for MA) to syntactically encode the items in sentence form.

Milgram and Riedel developed a *scoring system* for discriminating the quality of the *sentence mnemonics* generated by their subjects. The system looks as though it may be generally applicable. A sentence was scored one, if either one or both (rare) of the objects was omitted and was not implied by the context, e.g., "The *telephone* is ringing" (*barn* is omitted). A sentence was awarded two points, if both objects were present or implied by the context, e.g., "The *telephone* was up in the *barn*. A score of three was awarded to sentences, if an additional element was added, e.g., "The *telephone* was up in the *barn* and the sun was shining." The additional element was assumed to develop a better contextual relationship. A *context score* was also awarded for having a meaningful connection between the objects. If the terms were loosely connected in the sentence such that other nouns could be substituted for the target terms, with no loss of meaningful context, the sentence received a low score. For example, a sentence was scored one, if the relationship between the two objects was one of position, e.g., "The telephone is in the barn"; if separate, but unrelated actions were attributed to the objects, e.g., "Here is a *snowman* and the *flag* is red"; or if a relationship was precluded because either object was entirely omitted from the sentence. A sentence was scored two, if a verb combined both objects in a meaningful interaction, e.g., "The *snowman* is holding the *flag*." A score of three was assigned, if the interaction described in the sentence was *novel* or *optimally correct* for the visual compound. This creative context was usually achieved by introducing a third element that reportedly strengthened the associative bond between the terms, e.g., "The *telephone* is up in the barn so that the cows can call other cows."

MacMillian (1970) found that the sentence mnemonics generated by the young, educable *mentally retarded* children that they studied were usually *sentence fragments*, e.g., "the *cup* and the *soup*", that did not function as effective mnemonic devices. However, Ross and Ross (1978) reported that there was unequivocal evidence that paired-associate learning of young, educable mentally retarded children can be markedly improved by *short-term* (Taylor, Josberger and Knowlton, 1972) and *long-term* (Ross, Ross and Downing, 1973) *training* in the use of sentence mnemonics. Nevertheless, when these retarded children are required to link more than two objects together in a sentence, difficulties arise. The sentences they generate commonly link two objects together in a predicative relationship with additional objects being incorporated into the base sentence by means of conjunctions, e.g., The *train* ran over the *peach*, and the *guitar* and the *soap*. Such a sentence often facilitates recall of the first two items, but impairs recall of the remaining items. A study conducted by Ross (1974) indicated that educable, mentally retarded children in the primary grade generally performed better on a task recalling multiple objects illustrated in individual pictures when left to their own resources, than when instructed to use a sentence mnemonic strategy.

Ross and Ross (1973) experimented with two methods, *story modeling* and *observational learning*, to teach syntactic mnemonics to educable, mentally handicapped children (mean IQ approx. 69; mean CA approx. 104 months; mean MA approx. 72

months). In the story modeling approach, the child depicted in the story used a conjunctive, rhyming or sentence link to remember pairs of objects or events. The teaching technique used by the authors is parallel to the one they used in the previously reported study on teaching visual imagery. One of the stories used is reported below; questions and a game, as in the previous imagery study, followed each story.

> Bobby's class was playing *Take a Token*. In this game the teacher gave each child two words to remember. She gave Stevie *house* and *fire* and she gave Bobby *towtruck* and *car*. When the teacher said one of Stevie's words like *house*, then Stevie had to say his other word, *fire*. If Stevie could remember to say his word he got a token and two new words to remember. The first one to get three tokens won the game.
>
> Bobby's words were *towtruck* and *car*. Bobby tried to think of a way to remember that *towtruck* and *car* went together. Then he said to himself, "I'll make up a story with my two words in it, then I'll remember that they go together." Here is his story: *The towtruck pulls the car*. And he said it to himself two times.
>
> Just then the teacher looked at Bobby and said, "Towtruck," and quick as anything Bobby said, "car."
>
> Good word, Bobby!" said the teacher. "You didn't have to stop for a minute to think of your word, did you? Can you tell us how you remembered to say *car* when I said *towtruck*?"

The card and word games were not directly related to the story content. In the card games, a child was first shown pairs of cards of picture dominoes that went together. Then, she/he was either required to find a specific pair, or was given one member of a pair, and was required to find the other member. The word games followed the same general procedure. In all the games, the child was first supplied with syntactic encoding (*modeling*); next, she/he was instructed to formulate his/her own sentence mnemonic (imitation); and finally she/he participated without any instructions to use mnemonics (modeling removed). The word pairs used in the games varied from words having a strong relationship to each other, e.g., *bread* and *butter*, to words having a weak relationship, e.g., *train* and *peach*. Thus, a *shaping* procedure was used to provide a graded series of opportunities for learning to use mediational links. Modeling as an instructional technique is discussed in Chapter Ten.

A second method of teaching syntactic mediation examined by Ross and Ross involved *observational learning*. The experimenter read modified versions of the stories that did not require any verbal response from the subjects. She did not ask any questions about the stories. Using the game materials, the experimenter taught the subjects to play, and explained the score card procedure. A second adult, acting as a *model*, participated as a player and exhibited syntactic mediation strategies. Neither the model nor the experimenter made any comment about the model's use of mediational strategies. The model and the subjects continued to play the game for the next several weeks. The model also read the remainder of the stories to the children. In both groups, subjects participated in small group instruction and table games for three 20-minute periods for five weeks.

Both methods of instruction significantly improved the recall of the participating children beyond that of children in the control group. No significant difference in recall performance occurred between children in the two mnemonic groups. Furthermore, a *follow-up* two months later showed no loss of mediational efficiency in either group.

The discussion of mnemonic strategies is continued in the next chapter.

Chapter Four

Mnemonic Strategies: Three

This chapter is a continuation of the preceding two chapters. Additional mnemonic strategies are reviewed, as are methods of teaching application of the procedures, and supporting research evidence.

Loci, Pegword and Link Mnemonics

Loci, pegword and link mnemonic strategies employ *interactive visual imagery* to assist recall of a series of items on a list. During application of the loci method, an interactive image is developed to join the image of each of the individual items on a list to the image of each of a series of familiar, physical locations (*loci*). Similarly, with the pegword mnemonic, an interactive image is developed to join each of the items on the list to each of a series of *pegs*. Pegs are words that rhyme with numbers; these words, memorized by a learner prior to a particular memory task, may be used to assist recall of any list of items. With the link mnemonic, each of the items in a list is visualized interacting with each of the adjacent items in the list. All three mnemonic methods facilitate recall of the *serial order* in which a list of items was presented. In addition, the pegword method directly encodes the *numerical order* of each item in the list. To recall a particular item on the list that had been encoded by the loci or link methods, a performer must sequentially search each item in the list until the desired item is reached. However, when the pegword method has been employed, the performer may directly access any item in the list simply by referring to the corresponding pegword. Each of these mnemonic methods is discussed in the following paragraphs. Unfortunately, very little research data is available describing the use of these methods with children.

Loci mnemonics. The *loci method* of mnemonics was discussed earlier in the section on visual imagery. In the example described, a performer visualized an interaction between each of a list of grocery items, and each of a list of physical locations (loci) situated along a familiar route of travel. Spaghetti (list item) was visualized draped over the front gate (locus) leading to the individual's house, while apples (list item) were envisaged rolling down the inclined sidewalk (locus). A individual being instructed in the use of this method is usually advised to walk mentally along a familiar route, to identify a fixed sequence of distinctive and easily visualized, physical locations (loci) along the route and to visualize an interaction between each of the items on the list and each of the loci. When the items on the list are to be recalled, the learner is instructed to once again mentally retrace the route, look at each loci and identify the corresponding interacting item.

The method of loci may also be used to assist the recall of a *speech*. In fact, the loci method was first developed by Roman orators to remember the content and sequence of speeches. In this application, the content of a speech was reduced to a series of visual images in which each image representing an important word or idea in the speech was *visualized interacting* with each of the corresponding loci.

Crovitz (1970) conducted a study in which subjects were required to remember 40 words in sequence using a street map on which 20 loci had been established. The experimental subjects were told to visualize interacting images for each item and each loci. Because there were 40 items and 20 loci, the imaginary walk along the street route had to be taken twice. The average sequential recall was 34 out of 40 items; most subjects recalled more than 35 items. Apparently, having two items placed at each loci did not interfere with recall.

Once a series of *loci* have been identified, they can be *used repeatedly* to memorize and recall different lists of items. Each new set of interactive images tends to obliterate the old ones, that is, *retroactive interference* occurs. Thus, the method is most useful for short-term recall of a list of items. Not much *proactive interference* exists in which imagery developed for one list interferes with the recall of later lists (Bellezza, 1981).

Pegword mnemonics. The pegword mnemonic, or *hook strategy*, provides a system of remembering numbers, nouns and the numerical order of nouns. To employ the method, one must first remember a list of pegwords referring to tangible objects that may be readily visualized. Each pegword rhymes with one of the cardinal numbers. For example, *one* is a *bun*, *two* is a *shoe*, *three* is a *tree*, etc. The list of pegwords should be sufficiently well rehearsed so that given a number such as *eight*, one can rapidly recall the corresponding pegword *plate*; or, conversely, given a pegword such as *pen*, one can rapidly retrieve the corresponding number *ten*. Thus, given the numbers 2, 5, 8 and 3 to recall, one can translate the numbers into their corresponding pegwords, and employ *syntactic encoding* and *visual imagery* to visualize a *shoe*, stuck in a *hive* on top of a *gate* under a *tree*.

A more typical application of the method is to recall the numerical order of a list of items such as: 1. car, 2. apple, 3. book, etc. Once again, visual imagery is employed and the pegword and its corresponding list item are visualized as interacting with each other. For example, a *car* is visualized shooting out of the barrel of a *gun*(1); similarly, the image is conjured of a *shoe*(2) filled with apples. Thus, given any number, one could recall the corresponding item in the list. For example, given the number *two*, one would recall the previously learned pegword *shoe* and the interacting image of the apples; thus, item two is an apple. Also, using the reverse operation, given an item in the list, e.g., *car*, one can rapidly recall its numerical position in the list, e.g., car shooting out of a gun (1). The pegword also facilitates sequential retrieval of each of the items in the list in their numerical order. The pegwords most commonly employed are listed below; the words in parentheses are alternative pegwords. Pegwords eleven to twenty were developed by Bower and Reitman (1972).

one = bun (gun)	11 = penny one, hotdog bun
two = shoe	12 = penny two, airplane glue
three = tree	13 = penny three, bumble *bee*
four = door	14 = penny four, grocery store
five = hive (knives)	15 = penny five, big *bee* hive
six = sticks	16 = penny six, magic tricks
seven = oven (heaven)	17 = penny seven, go to heaven
eight = gate (plate)	18 = penny eight, golden gate
nine = line (wine)	19 = penny nine, ball of twine
ten = pen (hen)	20 = penny ten, ball point pen

Several considerations must be made in the choice of suitable pegwords. Bellezza (1981) recommended that, if more than one stimulus is being encoded in any mnemonic operation, each specific encoding should be discriminable from each of the others. For example, in the pegword mnemonic system, the rhyming pegwords 1 = *bun*, and 2 = *shoe* are discriminable auditorially, visually and semantically. However, in some renditions of the pegword mnemonic, various confusions may arise. For example, the visual image of 4 = *door* and 8 = *gate* may be confused because the visualized images of a gate and a door share common characteristics. The images would be more discriminable, if 4 = *door* and 8 = *plate*. Confusion may also exist between the numbers from 1 to 10, and the corresponding numbers from 11 to 20. For example, although the numbers *2* and *12* refer, respectively, to *shoe* and *glue*, the numbers 1 and 11 both refer to a *bun*. A similar situation may occur between the numbers 8 and 18 (*gate*), and 10 and 20 (*pen*). Also, both the numbers 13 and 15 refer to *bees*. Additional problems may occur for some age levels with the abstract nature of the pegwords. For example, both the numbers 7 and 17 refer to heaven.

Whether or not, and how, any of these or other variables influence the effectiveness of recall can only be determined by controlled experimental analysis. Paivio (1968), for example, studied the effects upon the recall by *college students* of *abstract*, rhyming pegwords: 1 = fun, 2 = true, 3 = free, 4 = fore, 5 = live, 6 = tricks, 7 = given, 8 = fate, 9 = time and 10 = sin. The result of the study clearly demonstrated that recall was better when a concrete or an abstract pegword method was used than it was when no pegword mnemonic was used. Given directions to imagine the abstract or concrete words (depending on the respective experimental group) interacting with the items in the recall list, recall increased dramatically over the condition in which no pegword was used. Alternatively, the use of the pegwords, either concrete or abstract, *without imagery*, had no beneficial effect on recall. If anything, without imagery, recall tended to be lower with the use of the mnemonic than under the conditions in which no mnemonic was used. This study illustrates the importance of imagery in the use of the pegword mnemonic. Paradoxically, however, the study also shows that whether the pegwords are concrete or abstract is of little consequence with the college population studied. This observation is in contrast to the evidence produced by Paivio (1971) in other studies showing that concrete words are easier to visualize and lead to better retention than are abstract words. Whether the results of these studies may be generalized to the performance of children remains to be demonstrated.

The *rate* at which items to be recalled are presented to college subjects influences the effectiveness with which they can employ pegword mnemonics. Bugelski, Kidd and Segmen (1968) found that subjects using the pegword system performed better than control subjects did only at the slower presentation rates of four and eight seconds per item. At rapid rates of presentation, there is presumably insufficient time to indulge in the encoding necessary for success.

The list of *pegwords* that one initially memorizes can be *used repeatedly* to assist the memorization of a number of different lists of items. However, *retroactive interference* may occur in which the learning of one list may interfere with the recall of previously learned lists. Therefore, the pegword mnemonic is most useful for short-term recall. Alternatively, as Bower and Reitman (1972) have demonstrated with college students, a *cumulative pegword mnemonic* may be employed in the recall of items from several lists. In this procedure, one learns the first list of items applying the pegword mnemonic in the usual manner. However, when the second and each of the successive lists are memorized, the first item in the second list is added to the image developed for the first item in the first list. Similarly, a cumulative image is developed for the second items in each list. For example, suppose the third word in lists one, two and three were, respectively, *swing, cigar* and *fish*. Using the pegword *three* = *tree*, a cumulative image is developed. For list one, the image may be of a *swing* hanging from a *tree*; for list two, the image may be elaborated to a *cigar* on a *swing* hanging from a *tree*; and for list three, the image may be of a *fish* smoking a *cigar* on a *swing* hanging from a *tree*. The results of the study indicated that subjects who used the *conventional* pegword method for each list suffered large amounts of retroactive interference. However, use of the progressive elaboration pegword method dramatically improved recall after one week. The loci and pegword mnemonics produced similar results in this study.

Link mnemonics. The Link mnemonic offers an alternative to the pegword, "one is a bun," method of recalling a list of items. Each of a number of items to be recalled is linked in a series of *overlapping images*. The overlapping series of images associating pairs of items in a sequence act like interlocking links in a chain. The method is employed in the following manner:

(a) Given a list of unrelated items, such as a shopping list: e.g., batteries, nylons, toothpaste, etc.,

(b) form a visual image of the first two items;

(c) form an interactive visual image between the first two items, e.g., visualize a nylon stocking filled to gross proportions with hundreds of flashlight batteries;

(d) visualize the third item;

(e) create an interactive visual image between the second and third item, e.g., visualize nylon stockings being squeezed from toothpaste tubes;

(f) continue the procedure until overlapping interactive visual images have been formed between each item in the list and each preceding and subsequent item.

Unlike the pegword mnemonic strategy, where one can directly access any particular item in a list by recalling the *pegword* with which the item was associated, with a link mnemonic, a particular item can be accessed only when recall proceeds sequentially through the list. Thus, recall of the image of batteries stuffed into a nylon cues the image of nylons being squeezed from toothpaste tubes. There is always a danger with this method that, if a *link* in the chain is *broken*, the remainder of the chain may be lost. This disadvantage is not found in the pegword mnemonic, as each item is coded individually. Roediger (1980) suggested a simple procedure designed to insure that the first item in a list is not forgotten. He suggested that rather than starting the chain with an interactive image between the first two items in a list, one should link the first item in the list with an object commonly found in the environment. This method provides a means of establishing the *primary associative link* discussed in Chapter Two.

In addition, the *pegword* strategy automatically codes the *numerical order* of each item. Although the numerical order of items may also be obtained, when a linking strategy has been used, decoding is less direct and is usually more difficult than is the case when a pegword strategy has been employed.

Roediger (1980) conducted a *comparison* of the effectiveness of several mnemonic methods used by *undergraduate* students. Control subjects were told to singly and cumulatively repeat high imagery words presented to them. Experimental subjects were taught to use imagery, loci, link or pegword mnemonics. Immediate recall, and recall after 24 hours, where credit was given for recalling a word in any order produced the following results:

[Loci; Pegword > link] > [Imagery; Rehearsal]

No significant difference was found between the loci and pegword methods, or between imagery and rehearsal. Recall after 24 hours, when credit was given only if a word was recalled in the appropriate numbered position, produced the following results:

[Link; Loci; Pegword] > [Imagery; Rehearsal]

No significant difference was found between the methods listed within each bracket.

Semantic Encoding

Semantic memory is based on the *knowledge* a person possesses about words, meanings, relations, concepts, symbols and rules, etc. (Brown, 1975). According to Tulving (1972) semantic memory is based on one's stable, long-term knowledge of language and how to use it. As described in Chapter One, Craik and Lockhart (1972) proposed a levels of processing model of memory. At a shallow depth, a stimulus is analyzed and stored in memory in terms of its surface, visual or auditory qualities. *Conceptual, semantic*, or *associative* analysis of a stimulus involves the greatest depth of processing, and according to Craik and Lockhart, leads to a stronger, more *elaborate* and durable memory trace.

Engle and Nagle (1979) conducted an interesting study of the effects of levels of processing on educable mentally handicapped students in grades five and six. The study is particularly noteworthy because of its use of *modeling* as an instructional technique, and the inclusion of *maintenance* and *generalization* measures of learning. Subjects were assigned to one of three experimental conditions. In the *semantic* condition, each subject was told that the best way to remember a word (concrete noun) was to think of its *meaning*, try to think of personal *experiences* with the object, think of *functions* of the object and try to remember other objects in the list within the same category. Note that although *categorizing* may be considered as a separate mnemonic technique that may be used independently, categorizing may also be a part of a semantic analysis of a word's meaning and conceptual and associative characteristics. Semantic encoding may also be conducted without categorizing.

Subjects in the *repetition* condition were told that the best way to remember a word was to repeat its label over and over again, either covertly or overtly. In the *acoustic* condition, subjects were encouraged to think of the sound of the word, and to repeat the initial sound over and over again, either overtly or covertly.

For each of the three conditions, *videotapes* were used to *model* the mnemonic strategy appropriate to each experimental group. The tapes depicted a woman experimenter and a subject using the mnemonic strategy during two trials of the experimental task. The subject in the tape was a college-age woman chosen to look and talk in a manner similar to the experimental subjects. In each 10 to 12 minute tape, the model's recall and clustering were perfect.

Before each tape, the experimenter explained to each subject that they would be taught how to remember better; the strategy used for the particular experimental condition was explained. Each subject was then shown the video and was told to learn the words in the same manner as demonstrated in the video. This session was then followed by the initial trial of the first training list consisting of 20 items presented at a rate of 10 seconds each. As each picture was presented, the experimenter prompted the child as to the strategy to be used, and asked the child questions relevant to the condition. Two additional trials followed. These trials involved different orderings of the same list, and the experimenter prompted each subject during input as on the first trial.

Post-tests were conducted immediately following instruction, seven days later and after seven months. The post-tests consisted of a *new* list of words; subjects were not reminded to use the strategies. These tests provided a measure of *maintenance* and *generalization* of learning. On the first and second post-tests, subjects in the semantic condition were superior to those in the repetition and acoustic conditions. The semantic strategy had almost as much effect after seven days as it did immediately following training. No significant difference in recall existed between subjects in the three groups seven months after training. However, the use of prompting on a second test was effective in quickly improving the performance of subjects in the semantic condition. In view of the previous discussion about the relationship between semantic analysis and categorizing, it is interesting to note that subjects in the semantic condition clustered at a rate greater than what would be expected by chance seven days after training, in the absence of any prompts to do so.

Bugelski (1970) described a second type of semantic mnemonic encoding in addition to that of analyzing the meaning and the conceptual and associative features of words. In the method described by Bugelski, an *abstract word* is *transformed* into a *semantically equivalent* word that has a higher imagery value. In an example provided by Bellezza (1981), the word *origin* is transformed into *egg*. Later, when the image of egg is recalled, it is decoded into the semantically equivalent word *origin*. Bellezza pointed out that decoding of this nature may be more difficult than decoding the image *dog* into the word *dog*.

Episodic Memory

Episodic memory, a term coined by Tulving (1972), is concerned with the storage and retrieval of personally experienced events or episodes. Recall of an episodic memory is usually reproductive—the event is recalled as it was experienced. For instance, one may recall the episode of eating a club sandwich (event) yesterday (time) at the Chablis Restaurant (place). Unlike semantic recall, with episodic recall one is not required to understand the meaning of the event or the relationship among its parts. In fact, the information coded in episodic memory may not be meaningful. For example, one may recall that a nonsense word *gloim* occurred at a particular point in a list of nonsense words. There is no meaning in either the word or its location.

In accord with Craik and Lockhart's (1972) depth of processing model, one would predict that episodic coding would involve *shallow processing* and that it would not produce durable memories. Wingfield and Byrnes (1981) described episodic memory as being highly susceptible to *interference* and readily subject to forgetting. Thus, episodic memory is not usually considered to be a mnemonic strategy.

On the other hand, in actual application, there is frequently an *interaction* between *episodic* and *semantic* methods that may lead to enhanced recall. For example, several months ago, I was introduced to my new neighbor Heinz (episode) in front of his house (place). I can still clearly recall the event (episodic recall). However, had I not combined episodic and semantic recall, I would probably not be able to remember that the low meaning and low imagery word, Heinz, was my neighbor's name. To me there was no readily apparent way to associate the word Heinz with the appearance or style of my neighbor. Luckily, I observed that the front door of his house is red, like the color of Heinz Ketchup (semantic encoding). Thus, to recall my neighbor's name, I recall the event of our introduction, visualize the front door (high imagery), associate it with Heinz Ketchup (high imagery) and recall my neighbor's name. This technique of combining imagery with episodic and semantic recall has been personally very useful. A review of the research literature, however, does not reveal that application of the method has been experimentally evaluated.

Phonetic Encoding

Phonetic encoding is a mnemonic technique involving the translation of an abstract and/or unfamiliar word into a similar sounding, more familiar, concrete, high imagery word. Craik and Lockhart (1972) have suggested that because *phonetic* encoding takes place at a more shallow level of processing than that at which *semantic* encoding is conducted, it will produce a weaker memory.

Using phonetic encoding, one might translate the name *Helen* into *melon*. Because of the high phonetic association of these words, if a melon were visualized, the name *Helen* would likely be readily recalled. The phonetic mnemonic does not necessarily provide a primary associative link between the original stimulus, the appearance of Helen and the image of a melon. Thus, if Helen were to appear, one might not readily think of a melon, and thereby recall the name Helen. However, if the phonetic mnemonic were used in conjunction with *semantic* encoding, a critical link between some characteristic of Helen and the image of a melon might be established. If, for example, Helen was *rotund*, one might have little difficulty thinking of a melon, and thereby recall the name Helen.

Phonetic encoding may also be used in conjunction with the *link* method of mnemonics. For example, the names *Frank, Don* and *Paul* may be translated into the similar sounding, high imagery nouns *crank, con* and *pole*. The link mnemonic may then be used to associate the images into interacting pairs of images, such as a *crank* being turned by a *con* to raise a *pole*. Phonetic encoding also forms the basis of the *keyword* mnemonic discussed in the next section. The keyword method is used to assist the recall of new vocabulary words and their meaning. For example, the French word for book is *livre* (pronounced leave). Using phonetic encoding, one may translate *livre* into *leaf* and visualize leaves pressed within a book.

Keyword Mnemonics

The keyword method of mnemonics developed by Atkinson and Raugh (1975) has direct application to the teaching of foreign and native language *vocabulary* and *meaning*. A number of additional educational applications, described below, have been studied.

In *foreign language instruction*, the keyword mnemonic involves the establishment of a *phonetic* and an *imagery* connection between a foreign word and its native language equivalent. The phonetic link reminds the learner of the relevant native language word, while the imagery link provides a clue to the meaning of the foreign word. The procedure is as follows. In the first stage, the learner associates all or part of the unfamiliar foreign word with a similar sounding English word, preferably a concrete noun. The English word is the *keyword* to which both the phonetic and imagery links are attached. In the second stage, a mental image is formed of the keyword interacting with a word representing the meaning of the foreign word.

The following *example* from Atkinson and Raugh demonstrates the procedure. In the first stage, the Spanish word *carta*, meaning *letter*, is associated with the similar sounding English word *cart*. Thus, the phonetic link is established between the foreign word and a similar sounding, concrete, English keyword. In the next stage, a mental image is formed of the keyword *cart* interacting with the word representing the meaning of the foreign word, *letter*. For example, a shopping cart may be visualized carrying a *letter*. Later when given the Spanish word *carta*, through phonetic association one may recall the English keyword *cart*, thereby evoking the image of the shopping cart, and the word *letter* representing the meaning of the Spanish word. Conversely, the learner, given the word *letter*, may retrieve the Spanish word *carta*. Obviously, selection of a suitable keyword is important. The keyword should (a) sound as much as possible like a part (not necessarily all) of the foreign word, (b) be concrete and readily form a mental image, (c) readily form a memorable mental image linking the keyword and the English translation and (d) be different from other keywords used to learn a list of foreign vocabulary words.

Following an extensive review of the literature in the use of the mnemonic keyword method, Pressley, Levin and Delaney (1982) conclude that the evidence is overwhelming that use of the keyword method, as applied to recall of vocabulary definitions, greatly facilitates performance. The keyword mnemonic method has been successfully employed with:

(a) abstract and concrete words;

(b) words from different grammatical classes: action verbs and a variety of complex (for children) English nouns, such as *surplus*, verbs, e.g., *persuade*, and adjectives like *quaint*;

(c) various languages, such as Spanish, Russian, Latin, French, German, Navajo, Hebrew, Malay, and English;

(d) subjects from three years of age to adults; good and poor vocabulary learners as well as native and foreign English speakers;

(e) keywords provided by the experimenter, or generated by learners. In many experiments, no significant difference between the two sources of keywords has been found, but the results have been inconsistent. Each procedure may have different effects upon various populations of learners. For example, McGivern (1981) found that children with greater vocabulary knowledge benefitted more from generating their own keywords than from keywords provided by the experimenter, whereas children with less vocabulary knowledge experienced comparable benefits from generated and provided keywords. As it becomes more difficult to derive keywords for particular types of vocabulary words, it is probable that experimenter provided keywords would prove more effective (Levin, 1981).

In addition, the following has been found:

(a) Several studies of children in the second and sixth grades and of adults have shown that providing pictures of the interaction between the keyword and the word representing the meaning of the foreign word have led to higher recall than having subjects generate their own images.

(b) With respect to older children and adults, the cost of constructing interactive illustrations as described in (a), above, outweighs the slight benefit produced by such illustrations. On the other hand, if the materials to be linked are complex and do not lend themselves to readily generated images, or are used with populations for which one or more of the steps in the keyword method are difficult, prepared illustrations may serve an advantage.

(c) The keyword method using *imagery* to link the keyword to the meaning word is slightly superior to the *sentence method* in which the keyword and the meaning word are linked together in a sentence mnemonic.

(d) The keyword method has been successfully employed with whole classrooms and small groups of elementary and junior high school students.

(e) The method is versatile and has been employed with grade eight students to attach a persons name to a number of pieces of biographical information (Levin, Shriberg, Miller, McCormack and Levin 1980; Lewisohn, Danaher and Kikel, 1977).

(f) The method produces better results than those obtained by other more conventional methods of teaching vocabulary, such as (a) learning the words in context, (b) finding root words and (c) learning synonyms and antonyms (Johnson, 1974); or (d) presenting vocabulary words in meaningful sentences, (e) having students discriminate correct from incorrect use of the words in sentences and (f) having subjects generate their own meaningful sentences (Pressley, Levin and Miller, in press).

McCarty (1980) and Lewisohn, Danaher and Kikel (1977) conducted studies demonstrating successful use of the keyword method to promote recall of *name-face associations*. Subjects in these studies generated keywords for names, e.g., *con* and *rat* for *Conrad*, and then formed an interactive image involving the keyword referent and a prominent facial feature. For example, one could imagine a prisoner, a *con*, riding a *rat* while sliding down a *nose*.

Teaching the use of keyword mnemonics. English-speaking children in the fourth grade have been taught a number of *abstract* English verbs, such as *persuade, hesitate, object, glisten* and *resolve*, using the keyword method (Levin, McCormick, Miller, Berry and Pressley, 1982). In this study, children were instructed to learn the meaning of the words by following two steps. The students were asked to learn a keyword (word clue) for each vocabulary word. The keyword was a word (or words) phonetically similar to a salient part (or all) of the vocabulary word (e.g., *purse* for *persuade*, or *he's a date* for *hesitate*). Each item was randomly presented on a 5" x 8" card that contained both the vocabulary word and the keyword. After all of the vocabulary items and keywords had been read once, each child was asked to supply the keyword when presented with just the vocabulary word typed on one side of the card. If a child hesitated, or gave a wrong response, the correct answer was immediately displayed as the experimenter turned the card over. This procedure was repeated twice for each student. Most children were able to respond without error at the end of two trials.

In the second stage of instruction, students were asked to learn the meaning of the twelve vocabulary words. The children were instructed to remember the content of a colored *line-drawing* (see Figure 4.1) that contained a representation of (a) the keyword interacting with (b) the definition of the vocabulary word. In addition, each 8.5 x 11-inch illustration had the vocabulary word and its definition printed at the bottom, along with the captioned dialogue of the two central figures in the illustration. One character's utterance contained the keyword, while the utterance of the other character contained the vocabulary word. The sentence was constructed so that the meaning of the vocabulary word could not be ascertained directly from the sentence. As each picture was displayed, the experimenter read the material at the bottom of the illustration and the two-sentence conversation. Each child was then given 15 seconds to study each picture.

In the *testing* phase of the experiment, each student was presented, in a random order, with each vocabulary word typed on a card and was asked the meaning of the card. If a child did not provide a definition of the word, the experimenter prompted the student by saying "... (vocabulary item) means when you ...?" Students were given as much time as they needed to respond to each item. The results of the study indicated that the children taught by the keyword method obtained 82.8 percent correct, while the control subjects, taught by an alternative, instructionally sound method, obtained only 55 percent correct. The article by

Figure 4.1. Shows Vocabulary Word "Persuade"
Interacting with Keyword "Purse." (Levin, McCormick,
Miller, Berry & Pressley, 1982, p. 124)

Levin *et al.* (1982) describes a second study in which the keyword method was successfully compared with several alternative methods for teaching vocabulary that are described in considerable detail in the report.

An adaptation of the keyword method has also been employed to teach fourth and fifth grade students the U.S. states and their capitals (Levin, Shriberg, Miller, McCormick and Levin, 1980). The adaptation involved *two steps* rather than the customary three step procedure. In the first step, the learner formed an association between the name of the state and the keyword for that state. In step two, using a different keyword, the learner formed an association between the name of the capital and the keyword for the capital. Finally, the two keywords are linked by a visual image, in this case, a line-drawing in which the two keyword referents are related to each other. The following teaching procedure was employed.

The students were first asked to learn keywords (word clues) for each of the states, for example, *marry* for *Maryland*. The entire list of 12 state-keyword pairs were read to each student, one pair at a time. As the experimenter held up a randomly selected index card with a state and keyword typed on it, she said, "The word clue for . . . (state) is . . . (keyword)." After all of the states and keywords had been read once, each child was shown the name of the state typed on another deck of cards, and was asked to supply the appropriate keyword. Correction procedures similar to those used in previously described studies were employed.

In the second stage of the study, similar instructional procedures were employed to *teach* a *word clue* for the capital city of each state. For example, for the capital of Maryland, Annapolis, subjects were taught *apple*. Because students would ultimately be tested on their recall of the correct capital for each state, testing in this phase was the reverse of that used in phase one. In this phase, students had to produce the name of the capital city, given the associated keyword, rather than produce the keyword, given the capital. Because it had been found that in foreign language vocabulary tasks, *backward keyword learning* is more difficult than the *forward* process, students were given up to five trials (in contrast to three trials in the state-keyword phase) to produce all of the capital cities upon presentation of the keyword.

In the final stage, subjects were shown a picture displaying the previously learned word clue for the state, and the word clue for the capital city. The students were told that they should remember those pictures to help them learn the state capitals, because later they would be asked to name the capital city for each state. In the pictures, the keyword for the state was related to that for the corresponding capital city as depicted in Figure 4.2. The experimenter said, "The capital of *Maryland* is *Annapolis*. Here is a picture of two apples getting married." Students were given 15 seconds to study the picture.

On the second day, after the subjects had been taught 12 states and capitals using the keyword method, they were given an additional 13 pairs of states and capitals to learn, in any manner they wished. This task was designed to see if the students would spontaneously employ the keyword approach on the new task.

*Figure 4.2. Shows Keyword for Name
of State Interacting with Keyword for
Name of State Capital. (Levin, Shriberg,
Miller, McCormick & Levin, 1980, p. 188)*

The evidence obtained indicated that the students did not *transfer* the keyword strategy. The one student who tried to do so applied the method ineffectively.

That transfer did not occur is not surprising. In the initial task of learning state names and capitals, the students were given two *experimenter-derived keywords* and an *experimenter-derived picture* depicting an interaction between the two keywords. In the transfer task, subjects applying the keyword method were required to derive two keywords and to develop an appropriate interactive picture. The transfer task required a number of skills that had not been taught in the first part of the study. Thus, the experiment did not evaluate transfer of skills learned to a new situation parallel to that in which the skills were initially learned; the task actually required the learning of previously untaught skills, and therefore cannot be considered a simple test of transfer.

Nevertheless, after learning the first set of states and capitals, the students in the keyword group obtained an average of 78 percent correct, while the control group had an average of 65.9 percent. On the second day of the study, students previously using the keyword method were allowed to use any method to learn a second set of states and capitals. Students previously in the control group were taught to use the keyword method. On the third day, both groups were given a test of the states and capitals learned on the first day. The students who had used the keyword method, at that time, recalled an average of 71.2 percent of the items, while the students in the control group recalled only 36.4 percent. Thus, it is apparent that the keyword method enhances both *acquisition* and *retention*. The data also indicate that a delayed (*maintenance*) rather than an immediate test of skills more accurately represents the benefit of the keyword method.

As was previously mentioned, there is a *sentence version* of the keyword method in which the keyword and the definition of the vocabulary word are placed in a meaningful sentence. Consider, for example, the Spanish word *carta* meaning (postal) letter. Using the keyword *cart*, a learner might generate a sentence such as, "The cart carries the letter" (Pressley, Levin and Miller, 1982). A study of college students by Pressley *et al.* compared the effectivenss of the *imagery keyword* and the sentence keyword methods in relation to three non-keyword techniques for learning vocabulary. The keyword methods were superior to the non-keyword methods, and the imagery keyword method was superior to the sentence method.

Pressley, Levin and Miller (1981) suggested that if the keyword method is to be employed in actual *classroom* rather then *experimental conditions*, some guidelines should be followed. They suggested that concrete stimulus support is required with children, especially those ten years of age and younger. For younger children, simple instructions to visualize may need to be supplemented by experimenter-provided illustrations of keywords and definition referents. As Paivio (1980) reported, children seven years of age or younger cannot use imagery effectively, when they have to construct their own images, but they can do so if interactive pictures are provided. Moreover, according to Pressley and Levin (1978), facilitation may occur only if subjects are provided with illustrations in which the interaction between the keyword and definition referent is made explicit. For example, Pressley and Levin presented lists of simple Spanish words to children in the second and sixth grade. The children in the second grade did not benefit from instructions to use an imagery-based version of the keyword method, when the keywords and translations were presented verbally, but did do so when the materials were presented pictorially. Children in the sixth grade could execute the keyword strategy regardless of the mode of materials presented.

Two additional studies of interest are briefly described in the following two paragraphs. Levin, Shriberg and Berry (1983) successfully used the keyword mnemonic with *prose* passages to teach students in the eighth grade to recall the *abstract attributes* of fictional towns. Abstract attributes such as *considerable wealth, abundant natural resources* and *advances in technology* were pictorially represented. The results of the study indicated that pictures in which the attributes were separately represented did not enhance recall; when the attributes were combined in a picture that incorporated the keyword, performance was dramatically improved.

In a study conducted by Mastropieri, Scruggs, Logan and Levin (1984), 300 mildly handicapped and gifted students as well as some nonexceptional junior high students were instructed in the use of the keyword mnemonic in social studies, science and language. Performance on all recall measures indicated that students who had received mnemonic instruction were consistently superior to students in both direct instruction and free-study conditions, typically by margins of two to one.

First-Letter Recoding

First-letter recoding involves using the first letter of several words to form a single word. For example, the first letter of each of the names of the Great Lakes, Huron, Ontario, Michigan and Erie, may be used to form the word *HOME* (Higbee, 1977). The reader may also remember the example provided in Chapter Two in which the trigonometric functions involving the *sine, cosine* and *tangent* were represented in the *acronym SOH-CAH-TOA*. The method may also be used in conjunction with a syntactic (sentence) mnemonic. For example, the first letter of each of the planets in order from the Sun: Mercury, Venus, Earth, Mars, Jupiter, Saturn, Uranus, Neptune and Pluto may be used as the first letter of each of the words in the following sentence, "Men Very Easily Make Jugs Serve Useful Nocturnal Purposes" (Higbee, 1977).

Bellezza (1981) reported that research on the *effectiveness* of the first-letter mnemonic has produced mixed results. Some studies have found that material coded by the first-letter mnemonic method was not always as well retained as when other methods were used. However, the first-letter mnemonic has been found to be superior to attempts to recall without the use of mnemonics (Bellezza, 1981). One possible source of weakness of the first-letter mnemonic is illustrated in each of the previously described examples. None of the encodings has a primary associative link with, respectively, the Great Lakes, trigonometry or the planets. Furthermore, interactive images are not readily formed between the word or sentence encoding, and the reference lakes, functions or planets. These weaknesses, however, would seem to be more a problem with specific applications of the method rather than a weakness of the approach, in general.

As with any mnemonic method, retrieval of information by the first-letter mnemonic will be improved if the encoded form of the information is associated with the referent information. For instance, retrieval may be improved by coding the grocery list: *p*eas, *s*quash, *c*elery, *t*urnips and *c*orn as CoST CuP rather than as CaT CoPS. In the first coding, *cost* relates to *store*, and *cup* relates to *cooking*; the second set of words do not relate to the retrieval referent stimuli, and may be more difficult to recall.

Number Related Mnemonics

Four of the better known mnemonic methods developed to aid recall of numbers are: (a) chunking, (b) identification of number patterns, (c) pegwords and (d) digit-consonant encoding. The use of *chunking* was discussed in an earlier section of this text. For example, a nine digit (or nine chunk) number such as 615372418 is difficult to recall, as it borders on the upper limit of the 7 (+ or -2) chunks of information that the average person can usually recall. When the information is reorganized into three chunks, 615-372-418, short-term recall is improved considerably. Chunking alone, however, does not usually lead to long-term retention.

Identification of *number patterns* involves the analysis of relationships between adjacent numbers. If a pattern can be identified, meaning, organization and predictability are added to an otherwise arbitrary sequence of stimuli. For instance, recall of the telephone number 4264860 may be enhanced by dividing the number into two chunks 426-4860. Recall may be further enhanced through identification of the "2-plus" pattern that relates all of the numbers: 2 + 2 = 4, the first number in the sequence; the third (6), fifth (8) and the seventh (0) numbers are each equal to the preceding number plus 2. The numbers in the second (2), fourth (4) and sixth (6) positions are calculated in the same manner. Thus, even if the number cannot be immediately recalled, knowledge of the pattern will permit reconstruction of the number.

Pegwords, as previously described, are high imagery words that rhyme with numbers. For example, the words, *bun, shoe* and *tree* rhyme with the numbers one, two and three. Thus, to remember that the third item in a list is *car*, one might visualize an interactive image between a *car* and *tree*. Then, to recall the third item in the list, one would recall three, the pegword *tree* and the interactive image between the *tree* and the *car*. These pegwords may also be used to translate each of the digits in a number into high imagery words and the words into a sentence. In this manner, pegword and syntactic mnemonics are combined. For example, the access number to a card operated computer banking system, 7985, may be translated into the pegwords: *heaven, line, gate* and *hive*. These words are then sequenced into a meaningful sentence, "*Heaven's line* (cued by the line on the back of the card) is in a *gate* (the card slot) to a *hive* (the buzzing of machine activity). This mnemonic encoding has several *associative links* to the *referent stimuli* that will strengthen storage of the coding in memory.

In 1648, Winckleman translated each of the ten numbers from 0 to 9 into a consonant *sound* (Paivio, 1971). One version of the *consonant-sound code* is as follows:

1	2	3	4	5	6	7	8	9	0
t,d	n	m	r	l	ch,sh	k	f,v	p,b	s,z
					g,j	(hard c)			

The rationale for some of these substitutions follows: *t* has one stroke like the number 1; n and m have 2 and 3 legs, respectively, corresponding to the numbers 2 and 3; *r* represents the number four because the *r-sound* is found in the word *four* in several languages; and the *l* corresponds to the Roman numeral for *50*. Some of the numbers are represented by more than one acoustic variant to increase the number of words that can be produced. Each number is translated into a letter. Words are then developed in which each *consonant* sound in the word unambiguously represents a number. For example, the date *1607* may be translated into the words: *dash a sack*, *d(1)ash(6) a s(0)ack(7)*. These words may be linked in a sentence together with the name of a person or event to which the date is related. Bellezza (1981) described the following example. Mr. Smith's telephone number, 546-4120, is coded into the words *large, red* and *nose*. Mr. Smith's name is translated into a high imagery keyword, *blacksmith*. Then an interactive image is developed and Mr. Smith with the large red nose is visualized working as a blacksmith.

The sentence "Satan may relish coffee pie" provides a method for recalling the consonant sound corresponding in order to each of the numbers in the consonant sound word encoding system (Bellezza, 1981). Note that "y" in the word *may* is not sounded and, therefore, does not represent a number.

Paivio and Desrochers (1979) conducted a fascinating study in which they combined *pegwords* and *digit consonant encoding* to assist *acquisition* and *rehearsal* of foreign language vocabulary. In this study 96 French pegwords were developed so that each *sounded* consonant in each word represented a letter in the same manner as described above: 1 = *t*he (ten); 2 = *n*oeud (knot) and 3 = *m*at (mast) . . .; 75 = *cle* (key) where *c* = 7 and *l* = 5. Only·high imagery words were selected. The first year *university students* participating in the study were given the list of 96 numbers, the corresponding French pegwords and the English translation of each pegword. Subjects were instructed to learn these keywords and the corresponding visual images for each number, to the point where each number presented suggested the French pegword and its visual image. Subjects were then given a list to learn, including 96 new French vocabulary words, and the corresponding English translation for each. For each of the new vocabulary words, the subjects were instructed to visualize an interacting image between the previously memorized pegword and the vocabulary word. Concrete and abstract words of low, medium and high familiarity were presented. One of the benefits of this mnemonic procedure is that an individual may mentally rehearse the list of new vocabulary words during any period in which she/he is not otherwise preoccupied with thought. For example, while walking to school, subjects could recall, in order, each of the numerical pegwords and the interactive image with the corresponding vocabulary word.

The authors reported that the method led to remarkably superior recall of both the French words and their English counterparts. The results were significantly better than those achieved by subjects who employed rote rehearsal strategies, regardless of the familiarity or concreteness of the vocabulary words. Subjects employing the method recalled three times as many French words using the interactive imagery as they did when they simply rehearsed the words together with their translations and associated pegwords.

Selection and Evaluation of Mnemonic Strategies
The following considerations, adapted from Bellezza (1981), provide a guideline for the selection and evaluation of mnemonic strategies.

1. Does the strategy enhance long- or short-term retention? For example, simple rehearsal does not lead to long-term storage.

2. How much training is required to master the strategy? For example, the digit-consonant technique may require considerable practice.

3. What level of cognitive functioning is prerequisite to acquisition of the strategy? Is the technique suitable to young children and developmentally delayed individuals?

4. How much time and effort is required to apply the strategy

in actual practice? Will time constraints make application impracti-
cal? Will the amount of work decrease motivation to apply the
strategy?

5. Is the strategy consistent with the learner's style? Some
techniques, regardless of their potential effectiveness, will not be
adopted by some individuals because of the nature of the strategy.

6. In what manner is information recalled? What are the
constraints with respect to speed of recall and the type of
information that is readily available? For example, some strategies
will not only permit recall of all of the items in a list, but also will
give direct access to the nth item, e.g., the peg word strategy.
Alternatively, when a story mnemonic is used, it may be necessary
to recall an entire story to retrieve the nth item.

7. Does the strategy interfere with comprehension? By relying
on a mnemonic technique, an individual may fail to see the
internal structure of information presented to him/her, and thus
fail to understand and remember it in terms of its underlying
schema. For example, Luria (1968) reported that the mnemonist
Shereshevskii would memorize sequences such as 4, 8, 12, 16 and
20 rather than notice the underlying rule.

8. Does application of the strategy interfere with concurrent
methods of learning?

9. Does application of the strategy result in interference with
other learned information? Does the strategy lead to proactive or
retroactive inhibition?

10. Does the strategy permit establishment of a primary
associative link? Can an association be established between the
recall demand cue (the event that indicates when recall is required)
and the first link in the mnemonic chain of storage and recall?

11. What is the generality of the strategy? Can it be used in a
variety of situations?

12. Does the manner in which information is stored facilitate
integration of related information? Sometimes the manner in
which information is coded transforms the information into a
unique form so that it becomes difficult to build a body of
associated information.

Chapter Five

Metamemory

Metamemory refers to *knowledge* about (a) one's *personal* memory storage and retrieval *capacity*, in relation to (b) particular memory tasks and to (c) mnemonic *strategies* that may be applicable to the task (Brown and Campione, 1977; Flavell and Wellman, 1976). Knowledge of one's personal memory capacity refers to an individual's awareness of his/her general memory *abilities* and *limitations*, as well as to information about one's current state, and its influence upon the ability to perform memory tasks. Knowledge of memory tasks refers to an understanding of the characteristics of tasks that affect one's ability to store and retrieve information. For example, task difficulty may be influenced by the amount of information to be remembered, whether the material is concrete or abstract, familiar or unfamiliar, and whether recall or recognition is required. Knowledge about memory strategies refers to one's knowledge about where, when and how to use particular mnemonic techniques, such as rehearsal, pegging, keyword or chunking. Thus, metamemory refers to knowledge about one's self, a task, potentially useful mnemonics strategies, as well as an awareness of the effect of the interaction of these variables in a particular time and place (Flavell and Wellman, 1977).

Application of metamemory involves:

    (a) deciding if it is likely that one may be required to recall currently available information that may not be present in future;

    (b) deciding on the relative importance of the information;

    (c) determining if long- or short-term retention is required.

    (d) predicting under what conditions the information may have to be recalled, e.g., recall or recognition, and the time available for retrieval;

    (e) examining the nature of the information to determine its memorability; reviewing its:

        —familiarity,
        —relationship to existing knowledge,
        —potential confusability,
        —organization,
        —magnitude,
        —concrete or abstract nature and
        —discriminating features;

    (f) deciding if it is likely that one will automatically recall the information, or whether a mnemonic strategy must be employed;

    (g) considering the amount of time available for processing;

    (h) reviewing the inventory of strategies; determining which strategies apply and reviewing the relative effectiveness of each method in the past;

    (i) adopting or modifying a strategy;

    (j) applying the strategy;

    (k) monitoring its effect; and

    (l) maintaining, modifying or abandoning the strategy in view of the feedback.

Distinguishing between situations that demand deliberate memorization skills and situations where memory will be more or less automatic is a particularly difficult task for a young child (Yendovitskaya, 1971). Similarly, spontaneous initiation of deliberate tactics of memorization, as a goal in itself, is atypical of the developmentally young (Brown, 1975).

The Development of Metamemory

    Preschool. Recognition memory is highly accurate throughout childhood. However, preschoolers rarely use mnemonic strategies to aid remembering. In fact, they may not even realize that the instruction to remember is an implicit invitation to be planful, and even if they do have this intention, they may not know how to fulfill it (Paris and Lindauer, 1976). For example, Appel, Cooper, McCarrell, Sims-Knight, Yussen and Flavell (1972) showed pictures to children of four, seven and eleven years of age under two instructional conditions: "to look at the pictures" or "to remember the pictures." The four-year-olds behaved the same way with both instructions, while other children employed study strategies when trying to remember. Myers and Perlmutter (1978) concluded from their study of memory *development* of children two to five years of age that there was little evidence of planful, deliberate use of mnemonic strategies or of age-related increases in the use of strategies in the age range studied. However, as Paris and Lindauer note, there is an important difference between being naive and being ignorant. *Preschoolers* can use strategies to aid recall, but appear to do so only when the strategy requires an external response or aid within the task that is highly familiar to them. Preschoolers will touch, point and look at a cup concealing a hidden object in order to remember it (Wellman, Ritter and Flavell, 1975) and will use spatial landmarks in trying to recall where someone lost an object (Acredolo, Pick and Olsen, 1975). Young children know that writing something on a note, tying a string around your finger or, better yet, having Mommy remind you are memory aids.

The nature of the *situation* in which children are asked to remember items may influence the nature of the response that they make (Paris and Lindauer), and influence the validity of the inferences that may be drawn about their behavior. For example, Istomina (1975), in a study described earlier in this text, presented a list of five words to remember to three- and seven-year-old children under two different conditions. In one condition, children were playing a *game* of grocery store and had to remember the items so that they could purchase them. In the other condition, children were simply told to remember the items. Children recalled nearly twice as many items in the *game playing* situation as in the *list learning* condition.

Flavell, Friedrichs and Hoyt (1970) found that over 50 percent of *preschoolers* unrealistically *predicted* the length of a series of pictures they could serially recall; fewer than 25 percent of second or third graders and very few fourth graders were unrealistic. Alternatively, Kreutzer, Leonard and Flavell (1975) found that even kindergarten children knew that a memory task was harder when one had a large number of items, whereas only older children knew that a recall task was harder when one had to learn two sets of words that were easily confusable.

Early school. Masur, McIntyre and Flavell (1973) presented students in the first and third grades and in college with a multi-trial, free-recall task to assess at which level the students would focus their *study-time* on items they had previously been unable to recall. On all trials but the first, the subjects were allowed to select only half of the total set of items for further study. Masur *et al.* found that students in the first grade and those in college did select previously unrecalled items for extra study, but this was not true of children in the first grade, who appeared to select items randomly.

Flavell, Beach and Chinsky (1966) presented pictures to children of five, seven and ten years of age and asked them to remember them over a brief delay. Few of the five-year-old children were observed to spontaneously rehearse the picture names, while most of the older children did.

Paris and Lindauer (1976) drew the following *conclusions* from their review of the literature. Before the age of nine or ten, on many memory tasks, children do not construct effective strategies that transform and reorganize information into consolidated chunks or units. They can profit when these relations are inherent in the stimuli or when directed to use appropriate strategies. Flavell (1970) described the problem as a *production deficiency* because it seemed to indicate a failure to produce a relevant activity rather than an inability to use the activity to mediate memory. Between five and twelve years of age, children show dramatic changes in their understanding of task parameters and generation of plans for remembering (Flavell and Wellman, 1977). Unfortunately, Paris and Lindauer report, there is not a clear picture of if, how or when metameory stimulates the development of memory strategies.

Teaching Metamemory

The majority of metamemory training studies conducted by
Ann Brown and her colleagues have been with *educable mentally
retarded* individuals of IQ 60 to 75. According to Brown (1978),
the general rationale for such studies with slow learning children
follows from a controversy concerning the benefit to memory
skills derived from training *specific* mnemonics. The general
picture to emerge is that educable mentally retarded children
readily respond to appropriate training and evidence a variety of
trained mnemonic skills accompanied by a satisfying improvement
in recall performance. Furthermore, there is some evidence of
maintenance. Brief instruction leads to temporary improvement;
however, less experienced memorizers show a marked tendency to
abandon a trained strategy when not explicitly instructed to
continue using it. Alternatively, a number of studies (cited in
Campione and Brown, 1978) have found that more *extended
training* can result in *durability* of a trained behavior for at least a
year, although the tendency of subjects to show such maintenance
does appear to be related to *developmental level*. Very young or
retarded individuals are more likely to abandon the strategy.
Unfortunately, evidence for *generalization* to new situations is
hard to find. The lack of convincing evidence of broad generalization of a trained mnemonic strategy indicates a poor *prognosis* for
obtaining educational benefits from such exercises, and this has
led some investigators to advance the view that efforts should be
directed at training *general* determinants of performance rather
than *specific* strategies. If one is interested in effecting improvement in a child's general performance on a variety of similar tasks,
then one must consider both the specific gains from training
(strategy use) and the general benefits (improved knowledge
concerning memory tasks) (Brown, 1978).

Brown (1978) reported on a metamemory training method
designed to improve *study-time* apportionment with *educable
mentally retarded* children. During pretesting, on each trial except
the first of a multi-trial, free-recall procedure, educable retarded
subjects were allowed to select half (6/12) of the to-be-remembered items to see if they would strategically select missed items
for extra study. Following pretesting, subjects were divided into

three groups for training, where the experimenter selected study items for the children. For the first group, the experimenter returned to the child those items missed on his/her prior free recall attempt. For the second group, the experimenter returned to the child the items he/she had recalled plus one new item (creeping strategy). The creeping strategy would enable the children to add just one extra item per trial, while permitting them to continue to review the previously recalled items. Thus, the students would gradually creep up to a better level of performance. This *creeping* technique appears to be similar in nature to the *shaping* procedure common to operant instructional programs. The third group of subjects received randomly selected items for review on each study trial. Following training, the children received posttests where they were again free, as on the pretests, to select whichever items they wished for study, with the restriction that they must not select more than six. The training results indicated that *younger children* benefitted from the imposed creeping strategy, but not from a condition where they were given either all of the missed items to review or a random selection of items to study. Alternatively, *older children* benefitted most from the condition where they were given all of the missed items to study, and little from the conditions where random items were studied or where the creeping strategy was used. According to the authors, the pattern of results obtained appeared to confirm that strategies, to be successful, must be compatible with the cognitive competency of the child.

Brown, Campione and Murphy (1977) conducted a study of *span estimation* with *educable mentally retarded* children of MA: 6 and of MA: 8. Each child was shown a series of cards with from one to ten items printed on each of them. Each card in the stack had one more item on it than was on the previous card. The child was asked to label the item(s) on each card as it was presented. The experimenter then asked "Suppose I showed you the card and said the name(s) of the picture(s) on it, and then covered it/them up; do you think you could say its/their name(s) back to me?" After the child responded, the instructions were repeated for each successive card in the series until the one containing ten items was presented, even if the subject had indicated that the number of items on a particular card was too long for him to recall. Following estimation on the seriated sets, the children were asked to estimate their spans on four ten-item sets, two categorized and two uncategorized. When the children had named all ten items on each card, the experimenter said, "If I covered them all up, how many do you think you could remember?" Following the establishment of each child's ability to estimate his/her recall capacity, all subjects were given two days of *training*. Half the subjects who were unrealistic in their estimations and half who were realistic received *explicit feedback*, and the remainder did not. Over the two-day period the subjects received ten lists, half *uncategorized* and half *categorized*. For each list, each child first estimated how many items she/he could recall, and then proceeded to attempt recall. The only difference between children receiving explicit feedback and the remaining children was that following each recall attempt, the experimenter told the subject, "good, you remembered N on that list" and placed N items on the left side of a toy bead counter. The child's score across the ten trials was, thereby, emphasized and always visible to him. The experimenter and each child reviewed this information repeatedly. The results of the study indicated that children (MA: 6) needed the explicit feedback before they would show any effects of training. While children (MA: 8) improved whether or not the feedback was explicit. The majority of children (MA: 6 and MA: 8) were unrealistic in their estimations. Following training in span estimation, children (MA: 8) improved under both explicit and implicit feedback conditions, while the younger children only benefited from explicit feedback. Three posttests of the effects of training revealed maintenance of training for the (MA: 8) subjects one year after training. However, the (MA: 6) subjects showed post-test improvement only on an immediate test. While long-term maintenance was found for older subjects, generalization to similar span estimation tests was not found.

Rather than *teach specific routines* tailored to the needs of a specific task, Campione and Brown (1978) attempted to train a more *general strategy*, such as, *self-testing*. As above, students of mean IQ: 70 and MA: 6-8 were asked to study a series of pictures until they felt that they could remember all of the pictures in order. Prior to intervention, performance on the task was exceedingly poor, and students regularly terminated study well before they were able to recall all the items. In the first phase of the study, two of the groups were trained in the use of *anticipation* or *rehearsal strategies* involving self-testing, while the third group was taught a *labelling strategy* that did not require self-testing. Anticipation involved saying the name of the picture on the next card in the series before looking at it, while sorting through the cards on successive passes. Rehearsal involved rehearsing the items in sets of three. Labelling involved simply labelling each item on successive passes through the deck of cards. As was expected, the subjects who simply labelled continued to perform poorly, while the subjects who had rehearsed or anticipated improved their accuracy significantly. For the MA: 8 subjects, the effects of training were *maintained* over one year, while the MA: 6 children reverted to pretraining levels of performance as soon as the experimenter stopped reminding them.

The second phase of the study, *generalization training*, took place about fifteen months after the end of the training sessions. This phase involved students who had successfully maintained adequate recall readiness for the list-learning task. The generalization task, thought to be representative of the type of study activity required in classrooms, asked each student to extract the *main ideas of prose* passages and recite the gist of the ideas in his own words. The research question asked was, would training on recall readiness on the simple rote, list-learning task help children on the more typical school study activity of preparing for gist recall of prose passages? These tasks were quite different; however, both of them required the same general *stop-check-study-recheck* routine.

During *training*, each subject was seen individually for a total of six days. No mention was made of prior testing. On each day the students studied and recalled two stories. The experimenter read each story to the students, and then the students read it back twice with the experimenter sounding-out and explaining any words with which the students had difficulty. The students were then told to read the stories over as many times as necessary to remember all that had happened.

The *results* of the study indicated that students trained in the use of task appropriate self-testing strategies did recall more than students in the control groups. Students previously trained in anticipation had a mean recall of 50 percent of the idea units in the stories; students trained in rehearsal recalled 49 percent; and both groups outperformed the labelling group that recalled a mean of only 35 percent of the idea units.

Brown and Palincsar (1982) recommended that rather than teach either *general* or *specific* skills, *intermediate* level skills or packages of skills may be more useful. Very specific skills, as previously described, are useful for the solution of very specific problems; however, these skills do not *generalize*. Alternatively, very general skills, although they generalize, may not be specific enough for the solution of particular types of problems. Newell (1979) describes a hierarchy of specific, intermediate and general skills.

Training studies may be *classified* into three broad categories: *blind, informed* and *self-control* (Brown and Palincsar, 1982). In blind studies trainees are not informed of the importance of the activities they are trained to use. The typical procedure in blind training is to tell the learner what they should do; however, the student is neither informed as to why he should act in a particular manner nor that the procedure aids performance. Blind training procedures fail to result in *maintenance* and *generalization* of the strategies trained.

Informed training involves instruction in the significance of the trained activity. For example, Kennedy and Miller (1976) showed that an instructed rehearsal strategy was more likely to be maintained in the absence of experimenter prompts, if it had been made clear to the student that the use of the strategy resulted in improved recall. Paris, Newman and McVey (1981) tested the effects of informing seven- and eight-year-old subjects of the benefits derived from using *grouping, labelling, cumulative rehearsal* and recalling by groups. The children were given a brief rationale for each of the procedures, and *feedback* was provided about performance after recall. During training, and on subsequent training probes, students who had been informed in this manner outperformed the students who had been uninformed.

The final category of training described by Brown and Palincsar was referred to as *self-control*. The main feature of this approach is the inclusion of explicit training of *general executive skills*, such as *planning, checking* and *monitoring*. The student is trained to produce and regulate the activity. Two studies of *mentally retarded* children MA: 8 (Brown and Barclay, 1976; Brown, Campione and Barclay, 1979) have produced *maintenance* over a one-year period, and *generalization* to quite different tasks. The younger children in these studies, MA: 6, showed only immediate effects of training and reverted to baseline levels of performance on maintenance probes. According to Brown and Palincsar, evidence is accumulating to suggest that an *ideal training package* would consist of practice in the use of task appropriate strategies, instruction concerning the significance of those activities, and instruction concerning the monitoring and control of strategy use.

Borkowski and Cavanaugh (1979) have described a number of steps that must be followed to achieve *generalization of executive functioning*.

> First, we need to identify several strategies each of which are operative in different learning situations. Second we need to train children on several strategies, making sure that they know when and how to apply them. Third, we need to train the instructional package so that common elements between training and generalization contexts are evident, and distractors minimal. Fourth, we need to develop child-generated search routines, probably through the use of self-instructional procedures, that encourage the child to analyze a task, scan his or her available strategic repertoire, and match the demands of the task with an appropriate strategy and retrieval plan. Fifth, we need to instruct children in such a way that we utilize whatever skills they possess, in order to bring each child to an awareness of the advantage of executive monitoring and decision-making in solving problems. Finally we may need to reinforce, in a very explicit way, successful executive functioning in order for it to come under the control of natural environmental contingencies, such as a child's good feelings about solving a difficult problem (p. 54).

Knowledge and Behavior

One of the *assumptions* underlying the training of metamemory is that there must be a close tie between what one knows about memory and how one goes about memorizing. Kail (1979), after review of the topic as it relates to children, concluded that metamemory, knowledge of particular methods of memory, will not automatically lead to activation of the associated memory behavior. Knowledge of mnemonic methods is necessary but not sufficient to induce the related memory behavior For example, Salatas and Flavell (1976) found that with children in the first grade there was not a relationship between *categorization* on memory trails and answers to metamemory questions about categorization.

Children may not be aware that categorizable sets of pictures are easy to recall and yet show category clustering in recall tests (Moynahan, 1973). Similarly, children who spontaneously group pictures by category during study may not identify this as a helpful memory strategy (Salatas and Flavell, 1976). Conversely, and perhaps most surprisingly, some children recognize the usefulness of a particular memory strategy, but do not employ it in actual test situations (Salatas and Flavell, 1976, in Waters, 1982).

Kramer, Nagle and Engle (1980) stated that there is currently little evidence indicating that teachers should concentrate on attempting to increase retarded children's knowledge of their memory system. *Metamemory alone appears to have little effect on memory performance (at least with developmentally young people).* In contrast, a study conducted by Waters (1982) found that with students in the eighth and tenth grade, knowledge about mnemonic strategies and their application was related to both reported use of mnemonics and performance on a paired associates learning task in the absence of specific training.

Results of various studies suggest that the *role of metamemory* in memory development *changes from the middle childhood years to adolescence*. While metamemory is not predictably related to the use of age appropriate strategies during elementary school, there is a positive relationship in later school years (Waters, 1982).

The failure to observe a strong relationship between metamemory and the use of mnemonic strategies could lead to the abandonment of efforts to improve metamemory in an effort to improve recall. Such an action would be regretful. If the statement made by Kail (1979) is valid, that knowledge of mnemonic methods is necessary but not sufficient to induce related memory behavior, then *training should focus not merely on teaching knowledge of mnemonic methods, but* also *on the application of that knowledge*. Methods of application and, as Ryan, Ledger, Short and Weed (1982) suggest, *generalization*, can be made an actual part of the training. Strategy use may be trained in multiple settings with a variety of tasks that require application and adaptation of the strategy. Prompts may be introduced to indicate when and how to apply a strategy. As the learner requires less assistance, the prompts may be systematically *faded* from use. *Cognitive behavior modification*, discussed in the next chapter, may be instrumental in teaching application of metamemory strategies.

Limitations of Metamemory Research Methods

Cavanaugh and Perlmutter (1982) have identified a number of limitations of metamemory studies that may account for some of the negative findings. These authors report that most investigations of the relationship between metamemory and memory have been *correlational*. Subjects were evaluated on some aspect of memory knowledge, and asked to perform a related memory task; then, measures of metamemory and memory performance were correlated. Studies based on this approach have yielded only moderate or low correlations between metamemory and memory. The first methodological problem is that correlational studies to date largely include only a *single index of metamemory*, usually *verbal self-report*. This is one of the weakest methods of assessing metamemory. The inclusion of only a few inquiries in interviews further compounds the problem. Finally, the rationale for selecting the particular questions that are used is often obscure. A *second short-coming* is that with only a few exceptions most of these studies only examined the relationship between metamemory and performance on a single task.

Brown (1978) has identified a number of problems associated with relying on *verbal reports* made by children. Reportedly, an experimenter responsible for running a study on which Brown was working asked her seven-year-old son how he would study a group of pictures to help remember them. He replied, without hesitation, that he would look at them; he always did that if he had to remember. Given the list, he carefully put all the pictures in taxonomic categories, spatially separated the categories, and proceeded to scan them systematically. Asked what he had done to remember, he replied that he looked at the pictures just like he said he would.

Another limitation of *self-reports* made by children comes from span-estimation studies. Brown reports that many of the children who would have been judged realistic in their estimations, if the experimenter had stopped at the first response, were quite happy to assert that a list of five was too difficult, while one of six was not, and to claim that seven was too many, but eight was okay. Whatever this indicates about a child's metamemory, it certainly suggests caution in accepting a single verbal response as a measure of awareness.

As was mentioned earlier, cognitive behavior modification may be a useful method for teaching the application of knowledge of mnemonic strategies. According to Campione and Murphy (1977), the elements of metacognitive processes include the ability to stop and think before attempting a problem, to ask oneself and others to determine if one recognizes the problem, to check solutions against reality by asking not "Is it right?" but "Is it reasonable?," to monitor attempts to learn, to see if they are working or worth the effort (cited in Meichenbaum and Asarnow, 1979). The similarity between these elements of metacognitive processes and the content of the *self-directing verbal statements* employed in *cognitive behavior modification* is quite apparent (Meichenbaum and Asarnow, 1979). The concern is with how one develops a training program to teach children to estimate task difficulty, to monitor and use a strategy, to adjust the strategy to task demands, and to make use of implicit and explicit information and feedback. How does one teach thinking, not so much *what* to think, but *how* to think? (Meichenbaum and Asarnow). The techniques of cognitive behavior modification are discussed in the next chapter.

Chapter Six

Cognitive Behavior Modification

Cognitive behavior modification is a therapeutic or *teaching technique* designed to teach and/or modify a person's internal, *self-directing, verbal statements* and thereby effect a change in his/her behavior. The procedure involves teaching an individual a sequence of covert, self-directing instructions designed to guide performance to successful completion. The technique includes elements of self-guidance, self-monitoring, self-evaluation, self-reinforcement, punishment and correction.

The approach is based on the assumption that the inappropriate or maladaptive performance of a problem child is the result of that child's use of poorly organized cognitions (subvocal speech, thoughts and images). The child is taught appropriate *cognitive strategies* that interrupt and inhibit maladaptive stimulus-response associations (Abikoff, 1979). Because the approach teaches self-regulation, it is believed that cognitive behavior modification will enhance *maintenance* and *generalization* of learning.

Cognitive behavior modification involves an integration of behavioristic techniques, social learning theory, cognitive psychology, developmental psychology and instructional design (Craighead, Wilcoxon-Craighead and Meyer, 1978; Mohoney, 1977). *The technique*, in various applications, may employ shaping, positive reinforcement, response-cost, prompting and fading and reduction of externally controlled reinforcers. In addition, the technique usually involves self-control, self-directing verbal statements, self-monitoring, self-assessment self-recording and self-reinforcement (Lloyd, 1980).

Applications

Cognitive behavior modification has been used in a variety of *applications* such as the following.

(a) Problem solving: McKinney and Haskins (1980); D'Zurilla and Goldfried (1971); Allen, Chinsky, Larcen, Lochman and Selinger (1976).
(b) Memory: Campione and Brown (1977); Brown (1974).
(c) Metacognition: Brown, Campione and Day (1981).
(d) Attentional deficits and impulsivity: Kendall and Finch (1979); Keogh and Margolis (1976).
(e) Development of social skills and the control of aggression, hyperactivity and disruptive behavior: Abikoff (1979); Craighead, Wilcoxon-Craighead and Meyers (1978); Craighead, Craighead and Meyers (1978); Douglas, Parry, Marton and Garson (1976); Camp, Blom, Hebert and van Doorinck (1977); Bornstein and Quevillon (1976); Palkes, Stewart and Freedman (1972).
(f) Reading comprehension: Abikoff (1979): Douglas, Parry, Marton and Garson (1976).
(g) Handwriting: Kosiewicz, Hallahan, Lloyd and Graves (1982).
(h) Arithmetic: Cullinan, Lloyd and Epstein (1980).

The following discussion focusses primarily on *educational applications* of cognitive behavior modification that have implications for the enhancement of memory. Although there have been relatively few studies of the use of cognitive behavior modification to improve memory, data from several sources appear to indicate that cognitive behavior modification may be used in several different way to *enhance recall*. For example, performers may be trained to:

(a) identify when mnemonic techniques are required;
(b) select suitable mnemonic techniques to fit particular situations;

(c) use a particular mnemonic technique in an appropriate manner or sequence; and

(d) use a particular technique to enhance comprehension and recall when reading, e.g., SQ3R.

The procedure may be used either to: (a) teach a new technique, (b) link a number of techniques already in a person's repertoire or (c) teach an individual where, when and how to employ an existing strategy. Asarnow and Meichenbaum (1979) assessed the efficacy of self-instructional training to enhance the *serial recall* of kindergarten children. The object of the training was to increase the children's tendency to *rehearse* during a 15-second delay in the presentation of a series of pictures. A question and answer format was employed in the self-instructional *training*. At the outset of training, the examiner supplied both questions and answers. As training progressed, the examiner supplied fewer questions, until the child was both asking and answering all questions. An example of the self-directing verbal statements follows. The procedure used resulted in *acquisition* and *maintenance* of the technique as evidenced at a one-week follow-up assessment.

> Now what is it I have to do? I have to find a way to remember the order in which the pictures are pointed to. How can I do that? Hmm. I know I can keep saying the names of the pictures over and over again until it is time to point to the pictures. Let me try it now. I have to remember three pictures. (Examiner pointed to the predetermined number of pictures and named each in turn.) That's right ... I just keep saying the names of the pictures in the right order. I won't forget the order of the pictures if I keep saying their names in the right order. (The examiner covered the pictures and continued to repeat the names of the pictures, saying "good" after each complete series.) Good, I knew I could do it. All you have to do is keep saying the names of the pictures—remembering which picture came first, second, etc. (p. 22)

Although self-instructional training has not been used frequently with *poor readers*, several studies have reported promising findings (Ryan, Ledger, Short and Weed, 1982). Bommarito and Meichenbaum (1978) used self-instruction training to improve the *comprehension* of students in the seventh and eighth grades. These children possessed the necessary word attack skills, but were one or more years below grade level in comprehension. *Training* was conducted in six 45-minute individual periods. Each child was shown:

    (a) how to analyze each comprehension task into manageable units;

    (b) how to determine the hierarchy of skills required to perform each task; and

    (c) how to translate these skills into self-directing statements that could be rehearsed.

The object of the *training* was to teach the learner how to guide his/her performance prior to, during and following reading a passage to enhance understanding. Students were taught to identify the main idea, watch action sequences and learn how the characters felt and why. After only six training sessions, the students showed improvements in *comprehension* of approximately one year. This improvement was *maintained* for a one-month interval.

A study by Short (1981) involved two groups of less skilled *readers*. These students were taught a self-instructional strategy focusing on the main components of *story grammar* (Stein and Glenn, 1977). In three sessions, the children performed as well as skilled readers on a *maintenance* task involving a difficult two-episode flashback story.

Development and use of cognitive treatment procedures has occurred partially in response to the limitations experienced with the use of other commonly used clinical interventions. For example, *maintenance* of treatment gains has frequently been disappointing following the termination of reinforcement with children having behavior problems (O'Leary and O'Leary, 1976). The frequent failure of treatment gains to *generalize* to nontreatment settings is another source of difficulty associated with contingency management interventions (Johnson, Bolstad and Lobitz, 1976; Kuypers, Becker and O'Leary 1968). Cognitive behavior modification has been developed to enhance the *acquisition, generalization* and *maintenance* of treatment effects.

General Cognitive Behavior Modification Training Strategies

In the following procedures, control over behavior is gradually *faded* from *overt* verbalizations made by an adult (external control) to *covert* verbalization made by a student (self-control). Cognitive behavior modification usually employs some variation of the following five steps.

(a) *Cognitive modeling:* an adult demonstrates the steps involved in performing a task while overtly expressing a number of self-directing, verbal statements that guide his performance through the task.

(b) *Overt, verbal prompting:* the child performs the same task as that performed by the adult, while imitating the verbalizations demonstrated by the adult. The adult assists the child to accurately imitate the procedures modeled.

(c) *Overt, self-prompting:* the child performs the task while instructing himself aloud; adult assistance is progressively faded.

(d) *Fading, overt self-prompting:* the child *whispers* the instructions to himself as he proceeds through the task.

(e) *Covert, self-prompting:* the child performs the task while using covert self-directing speech.

Over a number of *training* sessions, the package of self-directing statements *modeled* by the experimenter, and *imitated* by the child (initially aloud, and then covertly) is enlarged by means of *response chaining* and *successive approximations*. Also, over successive sessions, the *difficulty* of the training tasks is systematically increased through the introduction of increasingly more cognitively demanding activities (Meichenbaum and Burland, 1979).

During cognitive behavior modification training, students are taught a number of performance guiding *statements* related to, (a) problem definition, (b) planning strategies, (c) self-instruction, (d) self-monitoring, (e) error correction, (f) self-assessment and (g) self-reinforcement. Harris (1982) provides an example of the type of statements that are modeled by an adult and rehearsed by a child.

(a) *problem definition*: "What is it I have to do?" (b) *focussing of attention*: "I have to concentrate, think only about my work," (c) *planning and response guidance*: "Be careful . . . look at them one at a time." (d) *self-reinforcement*: "Good, I got it!" (e) *self-evaluation*: "Am I following my plan . . . did I look at each one?" and (f) *coping and error correcting* options: "That's o.k. . . . even if I make an error, I can back up and go slowly." (Harris, 1982, p. 6)

Meichenbaum and Burland (1979) described the following two examples of overt *verbalizations modeled* by teachers. The first set of instructions provide an example of *general task approach statements* that are aimed at the components of tasks in general. For example, "What am I supposed to do here?" and "What is the first step?" General, task approach statements may also be aimed at specific characteristics of a learner that interfere with performance, such as impulsivity. For example, "I must remember to work slowly," and "Think first."

The second set of instructions provides an example of *specific task approach statements*. These statements describe strategies that are relevant to the completion of a particular task.

I must stop and think before I begin. What plans can I try? How would it work out if I did that? What shall I try next? Have I got it right so far? See, I made a mistake there—I'll just erase it. Now let's see, have I tried everything I can think of? I've done a pretty good job!" (Douglas, Parry, Marton and Garson, 1976, p. 408)

Okay, what is it I have to do? You want me to copy the picture with the different lines. I have to go slowly and carefully. Okay, draw the line down, down, good; and then to the right, that's it; now down some more and to the left. Good, I'm doing fine so far. Remember, go slowly. Now back up again. Just erase the line carefully . . . Good. Even if I make an error, I can go on slowly and carefully. I have to go down now. Finished. I did it!" (Meichenbaum and Goodman, 1971, p. 117)

The majority of research using self-instruction to investigate school related problems has concentrated on problems like *impulse control*. Typically, this work has entailed little instruction in task specific strategies and more on general coping skills, such as, "Slow down," and "Look carefully at all your choices." As is discussed later, the use of either a general or specific strategy may affect *generalization* and *maintenance* of learning.

Meichenbaum (1977) has also suggested use of a coping skills training procedure called *stress inoculation training* that may be incorporated into cognitive behavior modification instruction. Burgio, Whitman and Johnson (1980) conducted a study in which stress inoculation training was used in conjunction with methods designed to increase the attending behavior of highly *distractible* retarded children. After attention to math and printing activities had been increased, in an attempt to establish immunity, the children were exposed to visual and auditory distractions commonly found in the classroom environment. The distractions included prerecorded voices and color slides. During the initial presentations of the distractions, the experimenter modeled the distraction-ignoring, self-guiding statements. In the final stages of inoculation training, other children were introduced into the training setting and were directed to play with noise producing objects.

An additional cognitive behavior modification strategy was also employed by Burgio, Whitman and Johnson (1980) during the modeling phase of their study, the experimenter would sometimes purposefully make an *error* on his task, and then verbalize a *failure coping, self-guiding statement*. Then, to supply an opportunity for the children in the study to verbalize the failure coping statement during their performance of the task, each task included a portion of increased difficulty that usually resulted in at least one error by the child.

Deshler, Alley, Warner and Schumaker (1981) have developed a set of training materials for teaching acquisition and generalization of *academic skills* to severely *learning disabled adolescents*. These procedures incorporate many of the features of cognitive behavior modification. The *acquisition* phase involves the following six steps of instruction:

Step 1. Analysis of current learning habits. The student is first asked to perform the target strategy or skill. At completion of the task, the teacher affirms with the student in a positive manner that she/he has either completed the task incorrectly, or that she/he has a skill deficit. The purpose of this step is to make the student aware of his/her ineffective habits and to provide motivation to adopt a new approach.

Step 2. Describe the new strategy. The steps involved in the new strategy are described to the student. For example, "First you will read a paragraph. Then you will stop reading and ask yourself some questions. As you think of a question, you will answer it yourself, or you will go back to the paragraph to find the answer. After you have answered all the questions you can think of, you will read the next paragraph. . . ." A rationale for each step is provided, and the advantages over the old strategy are described.

Step 3. Model the new strategy. The teacher models the strategy or skill in its entirety while *thinking aloud* so the student can witness all of the processes involved in the strategy.

Step 4. Verbal rehearsal of the strategy. Before the student is asked to demonstrate the strategy, she/he must learn the steps to an automatic level. The student is asked to verbally rehearse the steps. The aim is to transfer the teacher's instructions to the student who progresses from overt to covert verbal rehearsal.

Step 5. Student practices on controlled materials. As soon as the student demonstrates both understanding and mastery of the steps, the teacher should choose controlled materials (e.g., high-interest, low-vocabulary materials) for practice. A key component of this step is the repetition and practice required of the student to insure acquisition.

Step 6. Student practice in classroom materials. The student's regular classroom materials are used to achieve generalization. Instructional prompts and cues, liberally available in previous steps, are faded from use during this phase. Fading reduces the student's discrimination between the training environment and the regular classroom. In addition, as assistance is faded, the student becomes more active in use of the strategy.

Corrective feedback is an integral part of each of the foregoing steps. During each step, the student is given positive and corrective feedback, and is required to practice each step until it is performed to criterion with no prompts or cues from the teacher (Deshler, Alley, Warner and Schumaker, 1981).

Steps Involved in Developing a Cognitive
Behavior Modification Program

Harris (1982) recommends the following steps be taken *to determine the cognitions and strategies necessary* to successfully perform a task.

(a) The teacher or an expert performer should perform the task while examining and reporting upon his strategies.

(b) The teacher should observe and interview both adequate and inadequate performers to identify what possible factors may lead to poor performance.

(c) Cognitions should be identified that are involved in: (1) comprehension of the task, (2) production of appropriate strategies and (3) application and monitoring of these strategies. Various methods for assessing cognitions have been developed, for example, interviews, post-performance questionnaires, thought listing and think-aloud (Meichenbaum, 1979).

(d) Learner analysis is a complex, difficult and necessary task. Ideally, task and training requirements must be compatible with the learner's language development, learning style, knowledge, currently employed problem solving strategies, responses to behavioral antecedents and consequences, and the individual's intellectual level. Several studies (Bornstein, Bellack and Hersen, 1980; Ellis, 1976; and Santogrossi, O'Leary, Romanczyk and Kaufman, 1973) have found that children who fail to comply with typical environmental demands may not respond well to cognitive behavior modification training. *Oppositional children* may first require management programs designed to enhance compliance.

(e) The results of the learner analysis are combined with the results of the cognitive behavior task analysis to assist both the selection of individually suitable cognitive behavior modification components and the design of appropriate training procedures. Simple procedures, such as explaining a strategy or providing a model, may be all that is necessary when the task is simple or the learner's problems are relatively minor. As the goals of training become more involved and/or the learner's deficits are more significant, training becomes more complex, and multiple training tasks may be required.

1. Determine which cognitive behavior modification techniques, for example, imagery, modeling and/ or shaping, will be required.
2. Determine if a generic or specific task strategy should be employed.
3. Develop appropriate self-guiding verbal statements.

(f) If multiple components and procedures are to be used in training, it may be helpful to begin training on tasks with which the learner is relatively proficient. Then, progressively introduce new components and procedures as the learner demonstrates mastery of previously introduced material.

(g) Provide sufficient practice using interesting and varied materials to facilitate acquisition and generalization.

(h) Progressively fade external control as learner control of the task increases.

Component Analysis

Modeling. There is little data available that attests to the discrete effect of modeling when used in cognitive behavior modification with various populations of learners. Meichenbaum and Goodman (1971) found that with kindergarten and first grade children, modeling used in combination with *self-instruction* in which the children imitated the self-directing verbal statements modeled to them, was more effective than modeling used alone. Similarly, Burgio, Whitman and Johnson (1980) reported that, in a study of two retarded children (CA: 9 and 11; IQ: 46 and 70), modeling and *prompting* were not sufficient to train self-instruction behavior. To train these children in the effective use of a self-instructional chain, the authors found it necessary to use modeling, in conjunction with *shaping* and *verbal reinforcement*. Engelmann and Bruner (1974) have used a technique called *leading* in conjunction with verbal modeling to teach a chain of verbal responses. When modeling a verbal response, a teacher demonstrates the statement that the student is to make, then the student is given the opportunity to imitate the behavior modeled. If the response is long the teacher may model it in segments to facilitate imitation. Alternatively, a teacher may employ *leading* in which the teacher and the student repeatedly and in unison sound-out a chain of verbal responses. Engelmann and Bruner suggested that leading is a more powerful tool than modeling. They cite the example of teaching people to say the alphabet backwards; if the recitation is modeled, learning is slow; if the teacher uses leading, learning is much more rapid.

Harris (1982) made a number of recommendations designed to enhance the effective use of *modeling* in cognitive behavior modification training.

(a) The model should have a positive relationship with the student. Teachers, parents, paraprofessionals and peers can be used as effective models.

(b) The model should be enthusiastic and use self-statements with appropriate phrasing and inflection.

(c) In some cases, performance is improved by using a student who is being taught a cognitive behavior modification strategy to model the technique for another student (Pressley, 1979).

(d) Although live models are often preferable and most effective (Kendall, 1977; Ledwidge, 1978) alternatives may include a written list of steps and statements, tape-recorded statements, videotapes and cartoons (Harris, 1980, 1981; Lloyd, 1980; Meichenbaum, 1977).

In cognitive behavior modification, the self-directing verbal statements the learner is taught to make to himself are designed to function as a *chain* of verbal stimuli prompting the occurrence of particular behaviors at critical points in a sequence of performance. Methods of teaching behavioral chains are discussed more fully in other parts of this text; however, at this point it may be advantageous to review briefly some of the related considerations.

A *chain* is comprised of a number of stimulus-response links (S-R links). The *stimulus* in each link refers to the stimulus condition that naturally occurs during the performance of the task. Initially, this stimulus may not control the performer's behavior. The object of the cognitive behavior modification strategy is to introduce a self-directing verbal statement that does control the learner's behavior, and then *transfer* this *control* to the *naturally occurring stimulus*. Thus, the tasks involved in developing an effective instructional sequence include:

(a) identifying the response to be made at each step;

(b) identifying the naturally occurring stimuli that must eventually come to control each response; and

(c) selecting verbal statements that currently control the learner's responses.

The *verbal statements* that are selected must function as *prompts*. Prompts are stimuli that control an individual's behavior and that are temporarily introduced into instruction to facilitate performance of a response that would not otherwise be possible. Self-directing verbal statements are designed to be used in this manner. During the initial stage of learning, the statements are made overtly to assist the provision of feedback, shaping and reinforcement. As the statements come to be made rapidly, accurately and consistently, the learner is taught to make them covertly. In the final stage, after the learner has repeatedly performed the series of responses, the chain becomes automatic as each response through repeated association with the naturally occurring stimuli becomes attached to these stimuli and the verbal prompts fade from use. Engelmann and Carnine (1982) refer to the process by which overt verbal responses become covert and automatic as that of covertization. This topic is discussed later in this chapter.

Because of the important role of the verbal self-guiding statements, considerable care must be taken in the *selection* and use of *suitable statements*. In this regard the following suggestions are made:

(a) If the statements are to control the learner's behavior, each of the terms used should be well established in the learner's vocabulary. That is, the words should already control the responses the learner is required to make. Harris (1982) has suggested that the learner should be involved, as much as possible, in the design, implementation and evaluation of the cognitive behavior modification training program.

(b) If the learner is to remember the statements, then each statement should be as concise as possible, and be stated in a consistent form on each occasion.

(c) In addition, whenever the verbal prompt is being used, effort should be made to increase the stimulus value of the naturally occurring stimuli so as to associate the verbal prompt with these stimuli, and thereby, to foster transfer of stimulus control. As was mentioned earlier, the topic of teaching behavioral chains is discussed more fully in Chapter Ten.

Overt self-directing statements. What is the value of including overt self-directing statements in cognitive behavior modification training? Lovitt and Curtis (1968) assessed the effect of having children verbalize an arithmetic problem before writing the answer rather than simply writing the answer directly. Verbalization before responding enhanced performance. Meichenbaum and Goodman (1971) found that in a study of kindergarten children, overt verbalization of a modeled verbal statement was more effective than passive observation of a model. Two studies of the relationship between motor responses and self-instruction (Burron and Bucher, 1978; Higa, Tharp and Calkins, 1978) did not find that overt verbalizations had a direct effect on performance. Denney and Turner (1979) in a study of three- to ten-year-old children of normal intelligence found that strategy modeling with or without overt verbal imitation was equally effective. The authors suggested that, in fact, *overt verbalizations may interfere* with performance of the task.

Keogh and Glover (1980) suggested that with older children, when private speech becomes overt, self-direction may *interfere* with performance. For example, Kendler, Kendler and Carrick (1966) found that overt labelling facilitated problem solving for *kindergarten* children, but interfered with the performance of children in the *third grade*. Meichenbaum and Goodman (1969) found similar results with kindergarten and third grade children. Ridberg, Parke, and Heatherington (1971) found that combining overt verbal and nonverbal cues in training impulsive boys in the fourth grade worked better with *low IQ* than with *high IQ* boys. Keogh and Glover concluded that it appears that once a behavior has been mastered and is regulated by covert private speech, imposition of overt verbalization interferes with performance. Some students may find the use of overt verbal statements embarrassing and inhibiting.

Lloyd (1980) suggested that overt self-directing statements may interfere with performance on some academic tasks such as decoding, where *automaticity* rather than reflectivity is important. Meichenbaum and Asaranow (1979) point out that it is not the purpose of cognitive behavior modification instruction to teach learners to explicitly and consciously talk to themselves as they perform a task, but rather, as described above, to use the self-directing statements as a temporary means of establishing a new chain of automatic behavior that no longer requires verbal mediation. For example, one way for a *poor reader* to unlearn inefficient or faulty cognitive strategies and to develop efficient reading strategies is to deautomatize the reading act. Once the reading act has been deautomatized, the child can be taught how to employ new cognitive strategies that with practice will in turn become automatic (Meichenbaum and Asaranow, 1979). Thus, although performance of a task may be inhibited during the acquisition phase of a new set of responses when the self-directing verbal statements are being made overtly, the real test of the approach occurs when performance is evaluated after the newly acquired set of responses has been given the opportunity to become covert and automatic. For example, Malamuth (1979) trained poor readers in the fifth grade to overtly then covertly verbalize self-directing statements. These students improved more on a reading task than did children who had only observed modeling of self-guiding statements in the absence of overt verbal imitation of the statements.

An additional consideration to be made with verbalizations is to insure that there is a *correspondence* between *saying and doing*. Merely saying the right thing is insufficient, and some time may have to be spent shaping and developing correspondence between verbalizations and the behaviors they are to control (Meichenbaum, 1980).

Self-observation, evaluation and reinforcement. Self-observation involves an individual monitoring and recording his/her own behavior. Self-evaluation involves a subjective judgment of behavior against some criterion that may have been established by the individual or by another person. Self-reinforcement involves the dispensing of reinforcement to one's self upon achievement of the criterion. Administration of these three activities is the essence of self-control.

Nelson and Birkimer (1978) found that the effect of self-instruction was increased when accompanied by *self-reinforcement*. According to Craighead, Wilcoxon-Craighead and Meyers (1978), the efficacy of self-reinforcement is widely upheld. In many situations, self-reinforcement is at least as effective as external reinforcement.

Spates and Kanfer (1977) found that *criterion setting* was a most important component. Subjects trained in criterion setting in an arithmetic task improved significantly more than those trained only in self-monitoring, and more than control subjects who had not received training. The addition of other components (self-monitoring, self-reinforcement) to criterion setting did not enhance treatment effects. These results suggest that it may be important to specify clearly the criteria used to judge the adequacy of a behavior (Craighead, Wilcoxon-Craighead and Meyers, 1978).

Rosenbaum and Drabman (1979), after reviewing the literature, concluded that *self-recording* alone was effective with children, adolescents and mentally retarded individuals, in and out of classroom settings, at least in initiating a desirable change in behavior. The changes, however, are usually modest in magnitude. The authors suggest that to maintain the changes obtained by self-recording, reinforcing contingencies may be required. The majority of studies indicate that it may not be necessary to program for high levels of accuracy in self-recorded behavior to obtain desirable changes in target behavior (Rosenbaum and Drabman, 1979).

Rhode, Morgan and Young (1983) investigated the effect of *self-evaluation* in facilitating the *generalization* of appropriate classroom behavior of *behaviorally handicapped* children from a special education classroom to a regular classroom. Specific procedures were employed in this study to promote generalization and maintenance; these techniques are discussed in Chapter Nine. Briefly described here, students (CA: 6.5-10.9) were asked to rate their own academic work and behavior; their ratings were then matched with those of the teacher at the end of each 15 minute interval. Matching with the teacher was progressively faded from use. Contrary to the results of previously mentioned studies, the authors found that maintenance and generalization of higher levels of appropriate behavior were associated with accuracy of self-evaluation. The results of the study indicated that handicapped students as young as six years of age could accurately self-evaluate.

Following their review of the literature, Rosenbaum and Drabman (1979) made a series of recommendations to maximize the potential effectiveness of self-control training:

(a) Students should be taught self-observational procedures.

(b) Accurate self-observation can be prompted by initially requiring students to match their records with those of either a teacher or a trained observer, followed by gradual fading of the matching process.

(c) Once self-observation has been established, externally administered contingencies for desirable behavior change can be introduced.

(d) The control of these contingencies can then be transferred to the students.

(e) At the same time that self-determined contingencies are introduced, students can be taught to provide themselves with instructions and praise designed to guide their behavior.

(f) When the students are reliably controlling their academic and social behavior, explicit contingencies can be gradually withdrawn.

This multi-component approach would maximize the probability of *maintenance* of self-control skills after the training program has been removed. The approach would also contribute to the potential *generalization* of these skills across different situations.

Bryant and Budd (1982) concluded from their review of the literature that *component analyses* of the cognitive behavior modification training package have shown that training children in the use of self-directing statements leads to better performance on laboratory measures than was achieved by direct training using adult instructions, modeling and reinforcement in the absence of self-instruction. Keogh and Glover (1980), on the other hand, have suggested that the effect of any component in cognitive behavior modification training may depend on the nature of the child and the severity of the problem.

Age/Handicaps and Cognitive Behavior Modification

There is evidence that *young children and mentally handicapped* individuals are neither aware of nor efficient in the use of verbal strategies (Pressley, 1979). Mentally handicapped and young children can be taught to use mnemonic strategies, but they often fail to use them spontaneously (Bender, 1977; Campione and Brown, 1977). Other evidence suggests that mentally handicapped individuals do possess and use mediational strategies (Friedman, Krupski, Dawson and Rosenberg, 1977) and that a trained mediational strategy will maintain over time and generalize to similar tasks (Wanschera and Borkowski, 1974, 1975).

At what specific ages and at what specific levels of functioning can normal and handicapped individuals benefit from cognitive behavior modification training? The techniques have been used successfully to teach self-directing verbal guidance to *children as young as four and five* years of age (Arnold and Forehand, 1978; Bornstein and Quevillon, 1976). Bryant and Budd (1982) used cognitive behavior modification training with four and five year old children. The technique produced an improvement in performance on various *preacademic* worksheets that transferred to the classroom environment.

In *summary*, cognitive behavior modification strategies have been used quite successfully with *preschool and handicapped children*. There are, however, a *number of factors*, in addition to age and general level of cognitive functioning, that may influence success of the technique. For example, as was mentioned earlier, compliance with naturally occurring environmental demands, level of language development and learning style may be influential. Although cognitive behavior modification has been used primarily in experimental and therapeutic environments, the procedures can be readily modified to fit into classroom situations.

Generalization and Maintenance of
Cognitive Behavior Modification

As was mentioned in the introduction, cognitive behavior modification was initially developed as a method designed to enhance generalization and maintenance of behavior change. The rationale behind the approach was that, if an individual is taught self-control in the form of a well established style of thinking that guides behavior, the effects will be pervasive. Most studies have found self-instructional training to be effective in improving children's performance in standardized *laboratory tasks* that were identical or similar to those used in training (Bryant and Budd, 1982). However, the critical question is, to what extent are skills acquired in one setting (a training environment) practiced in another setting (a classroom) in which no special contingencies have been established to either prompt or reinforce the behavior? An additional question is, if a behavior transfers from a training to a natural environment, for what period of time is the behavior maintained in that environment in the absence of special environmental modification?

Only a few studies to date have directly measured children's behavior in routine *classroom activities* as a means of evaluating the generalized effects of self-instructional training, and their results have been equivocal. Meichenbaum and Goodman (1971) observed no reduction in the inappropriate behavior of children in the *second grade* as a result of cognitive behavior modification training. Burgio, Whitman and Johnson (1980) provided self-instructional training to *developmentally delayed* children aged nine and eleven years. Their results did not produce a decrease in off-task behavior in the classroom until 15 or more sessions of self-instructional training. Douglas, Parry, Marton and Garson (1976), working with *hyperactive boys*, successfully used a lengthy training period of two one-hour sessions per week for a total of 24 sessions. As well, six sessions were conducted with the child's teacher, in addition to twelve with the child's parents. Treatment effects generalized to the natural environment.

Two studies have obtained very *successful generalization*. Bornstein and Quevillon (1976) taught *disruptive preschoolers* to use a self-instructional procedure that led to large increases in the children's on-task behavior in the classroom. The improvements were maintained in postchecks after trainining was completed. Bryant and Budd (1982) worked with three children *ages four* and *five* who had demonstrated poor independent work performance, noncompliance and inattention. Following the cognitive behavior modification training, all three children demonstrated marked increases in accuracy on worksheets that were similar to those used during the self-instruction training. Two of the three children also increased their accuracy on worksheets that were dissimilar to those used during training. Several features of this study appear to have led to an increase in generalization. Three different types of worksheets similar to those used in the classroom were used during training. At the end of each of the ten minute daily training sessions, each child was told that saying the things she/he had been practicing would help in the classroom when doing worksheets; use of the technique was not, however, actually prompted or reinforced in the classroom. The authors interpreted the variability in improvement among the three children as an indication of the importance of considering individual child variables.

Equivocal results are difficult to interpret because of differences in training techniques, group composition, behaviors studied and assessment measures (Abikoff, 1979). The *results* obtained appear to be a *function of* the number and breadth of tasks trained, the relationship between training and target tasks, whether general or specific strategies were taught, the number, frequency and duration of training sessions, and whether new skills or application of existing skills were being taught.

O'Leary (1980) pointed out that in some *studies in which generalization did not occur*, there were wide differences between the training tasks such as "Matching Familiar Figures" and answering comprehension questions. O'Leary suggested that, if transfer to specific *target tasks* is desired, training should be specific to the particular demands of the target task. Alternatively, if *generalization* is desired, *generic methods* should be taught and practiced with a broad variety of tasks. Kendall and Wilcox (1980) examined the differential effects of variations in the type of self-instructions taught to children. *Concrete* training emphasized self-instruction that applied to a specific task, whereas *conceptual* training was broad and could be applied to a variety of tasks. Among the results, the observed changes in the classroom (teacher's *blind ratings*) were stronger for the conceptual training group (Kendall and Braswell, 1982).

After reviewing a number of studies, Harris concluded that maintenance of change is easier to attain than generalization (Harris, 1982). Harris made the following suggestions for *enhancing maintenance and generalization*:

    (a) Develop training procedures and behaviors that can be maintained by natural contingencies after transfer to a new environment or situation.

    (b) Provide training that is prolonged and in-depth, and conducted by several individuals across a variety of tasks, materials, modalities, settings and conditions.

    (c) Make sure that stimuli common to the generalization setting(s) are also present in the training mileau.

    (d) If distractors will be present in the generalization setting, include in the training gradual inoculation against distractions, and include coping strategies for handling distractions.

    (e) Tell students to generalize, and reinforce them when generalization occurs.

    (f) While teaching self-regulatory behavior, gradually fade prompts to facilitate transfer of control to the student.

    (g) Make use of delayed and intermittent reinforcement during training to strengthen learned skills and behaviors.

    (h) Require similar (but not necessarily identical) cognitions and skills in the training and generalization tasks.

    (i) Gradually adapt training materials and setting to the terminal goal. Training a child to cope with frustration on a maze task is not likely to ameliorate aggressive tendencies with peers, without including intermediate steps in the instruction.

    (j) Provide feedback about the purpose and usefulness of the strategies taught as well as feedback on the learner's performance.

    (k) Gradually increase the demand for mental involvement in the training tasks.

(l) Actively involve the student in the development of training and the acquisition of new strategies and skills.

(m) Emphasize consistency and precise strategy use during the initial phase of strategy instruction; then train "loosely."

(n) Facilitate generalization by attributing observed changes to the student's own efforts.

Covertization

Engelmann and Carnine (1982) have described in detail a process referred to as covertization. Covertization refers to the progressive *fading of overt verbal prompts* made by a teacher during successive demonstrations of the steps involved in a problem solving sequence. As is the case with cognitive behavior modification training, the teacher initially *prompts* each step in the sequence, then the learner performs the sequence while being prompted by the teacher. The teacher systematically reduces the amount of prompting. If the learner continues to perform the operation in the absence of prompts from the teacher, it is assumed that the prompt has become covertized and that the learner subvocally prompts himself to perform. At the end of instruction, all responses are to be prompted covertly by the learner without assistance from the teacher. If well designed, the transition from highly covertized instruction to independent work should be relatively *errorless*. The following discussion provides a brief review of the techniques that Engelmann and Carnine have used to achieve covertization. For a more complete discussion of the topic, the reader is referred to an excellent textbook by these authors, *Theory of Instruction: Principles and Applications*.

In the following *example*, each step of the problem being solved is initially prompted by the teacher. Four covertization phases follow after the learner has responded successfully to about eight applications of the initial demonstration. During each covertization phase, various verbal prompts provided by the teacher are either eliminated, regrouped, included in a broader form or modified into equivalent forms.

Original problem: $\Box$ = / / / /

Phase 1. Initial fully prompted sequence

 a. Teacher: Touch the equal sign.
    Learner: (Touches.)

 b. Teacher: What's the rule about the equal sign?
    Learner: We must end up with the same number on this side and on the other side.

 c. Teacher: Touch the side you can start counting on.
    Learner: (Touches side with the lines.)

 d. Teacher: Count how many are on that side.
    Learner: (Touches each line as be counts: "One, two, three, four.")

 e. Teacher: How many did you end up with on this side?
    Learner: Four.

 f. Teacher: So how many must you end up with on the other side?
    Learner: Four.

 g. Teacher: Write 4 in the box.
    Learner: (Writes.)

Phase 2. First covertizations

 a. Step a, from above has been eliminated.

 b. Teacher: What's the rule about the equal sign?
    Learner: We must end up with the same number on this side and on the other side.

 c. Teacher: Touch the side you can start counting on.
    Learner: (Touches the side with vertical lines.)

    d. Teacher: Count how many are on that side.
       Learner: (Touches each line as he counts: "One, two, three, four.")

    1. Teacher: Make the other side equal.
      Learner: (Writes 4 in box.)

Step 1, above, is an *inclusive step* incorporating steps e, f and g from phase 1. The wording is not identical to the original. The replacement step simply functions as the three steps had in the original sequence.

Phase 3. Increasing covertization
    b. Teacher: What's the rule about the equal sign?
      Learner: We must end up with the same number this side and on the other side.

    c. Teacher: Touch the side you start counting on.
      Learner: (Touches side with lines.)

    2. Teacher: Count the lines and make the other side equal.
      Learner: (Counts lines and writes 4 in box on the other side.)

Step 2, above, illustrates *regrouping* of steps d. and 1. from phase 2.

Phase 4. Increasing covertization
    Teacher: You're going to make the sides equal in this problem. First you're going to touch the side you start counting on. Then you're going to count everything on that side. Then you're going to make the other side equal. Do it.
    Learner: (Counts the lines and writes 4 in box.)

In this phase, pairs of *equivalent instructions* have been developed. For example, the first sentence is equivalent to the sentences that follow.

Phase 5. Final stage of covertization
>   Teacher: Make the sides equal in this problem.
>   Learner: (Completes the problem.) (p. 238)

The following discussion provides a brief review of some of the considerations involved in determining which of several *types of covertization techniques* to employ in various situations. For a thorough consideration of the topic, the reader is referred to Engelmann and Carnine's text.

Eliminating steps. Steps may be eliminated from subsequent phases of instruction after the performer has completed many problems in the same way while maintaining an acceptable rate, consistency and accuracy of response. Also, steps may be eliminated that make the sequence awkward. Note, however, that eliminating steps may not always be the best approach to covertization, and may give rise to various problems. In this case, other procedures should be considered.

Regrouping steps. When steps are regrouped, a single step provides the information that had been conveyed by two or more separate steps in the earlier phase of instruction. The general rule for regrouping steps is to combine those steps that lead to the same goal, or that are part of the same fixed series of steps. The regrouped step should contain the same words as in the original steps except where the revision becomes awkward or too highly prompted.

Inclusive steps. Inclusive steps involve new wording. The wording presents less detail than in the original instruction, but results in the same set of behaviors. Inclusive steps cover behaviors that had been treated as two or more steps in the initial phase. The difference between inclusive and regrouped steps is that when steps are regrouped, the resulting steps tend to contain the same words as in the original. In inclusive steps, more general wording is introduced.

Equivalent pairs of instruction. The use of equivalent pairs of instruction is more complicated than is the use of the other covertization techniques because the strategy generally requires three covertizations. Equivalent pairing is necessary when the instructions that are to appear in a later covertization do not appear in the earlier phase.

If the final instruction "B" does not appear in the original sequence, then equivalent pairing is required. Equivalent pairs consist of two instructions, one that the learner has mastered "A" and another that calls for the same behavior, but does so with unfamiliar instructions "B."

The general procedure is first to present the instructions in the "A-B" order, then in the "B-A" order and then finally to present only "B." For example, in the "A-B" pairing, the learner responds to the familiar "A": "You're going to tell me the opposite of *big*," following which the teacher immediately introduces the unfamiliar "B"; "That's an *antonym* for *big*." The learner does not have to respond to the meaning of the word antonym.

In the "B-A" pairing, the word *antonym* is presented first, and because the learner is now required to attend to it, the potential for learning its meaning is increased. Finally, when the meaning of antonym has been acquired, instruction "B'. may be presented alone.

The structure and organization of the covertization procedures are in considerable contrast to the apparent *imprecision* of the cognitive behavior modification procedures. Most of the examples of self-directing verbal statements that have been reported in the literature are verbose, poorly structured and inconsistent. In general, application of the techniques of task analysis, shaping, prompting and fading, modeling and chaining has been crude. On the other hand, cognitive behavior modification has achieved some limited success, and continues to be *potentially useful* both for teaching application of mnemonic strategies, and maintenance and generalization of a variety of academic and nonacademic skills. To assist realization of these potentialities, however, the method requires a more skillful application of its instructional procedures, and incorporation of some of the precision of *direct instruction*. Chapters Nine, Ten and Eleven provide a review of a variety of related instructional techniques.

Chapter Seven

Prose Recall and Comprehension: One

This chapter is the first of two that provide a review of (a) methods used for the structural analysis of narrative and expository prose; (b) the features of written prose that influence retention; (c) adjunct aids used to improve recall: questions, advance organizers, marginal notes, and pictures; (d) mnemonic strategies available to readers: notetaking, underlining, and review; and (e) memory enhancing instructional techniques used by teachers: instructions, questioning and prereading preparation. The discussion introduces the variety of characteristics of prose that have been studied in relation to their influence upon recall. Procedures, problems and the results of research are reviewed. A number of practical methods for improving prose recall are discussed that are of value to teachers, instructional designers, publishers and students.

For memory researchers, prose recall is a relatively new area of study. Research in this area is particularly important to students in upper elementary, secondary and higher levels of education, in which correspondingly more information is transmitted through the medium of *print*. At the early levels of elementary school, instruction depends more on the comprehension and recall of *oral prose*. Unfortunately, this research is still at a relatively early stage of development, and *research findings*, in many cases, must be

138

considered *tentative*. When applying the results of this research, practitioners should validate the application with particular students, materials and circumstances.

To assist the reader's understanding and appreciation of this area of study, the following paragraphs provide a review of some of the *methodological problems* associated with the research on prose recall. For example, in studies involving young or exceptional children, some researchers have substituted oral for written prose to obtain a measure of comprehension and recall that is not influenced by an absence of adequate reading decoding skills. An oral presentation of prose insures that each listener receives the complete prose message once.

Is the *comprehension* and *recall* of *oral* and *written prose* equivalent among young and exceptional children? According to Levine and Lesgold (1978), there is substantial documentation indicating that among skilled decoders, the comprehension demands and performance associated with reading are similar to those involved in listening. Johnson (1981) suggested that, in general, *listening comprehension* exceeds *reading comprehension* through the early years, reaches a point of equality as reading ability increases, and often comes to be less adequate than reading comprehension in the mature reader.

Some researchers have studied the performance of children on *passages* of prose that are considerably *shorter* than those with which the children are characteristically presented. For example, Koenke and Otto (1969) used 198-word passages with children in the third and sixth grades. Flagg, Weaver, Fenton, Gelatt and Pray (1980) used passages 73 words in length. Levin and Divine-Hawkins (1974) presented one line of prose per page to children in grade four.

The majority of research has been conducted in artificial, laboratory-type settings where formats and materials often bear little resemblance to usual classroom conditions. In a study of the effects of pictures on prose, children in grades k, 2 and 3 were presented with *one picture for each line of prose* (Guttman, Levin and Pressley, 1977). Some researchers have used computer terminals and slide projectors to present one or more lines of prose (e.g., Rigney and Lutz, 1976). To what extent are the results of these studies representative of the comprehension and recall of prose by children performing under typical classroom conditions?

Most of the research has been conducted on *narrative passages* of the type common to basal readers. Research on *expository* passages typical of instructional texts has been rare, and only a few studies of *descriptive* prose have been reported. Fictional narrative passages have typically been used in research because they are interesting, and hold children's attention. Also, when unfamiliar, fictional passages are used, an experimenter can control for knowledge that might have been acquired before the passage was presented. In addition, narrative passages usually have a very predictable structure that can be described by a *story grammar* that facilitates analysis of the amount and type of comprehension and recall.

Baker and Stein (1981) suggested that it is particularly important to assess performance on *expository* passages of children in the third and fourth grade who have mastered basic decoding skills but who are not yet fluent readers. It is at this time that children are expected to read expository prose in their *social studies* and *science* books. According to Baker and Stein, there is ample evidence to show that children understand *narrative* quite well at an early age, yet there is little information on how well they understand expository prose. It is possible that a particular child may be quite capable of performing a certain mental operation, such as making an inference with narrative, but not with expository prose (Baker and Stein). Similarly, children may understand the logical structure of narrative text before that of expository text. As mentioned previously, *stories* have a conventional structure, while the structure of expository text is variable and generally poorly defined. According to Berkowitz and Taylor (1981), it is because each expository passage has a unique structure that students are unable to readily discern the structure and use it as a memory schema. Thus, children characteristically have more difficulty reading and remembering exposition than they experience with narrative prose. Also, as Baker and Stein (1981) have indicated, narrative prose is usually more concrete and has events and characters with which children can identify. In contrast, expository material is typically abstract and concerned with difficult and often unfamiliar concepts and situations.

Berkowitz and Taylor (1981) conducted a study of readers in the sixth grade *comparing* their *memory of expository and narrative passages*. The passages studied were controlled for differences in familiarity of topic and organization of main ideas and details. The children recalled significantly more information from the narrative passages than they did from the expository passages having a familiar content. Thus, it appears that even when other factors are controlled, the structural variability of expository passages does not facilitate recall. In *summary*, the information in the foregoing paragraphs indicates that it is not valid to generalize the results of studies of narrative passages to expository prose.

Another limitation of prose memory research is that most of it has been conducted with high school and college students (Levin and Pressley, 1981). Because of the cognitive-developmental *differences between older and younger students*, it is unwise to conclude that strategies found to be effective at one developmental level will be similarly effective at another level (Levin and Pressley, 1981).

An additional complication arises with the attempt to *discriminate memory* and *comprehension*. Memory tests are frequently used as an index of comprehension in the belief that poorly understood information will not be well remembered. Conversely, a reader with a poor memory cannot adequately describe previously comprehended information.

Rather than *testing for comprehension* in the presence of the reading material, experimenters typically present the material, remove it, and then test for memory. *Free recall* tests require subjects to produce everything that can be remembered about the material. These tests are similar to essay questions students receive on exams. *Probed recall* tests require subjects to provide specific information about the material, and are often in the form of "wh" questions. These tests are analogous to short-answer exam questions. *Recognition tests* require subjects to discriminate from response alternatives, statements that are identical to, or consistent with, the previously read passage. Such *objective* tests correspond to multiple-choice or true-false items often found on standardized tests (Baker and Stein, 1981).

Difficulties can arise with attempts to *interprete* the *results* of *prose memory-comprehension tests*. A reader may have good comprehension while reading, but later be unable to recall all of the material. Possibly, also, information comprehended while reading and recalled later may not be reported by an individual, who may consider some of the information trivial and unworthy of mention.

Inferences that have been drawn by a reader may seem so obvious they are not reported. To avoid this problem, inferences are sometimes presented following the reading of a passage to see if they are *falsely recognized* as part of the original material. This technique, however, introduces another problem. There is no way of knowing whether the reader drew the inference as a result of initially reading the material, or merely recognized the inference as plausible after it had been presented (Johnson, 1981).

Anderson (1972) *compared recognition* and *recall* tests of comprehension and recall. Students can be given recognition tests in which they match, judge propositions true or false, or select answers from sets of alternatives. Recall tests may involve completion, short-answer or essay type responses. The choice between recognition and recall tests is often rationalized in terms of convenience and objectivity in scoring, but these are inadequate grounds for selection, if *answering the two types of tests requires different processes*. It is generally agreed that *recognition tests are easier* than parallel recall tests. Performance on recognition tests is higher even after correction for guessing (e.g., Anderson and Myrow, 1971). The difference between the results obtained in these two types of tests cannot be attributed simply to the greater likelihood of correctly guessing an answer on a recognition test. In addition, Anderson and Myrow found that there was a sharper decline in performance over a retention interval on short-answer (recall) items than on multiple-choice (recognition) items. Anderson (1972) concluded that it is not safe to assume that recognition and recall tests measure the same thing.

Whether *test questions* are stated in a *verbatim* or *paraphrase* form may also influence the results of test performance. For example, where the original text stated "One evening Sue's family sat down to eat a big turkey for dinner," a verbatim question might be stated in the form "What did Sue's family eat for dinner one evening?" A paraphrase question might ask "What food was served at the girl's house at suppertime" (Levin and Pressley, 1981). A verbatim question is developed by taking a statement from a text in a literal word-by-word form; an element of the statement is then deleted. The statement is phrased as a question and the student supplies (recall) or selects (recognition) the deleted element in a form identical to the original statement (Anderson, 1972). Two statements are defined as *paraphrases* of one another, if (a) they have no substantive words (nouns, verbs or modifiers) in common, and (b) they are equivalent in meaning. A paraphrase question relates to the original statement only with respect to meaning. Anderson suggested that verbatim questions could be answered correctly by recalling surface (*orthographic* and *acoustic information*) and are, therefore, a measure of rote recall, whereas answers to paraphrase questions have to be responded to at a *deeper semantic level* as described in the Craik and Lockhart (1972) model. Thus, answers to *paraphrase questions* reflect both *recall* and *comprehension*.

Bormuth, Manning, Carr and Pearson (1970) studied the responses of children in the fourth grade to four types of questions. An example of an original statement in the text was "The boy rode the steed." The children correctly answered 77 percent of the *verbatim questions*, such as "Who rode the steed?"; 71 percent of the *transformed verbatim* questions, such as "By whom was the steed ridden?"; 69 percent of the *partial paraphrase* questions, such as "Who rode the horse?"; and 67 percent of the *transformed partial paraphrase* questions, such as "By whom was the horse ridden?" In addition to using questions following reading to assess recall and comprehension, questions are also used before, during and after reading to enhance recall and comprehension. Use of questions in this manner is discussed in the next chapter.

Structural Analysis of Expository and Narrative Prose

Expository analysis. Meyer's method of prose analysis (Meyer, 1975; Brandt and Bluth, 1980) is a systematic, theoretically-based procedure for identifying an author's structural organization of expository text. The analysis reveals the *superordinate* and *subordinate relationship* among ideas and the logical relationship between the elements. The *analysis* has *several purposes*. The analysis of a prose passage in terms of the hierarchic and logical relationships permits an assessment of (a) the amount and type of a reader's comprehension and recall, (b) a reader's use of the author's organization for encoding and retrieval and (c) the similarities and differences between various passages. Meyer's method of analysis has also been used to classify five basic types of organizational patterns used by authors to structure expository text: (a) *problem-solution*, (b) *comparison*, (c) *antecedent-consequent*, (d) *description* and (e) *collection*. Meyer, Brandt and Bluth (1980) suggested that readers from upper elementary through high school should be taught to follow the organization of a passage to increase their retention.

Some of the *major steps* involved in *Meyer's analysis* of expository prose are described below. The first sentence in Meyer's (1975) *parakeet paragraph* is "The wide variety in color of parakeets that are available in the market today resulted from careful breeding of the color mutant offspring of green-bodied and yellow-faced parakeets." The *first step* of the procedure is to analyze complex or compound sentences into simple sentences or *propositions*. In Meyer's example, the first sentence in the paragraph was analyzed into three separate sentences; (a) "The wide variety in color of parakeets (exists)"; (b) "Color mutant offspring of green-bodied and yellow-faced parakeets were carefully bred"; and (c) (Parakeets) are available on the market today." Propositions are commonly known as either *dependent* or *independent clauses*. For example, "I went to the store" is a proposition and a simple sentence. The *compound sentence*, "I went to the store and applied for a job" contains two propositions (Pearson and Johnson, 1978). A sentence containing a subject and a verb is an independent clause. A dependent clause is a group of words having a subject and verb but not expressing a complete thought.

The *second step* in Meyer's analysis involves diagramming each of the propositions, as illustrated in Figure 7.1., to demonstrate the hierarchic or superordinate and subordinate relationship of

Figure 7.1. Meyer's Analysis of Sentences. (Meyer, 1975b, p. 46)

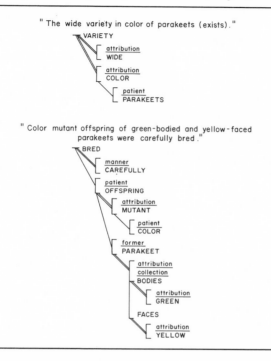

each element of the sentences. Capitalized words are from the text of each sentence. Solidly underlined words describe the nature of the relationship between the elements. Indentation indicates successive levels of subordination. Additional details of the analysis may be obtained from Meyer (1975).

Figure 7.2 illustrates Meyer's *top-level structural analysis* of the *supertanker passage* quoted below (Meyer *et al.*, 1980). Levels one and two in the content structure are labelled the message. The supporting major details are located in levels three and four, while minor details are located in levels five and lower. *Nodes* in the structure contain content words (capitalized) from the passage. The lines among the nodes show spatially how the content is organized. The solid, black line indicates the superordinate propositions referred to by Meyer as the *top-level structure*; this is the information placed *high* in the passage. Other propositions are

*Figure 7.2. Meyer's Top-Level Content Structure
of the "Supertanker" Passage.
(Meyer, Brandt & Bluth, 1980, p. 76)*

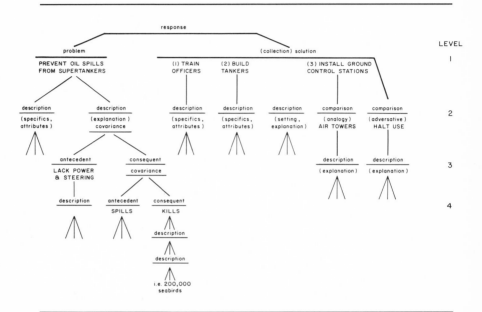

subordinate and are placed *lower* in the structure. The labels
(lower-case words) in the structure are referred to in their entirety
as the *content structure* by Meyer (1975) and as the *semantic
structure* by Frederiksen (1975).

Supertankers

A problem of vital concern is the prevention of oil spills from
supertankers. A typical supertanker carries a half-million tons of
oil and is the size of five football fields. A wrecked supertanker
spills oil in the ocean; this oil kills animals, birds, and microscopic
plant life. For example, when a tanker crashed off the coast of
England, more than 200,000 dead seabirds washed ashore. Oil
spills also kill microscopic plant life which provide food for sea
life and produce 70 percent of the world's oxygen supply. Most
wrecks result from the lack of power and steering equipment to
handle emergency situations, such as storms. Supertankers have

only one boiler to provide power and one propeller to drive the ship.

The solution to the problem is not to immediately halt the use of tankers on the ocean since about 80 percent of the world's oil supply is carried by supertankers. Instead, the solution lies in the training of . . . (Meyer, Brandt, and Bluth, 1980, p. 102).

Meyer (1975, 1977) hypothesized that *information* from a text is *organized by a reader* in a manner similar to that of the structure of the text. In *free recall*, retrieval is assumed to begin at the top node and proceed downwards from node to node along the links. If a link between nodes is missing, all information lower in the structure is inaccessible to retrieval. In this manner, information near the bottom of the content structure is less likely to be accessible, because its retrieval depends upon the presence of more links. In *cued recall*, the cue provides nodes, and gives access to information that otherwise would be inaccessible.

Several studies have been conducted in an attempt to *validate Meyer's analysis* of expository prose. Meyer (1975, 1977) conducted studies with *undergraduate students* to show that the *probability of recall* of information is a function of its *height* in the content structure of a passage. Meyer constructed two passages with an identical target paragraph embedded in each. The paragraph was placed high in the paragraph structure of one passage and low in the structure of the other; its serial position was the same in both paragraphs. On *tests of immediate recall, delayed free recall and delayed cued recall*, the two passages were recalled equally well; however, the recall of the target paragraph varied as a function of its placement in a sub- or super-ordinate position. In fact, in the 1977 study, results showed that there was almost twice as much recall of the information when it was placed in an important rather than a structurally unimportant position. Thus, knowing the *height of information* in the structure of a passage *indicates* the *likelihood of recall* of that information. This knowledge is vital to teachers, authors and instructional designers. *Important information* should be located high in the structure of a passage. When important information is located low in the structure, it may not be recalled unless special attention is drawn to it.

   Meyer, Brandt and Bluth (1980) conducted a study of students in the *ninth grade* to determine *if readers* at this level when recalling the content of a passage would employ *top-level structures* of the same type as those employed by authors in well organized text. Meyer *et al.* hypothesized that good readers would employ the systematic, organized strategy both for *encoding* and *retrieval* of information but that the structure would not be used by *poor readers*. These researchers found that of the students studied, less than 50 percent in the ninth grade used the top-level structure at least once in their reading and recall. Only 22 percent used it consistently on the four recall trials. Most of the students having high reading comprehension skills used the structure for oganizing their recall, while most students with low comprehension did not employ the structure. Those students that did use the structure recalled much more information from the passage. Taylor (1980) examined the use of top-level structure of a narrative passage by *adults* and by students in the *fourth* and *sixth grades*. Use of the top level structure by students during immediate recall was 82 percent for adults, 47 percent for good sixth grade comprehenders and 12 percent for good fourth grade comprehenders. The results of this investigation suggested that children's memory for expository material is enhanced if they follow the top-level structure of the text to organize their recall. The good and poor readers in the sixth grade who patterned their delayed recall after the top-level structure of the text passage were able to remember more than their peers who did not follow the organization. In contrast with Meyer (1975 and 1977), Taylor found that although differences in sensitivity to text structure did appear in subjects' organization of delayed recall, neither children nor adults demonstrated sensitivity to text structure in the form of *differential recall of superordinate versus subordinate concepts*. Apparently, general concepts were no more memorable than details in this short expository passage. Taylor suggested that because learning from reading becomes important in the upper elementary grades, children in these grades will probably benefit from instruction in following the organization of expository material through techniques such as *outlining* and noting top-level structure of expository text.

Bartlett (1978) examined the effects of *teaching* students in the *ninth grade* to identify and use an author's top-level structure. The intervention lasted for one hour per day for five days and focussed on how to identify and use four types of top level structures. The instruction and use of top-level structure led to an increase in *free recall* of prose passages. Students with a wide range of abilities, including those who had obtained low recall scores on the pretest, benefitted from the instruction. The *improvements* were *maintained* for three weeks following training.

At what *age* does *awareness* of the structure of a passage begin. Christie and Schumaker (1975) presented to children in *kindergarten* and in the *second* and *fifth grades* a passage containing sentences that were logically related to the main theme, and an equal number of randomly placed sentences that were thematically irrelevant. The results indicated that children at each grade level recalled significantly more thematically relevant than irrelevant sentences. Apparently, even kindergarten children are capable of using the high order relations of sentences that are thematically relevant. Similar results were obtained by Brown and Smiley (1977) with *eight-year-old children.* Brown's (1975a) research demonstrated that children as young as *four years of age* understand logical relationships expressed either *verbally or pictorially*, and that they use these relationships to enhance recall. Thus, evidence exists that beginning readers have the skills prerequisite to understanding logical structure in prose. Baker and Stein (1981) concluded from their review of a number of studies that children's knowledge about logical relationships and structures greatly influences their memory for prose material. Those passages that are organized according to an underlying structure are better remembered than arbitrarily sequenced or disorganized passages. Meyer, Brandt and Bruth (1980) suggested that competence with *narrative structure* precedes competence with *expository structure.* Use of the structure strategy may progress in the following sequence with different types of passages: *narrative*, then *expository*: description, antecedent/consequent, problem/ solution and comparison passages.

Kintsch (1974, 1982), and Kintsch and van Dijk (1978) have also developed a *model of text comprehension* and recall. In addition, the model describes some of the mental operations underlying comprehension, recall and summarization. The surface structure of a discourse is interpreted as a set of *propositions* that are ordered into a linear or hierarchic sequence on the basis of various *semantic relations* among the propositions. Kintsch analyzed the semantic structure of a passage at two levels: (1) the *microstructure* involving the relationship between individual propositions and (2) the macrostructure. The *macrostructure* characterizes the *topic of discourse* as a whole, and transforms the propositions of a text into a set of macropropositions that represent the *gist* of the text.

The model also describes the manner in which *sentence and phrase boundaries* are used to *chunk* the text in *short-term memory*. Part of the short-term memory is viewed as a short-term memory *buffer* of limited capacity. When a chunk of propositions is being processed, a number of propositions are selected and stored in the buffer to be connected later with incoming information. This process provides coherence (Kintsch and van Dijk, 1978).

Narrative analysis (story grammar). Unlike expository prose, in which each passage has a unique structure, narrative prose, despite variations in content, appears to have a *stable organizational schema* among the types of information and logical relations found in stories. In previous *investigations* of story recall, a story grammar was used to classify each event in the text. This analysis was then used to determine which types of events were the most frequently recalled. The results, when compared across a wide range of stories, adults, children and cultures, showed strikingly similar patterns of recall for story constituents (Nezworski, Stein and Trabasso, 1982).

Story grammars are methods of analyzing the content of narrative passages to determine the function of each sentence, and causal or temporal relations among the constituents. There are several methods of story grammar analysis that differ somewhat as to the identification of the constituents in a story; however, the similarities are more common than the differences (Nezworski, Stein and Trabasso, 1982).

Stein and Glenn's (1979) *story grammar* has two major *components*: (1) categories that specify the different types of information in a story and (2) logical-causal relations that describe how the categories are connected to each other. A story is analyzed into two units, the *setting* and the *episode*; see Table 7.1. The *setting* introduces the *protagonist* and other characters, provides background information, sets the locale and time, and describes personal states, traits and habitual actions or dispositions. The *episode* consists of five categories plus the relations connecting the categories. The first category of the episode is the *initiating event*, defined as an event changing the state of affairs in the environment and evoking an *internal response* in the protagonist. Internal responses include affective reactions, goals or desires, and thoughts or cognitions. These responses motivate the protagonist to make an *attempt* to satisfy goals or desires. The attempt represents overt actions that the protagonist performs to satisfy goals. These attempts result in direct *consequences* indicating whether or not the protagonist attained the goals. The direct consequences also produce a *reaction* in the part of either the protagonist or other characters (Nezworski, Stein and Trabasso, 1982).

The story analyzed in Table 7.1 is considered to be a *well formed story* because it contains all of the requisite categories, arranged in a logical sequence. In reality, few stories have a structure as simple as the one described. Most stories contain many episodes connected by various types of logical relations. Similarly, stories may also contain incomplete episodes, where one or more of the basic categories is omitted. However, if too many categories are missing and/or the logical connections are vague, readers will not be able to construct an adequate representation of the story. Such stories are not considered to be well formed (Baker and Stein, 1981).

An analysis of story recall indicates that story *events* are *recalled* in a regular temporal sequence with information in certain categories being recalled better than others. Settings, initiating events and consequences are retrieved most frequently; attempts are intermediate in recall, while internal responses and reactions are least frequently recalled (Nezworski, Stein and Trabasso, 1982). The exceptions to this pattern are the major goals (internal responses) that tend to be recalled with high frequency (Stein and Glenn, 1978), while minor settings (other than the protagonist's introduction) are not recalled very frequently (Mandler and Johnson, 1977; Stein and Glenn, 1979).

Table 7.1

Stein and Glenn's Story Grammar:
Analysis of a Well Formed Story

1. SETTING	1. Once there was a big grey fish named Albert.
	2. who lived in a big icy pond near the edge of a forest.
2. EPISODE	
a. Initiating Event	3. One day, Albert was swimming around the pond
	4. when he spotted a big juicy worm on top of the water.
b. Internal Response	5. Albert knew how delicious worms tasted
	6. and wanted to eat that one for his dinner.
c. Attempt	7. So he swam very close to the worm
	8. and bit into him.
d. Consequence	9. Suddenly, Albert was pulled through the water into a boat.
	10. He had been caught by a fisherman.
e. Reaction	11. Albert felt sad
	12. and wished he had been more careful.
	(Baker and Stein, 1981, p. 158)

Stein and Glenn (1978) presented children in the *first* and *fifth grade* with *oral stories*; recall of specific statements was stable over grades. In order from most to least recalled categories were major settings, initiating events, consequences, and internal responses. The only consistent developmental difference was that children in grade five recalled more internal responses than did children in grade one.

A major prediction derived from story grammar analysis is that stories that conform to the prototypical structure will be remembered better than those that do not. Stein and Glenn (1977) tested this hypothesis by examining the effects of *category deletions* on the story recall of children in the *first* and *fifth* grade. In general, the category deletions did not have the anticipated disruptive effect on recall, except when the initiating event of the story was deleted. Also, first graders showed decreased recall when the consequences were deleted. It is interesting to note that when

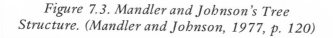

Figure 7.3. Mandler and Johnson's Tree Structure. (Mandler and Johnson, 1977, p. 120)

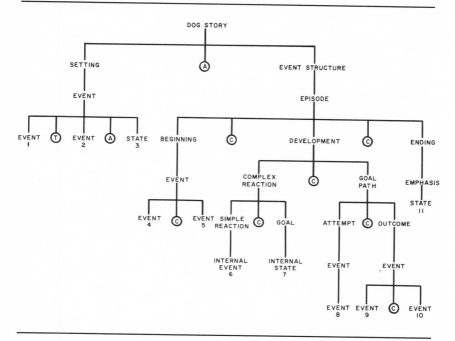

the most frequently recalled categories (*initiating events and consequences*) *are deleted*, the most new or fabricated information is added to recall. Similarly, the deletion of these categories produced the largest decrement in accurate recall. The added information was often of the same category type as that which had been deleted, indicating that young children do have knowledge to make deviant stories conform (Baker and Stein, 1981).

Baker and Stein report that the research dealing with children's understanding of story structure indicates that children, even *four and five years old*, do know what kind of information belongs in stories. Children have excellent comprehension of stories that conform to the structure specified by the grammar. However, their *comprehension* is *impaired* when stories deviate from the grammar. The impairment is greater for young children than for older children and adults. One of the major observations apparent in the research is that knowledge of the structure of stories is critical to an understanding of them. An important practical application of this research is to use the story grammar as a *model for the development of instructional materials.* According to Bruce (1978), many of the materials currently prepared for beginning readers are sometimes little more than strings of sentences, lacking the conflicts and goals that are such crucial elements of stories (Baker and Stein, 1981).

Mandler and Johnson (1977) have also developed a method of analyzing the underlying structure of simple stories—*folk tales, fables and myths.* The authors employ a type of *tree structure* similar to that used by Meyer, Brandt and Bluth (1980) to represent the basic elements of a story, and the interrelationship between the elements. The representation is outlined in the form of a *grammar* consisting of rewrite rules defining the elements and their relationships. Table 7.2 displays a sample story of a dog. The grammar of rewrite rules used to analyze the story is shown in Table 7.3. The tree structure resulting from the analysis of the dog story is displayed in Figure 7.3, where the elements of the story and their interrelationships are depicted.

Mandler and Johnson's story grammar (Johnson and Mandler, 1980; Mandler and Johnson, 1977) described six major categories of narrative information: *setting, beginning* (a precipitating event), *reaction* (the protagonist's reaction and setting a goal), *attempt* (the effort to achieve the goal), *outcome* (the success or failure of the attempt) and *ending* (the long-range consequence of the action sequence or the added emphasis). The beginning through the ending make up an *episode. Rules* in the grammar specify temporal relationships between categories and delineate how complex stories can occur through options such as embedding of episodes.

Tierney, Bridge and Cera (1978-79) when discussing discourse analysis of children wrote that studies by Meyer and McConkie (1973), Meyer (1975), Clements (1975), Marshall (1976), Marshall and Glock (1978-1979), McKoon (1977), Rumelhart (1976), Thorndyke (1977), Mandler and Johnson (1977) and Kintsch (1977) have provided substantial evidence indicating that the hierarchical structure of the text influences the extent and type of

Table 7.2

Dog Story

---

1. It happened that a dog had got a piece of meat
2. and was carrying it home in his mouth.
3. Now on his way home he had to cross a plank lying across a stream.
4. As he crossed he looked down
5. and saw his own shadow reflected in the water beneath.
6. Thinking it was another dog with another piece of meat,
7. he made up his mind to have that also.
8. So he made a snap at the shadow,
9. but as he opened his mouth the piece of meat fell out,
10. dropped into the water,
11. and was never seen again.

(Mandler and Johnson, 1977, p. 119)

---

information recalled and, further, that it enables one to predict where distortions, omissions and additions in recall will occur. A poorly constructed or vaguely written text makes greater demands upon the reader, who has to infer the missing structural elements to form a coherent semantic interpretation.

Fitzgerald and Spiegel (1983) conducted a study of children in the *fourth grade* to determine (a) if they could *be taught* an understanding of story grammar, and (b) if this knowledge of story grammar would improve *comprehension*. The children received two phases of instruction. The *first phase* was of short-term intensive instruction, consisting of six 30- to 45-minute sessions conducted over a two-week period. The *second phase* was long-term, intermittent instruction with *distributed practice* consisting of a ten 30- to 45-minute sessions over a five-week period. The instruction had two purposes: (a) to teach the story structure and (b) to increase the childrens' awareness of the ways in which knowing the structures of stories can help them understand stories in general.

During *phase one*, each lesson focussed on one story constituent and its temporal relationship to other story parts. In a typical phase one lesson, the instructor first gave a review of the story parts learned in previous lessons and an overview of the new lesson. Next, the instructor told about the story element (e.g.,

Table 7.3

Summary of Rewrite Rules for a Simple Story Grammar

Fable ———> story and moral
Story ———> setting and event structure
Setting ———>   state (and event)
                        event
State ———> state ((and state)n)
Event ———> event ((and then clauses   event)n) ((and
                state)n)
Event Structure ———> Episode ((then episode)n)
Episode ———> beginning cause development cause ending
Beginning ———>   event
                        episode
Development ———>   simple reaction cause action
                                complex reaction cause goal path
Simple reaction   ———> internal event ((cause internal
                                event)n)
Action ———> event
Complex reaction ———> simple reaction cause goal
Goal ———> internal state
Goal path ———>   attempt cause outcome
                                goal path (cause goal path)n
Attempt ———> event
Outcome ———>   event
                        episode
Ending ———>   event (and emphasis)
                        emphasis
                        episode
Emphasis ———> state

(Mandler and Johnson, 1977, p. 117)

attempt) by describing it, pointing out the element in a story on a wall chart, and giving two or three other examples of the element that would be appropriate for the story on the chart. Then, the instructor elicited two or three oral examples of the story element from the children. Next, the instructor gave *non-examples*, and asked why these were not good examples of the element being studied. The non-examples might be different story parts (e.g., an outcome for an attempt), or they might be the right story part but misplaced within the story. Last, the students participated in one or more *group or individual activities* designed to reinforce understanding of the element being taught that day. Examples of *reinforcement activities* were prediction and macrocloze tasks. For *prediction* tasks the students read part of a story (e.g., setting and beginning) told what part should come next, and provided an appropriate example of that part. In the *macro-cloze* activities, the children filled in missing chunks of stories after reading or listening to an entire story. For example, a story might contain a setting, beginning, reaction, outcome and ending. After reading the story, the student would identify what part was missing and supply an appropriate attempt.

Phase two instruction consisted of individual and group activities designed to provide continued reinforcement of knowledge of story constituents and to make the children aware of the relationship between comprehension of a story and knowledge of specific story parts and their temporal relationships. *Scrambled story* tasks required students to reorder stories in which the story had been jumbled. In the sorting tasks, the students sorted sentences and phrases from the story into piles to show which pieces went together. The students then ordered the piles to make a well sequenced story. In the *retelling activities*, the children recalled stories they had just read or heard and discussed ways in which the stories deviated from well formed stories, such as through the omission of necessary elements or additions of extra elements.

To emphasize the *relationship* between thinking about *story parts* and *understanding* a story, students read stories, identified the story parts, and then asked and answered questions designed to tap information from each story part. When answering questions, they would identify which story part contained that answer.

The *results* of the study indicated that the instruction did enhance story structure knowledge of children in the fourth grade who were average and below average readers. Furthermore, knowledge of story structure had a strong positive effect on both literal and inferential reading comprehension. These effects were realized during the first phase of instruction. The relative ease with which the results were obtained suggests that the instruction is practical, and that it could be readily incorporated into most classroom programs (Fitzgerald and Spiegel, 1983).

Gordon and Braun (1983) have described a number of excellent instructional procedures for teaching story grammar to children. Their suggestions are paraphrased below.

(a) Begin with an ideal story, one having each of the story grammar elements. Use a diagram of the story, as in Table 7.1 above, and fill in story information under each category as content is elicited from the children. Give the children copies of the diagram minus the story information. They then write the paraphrased story content on their own copies.

(b) Set reading purpose by posing schema-related questions prior to having children read a story segment. Elicit responses to the questions after the reading.

(c) Have the children identify the *major setting* in each of three different stories, then the *starter event* of the first *episode* in each of three different stories, and so on, before trying to identify all story components in one selection. Thus, the structural elements are held constant, while story content is varied.

(d) When children can associate story content with specific text structure categories on the diagrammed stories, begin asking story-specific questions. Continue to expect paraphrased story content as answers.

(e) Gradually introduce less well organized narratives, so children will learn that not all stories are ideal in structure.

(f) To help children handle structural variability, use the macrocloze technique on transparencies, and individual structure sheets for less well organized stories. In macroclose, some categories already contain story content, while others are left blank for the children to complete.

(g) Guide children to start asking their own schema-related or story-specific questions before reading. Have them read to find answers for their own oral or written questions. The authors also provide a number of procedures for transferring story knowledge to stories written by the children.

Constituent Features of Prose Affecting Recall

Readability. Readability refers to the difficulty experienced in reading a passage of text. Over the years, a number of formulas have been developed (e.g., Dale and Chall, 1948; Fry, 1968; Spache, 1953) to calculate readability in terms of grade level. These formulas have evaluated general factors such as the vocabulary, sentence structure and content of prose passages. Specific factors evaluated have been: frequency of pronouns, subordinate clauses, prepositional phrases, number of syllables, abstract words and affixed morphemes. In addition, Bormuth (1968) and Botel and Granowski (1972) have evaluated features like syntactic complexity. Criticisms have been directed at each of these formulas (Durkin, 1974).

Word frequency refers to how often a word is used in the language. Word frequency significantly influences readability. For example, Marks, Doctorow and Wittrock (1974) created two versions of a story read by elementary school children. Comprehension and retention nearly doubled, when only 20 percent of the words were changed from less- to more-frequent diction. The *abstract* quality of the words in a passage is defined in terms of whether words such as *dog, platypus* and *divan* have concrete referents. Words like *love, pity* and *parsimonious* have abstract referents and are more difficult to comprehend and recall. These observations are consistent with those made by Paivio, Yuille and Madigan (1968) that words with concrete referents that lend themselves to visual imagery are more memorable than abstract words.

Sentence length and *complexity* also influence readability. Some theorists have suggested that sentence length should be kept at a minimum. Prepositions, adjectives and adverbs should be used sparingly, and coordinating conjunctions should be replaced by periods (Bormuth, 1979).

Valentine and Francks (1979) have made several recommendations regarding the simplification of *social studies text*. One of their suggestions is to use *chunking* to facilitate assimilation of new and unfamiliar vocabulary and concepts into memory. According to the authors, students cannot effectively struggle with new vocabulary, complex syntax and abstract social studies concepts without assistance. The authors suggested that a common reaction for readers is to ignore anything that has no meaning for them. As a result, some information is never processed, and, therefore, cannot be recalled for later use. An example follows of *paragraph simplification* and *chunking* suggested by Valentine *et al.*; no evidence is reported as to the effectiveness of these procedures. *Segmenting paragraphs* or *chunking* is further discussed in Chapter Eight.

A Reindeer Stampede (Original Form)

Suddenly, a boy ran into the cave, shouting that a herd of reindeer had been spotted nearby! The men and boys in the cave put aside what they had been working on. They lit torches at the fire and rushed out of the cave (Yohe, 1971, p. 50, in Valentine and Francks, 1979).

The first paragraph is the form in which the material was originally printed in the text. The sentences that follow illustrate the revisions.

A Reindeer Stampede (Revised Form)

Suddenly a boy ran into the cave.
He was shouting,
    "I saw some reindeer!"
Men and boys were in the cave.
They stopped working when the boy ran in.
There was a small campfire in the cave.
The people used this fire for cooking and for supplying heat.
This time they used the fire to light torches so they could see when they went outside.
They ran outside the cave with the torches. . .
    (Yohe, 1971, p. 50, in Valentine and Francks, 1979)

Britton, Glynn, Meyer and Penland (1982) have described a more systematic method for *reducing* the *structural complexity* of prose. *Basic English* is a technique for reducing the structural complexity of textual material, while preserving its meaning (Ogden, 1943, Richards, 1943; Richards and Gibson, 1974). Basic English is a simplified form of Standard English in which a vocabulary of approximately 850 words is used to communicate all ideas; for specialized fields like science, the total vocabulary may be increased to 1000 words. This reduction in vocabulary is possible for three reasons. First, a relatively small number of words accounts for most of the words used in English text. For example, the 100 most frequent English words account for about 47 percent of the words occurring in written English (Kucera and Francis, 1967). Secondly, many English words are rarely used. In fact, about 41 percent of the words occurring in a million word sample appear only once (Britton, 1978; Kucera and Frances, 1967). Thirdly, rarely used words can usually be replaced by frequently used equivalents (Ogden, 1943, 1970). Basic English dictionaires are available (Ogden, 1943, 1970) both for words in general use (Ogden, 1970) and for the specialized words in science (Graham, 1966). A major part of the reduction in vocabulary is achieved by replacing the *verbs* with simplified two-word equivalents of one of the 16 basic verbs and a preposition or other word. For example, the verbs *to enter, climb and descend* can be replaced with *go in, go up and go down*. A similar economy can be achieved by dispensing with fine shades of meaning that are carried by rarely used verbs. For example, *made up* could be substituted for *prepared*, and *cut up* could replace *minced*. Britton *et al.* claim that complex technical texts can be translated into Basic English without loss of meaning. Also, Basic English uses a smaller number of *syntactic rules*, and the rules of syntax are less complex in the Basic English versions of a prose passage (Britton, Glynn, Meyer and Penland, 1982).

The following four paragraphs illustrate four variations of the same prose material that Britton *et al.* tested on *undergraduate students*. The paragraphs combine simple or complex syntax, and common or rare words.

Common words and simple syntax

The people of this truly colorful country have from their earliest days called themselves "Thai" (free). And the land in which they live, they themselves call "Muang Thai" (land of the free) or "Prathet Thai" (country of the free). Consequently, the people prefer to be called Thai, not Siamese, and prefer their country to be called Thailand, not Siam.

Common Words and Complex Syntax

The people of this truly colorful country have, from their very earliest days, called themselves "Thai" (free), and the land in which they live, they themselves call "Muang Thai" (land of the free) or "Prathet Thai" (country of the free). That the people prefer, consequently, to be called not Siamese, but Thai, is paralleled by their preference for their country to be called not Siam, but Thailand.

Rare Words and Simple Syntax

The populace of this veritably picturesque monarchy have from the incipiency of their annals referred to themselves as "Thai" (free), and the land inhabited by them is referred to by the residents as "Muang Thai" (land of the free) or "Prathet Thai" (country of the free). Consequently, the people favor being called Thai, rather than Siamese, and favor their homeland being called Thailand rather than Siam.

Rare Words and Complex Syntax

The populace of this veritably picturesque monarchy have, from the incipiency of their annals, referred to themselves as "Thai" (free) and the land inhabited by them is referred to by the residents as "Muang Thai" (land of the free) or "Prathet Thai" (country of the free). That the people favor, consequently, being called rather than Siamese, Thai, is paralleled by their preference for their homeland's being called, rather than Siam, Thailand. (Britton, Glynn, Meyer and Penland, 1982, p. 55.).

Recall tests that followed each passage illustrated that significantly more questions were answered correctly with text using common words than with texts using rare words. Also, more questions were answered correctly with the simple syntax versions.

There are *problems* associated with writing everything in short, simple sentences. Sometimes simplification leads to a change in the message. Also, some messages may be more effectively communicated by long, complex sentences. In the example below, if students are to answer question (a) they may be assisted more if they have been presented with message (b) rather than message (c).

   (a) Why did the peasants revolt?
   (b) The peasants revolted because the king raised the taxes.
   (c) The king raised taxes. The peasants revolted.
                    (Pearson and Johnson, 1978, p. 16)

   Bransford (1979) pointed out that the ability to abstract the overall idea of a passage involves more than the ability to remember individual sentences. Comparison of individual sentences may not be of major relevance when discussing readability. Moderate levels of *syntactic complexity* may enable readers to *integrate information* and abstract overall ideas. Sentences that are syntactically simple may actually make it harder for students to interrelate sentences and form holistic, integrated structures. For example, a story in a reading book for children in the fourth grade discussing Indian houses contained statements somewhat like the following: "The Indians of the Northwest Coast lived in slant-roofed houses built of cedar plank. . . . Some California Indian tribes lived in simple earth-covered or brush shelters. . . . The Plains Indians lived mainly in teepees. . . ." The story provided no information that the nature of the houses related to the climate and geography. Thus, children may have difficulty inferring the relationships between houses and their surroundings. As a result, *comprehension* and *memory* may suffer. In short, some attempts at simplification are not simplifications at all (Bransford, 1979). Furthermore, Pearson (1974) observed that children actually prefer moderate degrees of syntactic complexity to syntactic simplicity.

   Repetition of ideas within a prose passage influences the probability of *recall*. Research has found that the number of repetitions of word concepts is positively related to the probability that the concepts will be immediately recalled (Kintsch, Kosminsky, Streby, McKoon and Keenan, 1975). Both the *timing* and *nature* of the *repetition* may be important. An idea that is immediately repeated may be less well retained than an idea repeated after some time interval. The degree of similarity between a repetition and the first occurrence of the idea may be important. If the contexts are quite dissimilar, the idea may not appear to be related to its previous encoding, and hence, no effect on recall would be expected. If the contexts are very similar, the old retrieval pathways would be used and, therefore, strengthened. The best situation may be that in which the *contexts* are of *intermediate similarity*, as new links to the to-be-remembered material would be created in addition to strengthening existing links (Gagné, 1978).

Kintsch and Vipond (1978) analyzed the readability of text in terms of the number of *resource consuming operations* required to read the passage. The operations studied were the number of long-term memory searches and the number of inferences required. The assumption was that each of these operations disrupted the automatic comprehension processes and added to the difficulty of reading. The authors also suggested that the readability of a passage is also a function of the nature of the reader, in particular, a reader's *short-memory capacity* and the *proposition selection strategy* that she/he employs. The selection strategy determines which of the propositions read are put into the short-term buffer. Thus, according to Kintsch and Vipond, readability is not a property of a text alone, but of an interaction between the text and a reader.

Signalling. Signals are special words and phrases used by authors attempting to cue readers to the relative importance, function and interrelatedness of ideas expressed in a prose passage. Meyer (1975) has identified four *types of signals*: (a) the specification of the structure of relations in the context structure; (b) prematurely revealed information abstracted from content occurring later in the text; (c) summary statements; and (d) pointer words.

Specification of the structure of relations on the content structure includes explicitly stated rhetorical predicates and other information contained in the content structure. Meyer (1975) offered the following examples of this type of signalling; the signals are *italicized.*

> *The problems are* the generation of electric power *and* the protection of the environment. *A related problem of equal*

magnitude is the use of finite resources. *The solution is* nuclear breeder reactors (p. 77).

In the following example, signalling provides an explicit statement of the number of subordinate content nodes under the superordinate node psychotherapy.

Two approaches exist. *One* is based on psychoanalytic theory, *and the other* is based on principles of learning (p. 78).

Prematurely revealed information abstracted from the content occurring later in the text is presented toward the beginning of a passage or paragraph. These signals use the same words, or paraphrase the wording of information stated later in the text. There appears to be two kinds of signalling of this nature. The first, illustrated in example (a) below, is the prior enumeration of topics to be discussed later in the text. The second, shown in example (b), prematurely states ideas or interrelationships among content that are pointed out later in the text.

(a) *These alternative sources are solar energy, nuclear energy, geothermal energy and laser fusion energy* (p. 78).
(b) The first technique (psychotherapy) *attempts to change abnormal behavior by teaching the patient alternate, more effective patterns* (p. 79).

Summary statement signals use the same wording or para-phrased wording for information already presented and located in the content structure. These signals appear at the end of a passage or paragraph.

Pointer words are words that explicitly inform the reader of the author's perspective of a particular idea. The words may focus on a particular point, or inform the reader of the author's opinion, as in the following example:

Unfortunately, a large number of professional people attempting to change the behavior of mental patients use one technique with exclusion of the other (p. 80).

Hittleman (1979) describes eight types of tasks involving "signals" that may facilitate a reader's understanding of sentences. Examples of four of these signals are described below:

(a) Signals for indicating *where* something is, or is done: *under, in, on, at, to, between, among, behind, in front of* and *through*.

The class had its morning recess *in the school gym*.

(b) Signals indicating *when* something is done or happens: *before, after, later, while, as, now,* and *then*.

Frank was able to get inside his house *before the thunder and lightning started*.

(c) Signals indicating *how* something is done: adverbial endings *-ly, like, as*.

They walked quiet*ly* up the steps.

(d) Signals indicating *"how long"* or *"how much"* something is: *for, about, almost, as long (much) as, until* (and information dealing with any sort of measurement).

The cat sat *for hours* waiting for the canary to leave its cage. (Hittleman, 1978, pp. 237-240).

Stein and Nezworski (1977) used *markers* (signals), such as "This happened because . . ." to indicate that the order in which events were mentioned deviated from the order in which the events actually occurred. Children frequently experience difficulty with *inverted constructions*. Stein and Nezworski found that for children in the *fifth grade*, signalled inversions were at least as well recalled as when the information appeared in correct order, and some inversions where actually better recalled. For students in the *first grade*, some inversions were recalled as in well-formed stories, but some were worse. Baker and Stein (1981) suggested that first graders are probably less familiar with *temporal inversions* as a stylistic device in stories and are less able to deal with them.

Meyer (1975) conducted a study of the effect upon *college students* of the four types of *signals* she had defined. Signalling did not increase the *recall* of passages to a significant level although recall scores for all but one of the four passages were higher with signals. There was a tendency for signalling to increase the recall of content to which special emphasis was given; however, the effect was not statistically significant. Meyer suggested that perhaps signalling effects were not found in this experiment because the types of signals that would produce the largest effect were not studied. Reportedly, too many disparate things were lumped together as signals. Also, according to Meyer, the signalling in the four passages studied tended to be at the top level of the content structure, which generally is already well recalled. An author's use of signalling may be more effective if signals are used with middle or lower level information to increase attention to this information, which is usually less well recalled.

Meyer, Brandt and Bluth (1980) conducted a study on the effect of *signals* upon readers in *grade nine*. The authors investigated whether or not one type of signal provided by an author, *explicitly stating the top-level structure of text* would facilitate use of this structure by students in their *written recall* and the amount of information recalled. Relationships at the top half of the content structure were signalled rather than subordinate relationships. Three types of readers were studied, those with either good, average or poor pretest comprehension. A with- and without-signal version of each passage was written. The with-signalling version of the *Supertanker passage* began, "A problem of vital concern is the prevention of oil spills from supertankers." The without-signalling version did not include the words *problem* and *solution*, and began with, "Prevention is needed of oil spills from supertankers." The results of this study indicated that for one passage, signalling had no effect on the performance of good, average and poor comprehenders. On another passage, containing one-third more signalling, use of the authors' top-level structure and total recall were greater with signals on the *immediate recall* test. However, the aid derived from signals was not apparent a week later on a delayed test. There is some indication that greater *amounts of signalling* assist the learning and immediate recall of students with deficient pretest comprehension skills who cannot employ the structure strategy without assistance.

The research evidence does not support the intuitive value assigned to the use of signals. However, no studies have been reported of the effect of *teaching* students to use signals. A signal provides information that may enhance comprehension and recall only if the potential value of the signal is recognized and used by the reader.

Chapter Eight

Prose Recall and Comprehension: Two

Publisher-Controlled Aids to Improve Prose Recall

Typographic cueing, segmenting, and chunking. Research related to the effects of typographic cueing has shown that cues (e.g., **bold-face type**, and <u>underlining</u>) provide an isolating effect by visually *highlighting* cued words. Highlighting increases the probability that cued information will be recalled (Wallace, 1965). Typographic cueing can be used to increase a reader's awareness of the *underlying structure* of prose. The reader's attention can be directed toward important content and away from less important features. Rennie, Neilsen and Braun (1981) studied the effect on students in the seventh grade of cueing superordinate structure with the use of *italics*. Subjects were given prior instruction regarding the meaning of topic, main idea and paragraph. *Italic cueing* had no effect on memory of passages with familiar content. However, poor achievers on a pretest benefitted from cueing of unfamiliar content. It seems that cueing may make important information more salient for poor readers. The authors suggested that, if lower level ideas were cued this might negate the effect of superordinacy on recall.

Cromer (1970) studied the effect of *spacing* as a typographic cueing device on the reading comprehension of *college students*. He tested three groups of readers. *Difference readers* had adequate intelligence, language skills and vocabulary, but had difficulty comprehending reading material because of an inferred mismatch between the individual's typical mode of responding, and the pattern of responding necessary for adequate reading. The *deficit readers* also had adequate intelligence and language skills, but were deficient in both vocabulary and comprehension. Cromer expected that, if the reading passages were preorganized into meaningful *word groupings, comprehension* for the difference group would be facilitated, while comprehension of the deficit and the *good* readers would be unaffected. A *phrasing* condition was employed in which words were grouped on the basis of punctuation, structure and meaning. The groupings were primarily based on Lefevre's (1964) criteria that the significant elements are *grammatical* and *syntactical structures*: noun and verb groups and clusters, clauses and sentences. Two conditions were compared; reading with a regular sentence format, and reading with a phrased format, such as "The cow jumped (space) over the moon." As predicted, good and deficit readers were not affected by the spacing. With spacing, there was no difference in performance between good readers and difference readers. Thus, phrasing significantly improved the *comprehension* of difference readers.

O'Shea, and Sindelar (1983) studied the effect upon the *comprehension* of children in the *first* and *third grades* of *segmenting* written prose. Segmenting was based upon the following criteria established by Klare, Nichols, and Shuford (1957):

    (a) Subjects and predicates of simple sentences were separated, and the object was also separated from the predicate.

    (b) Phrases (chiefly prepositional) were set off.

    (c) Noun modifiers, if short, were linked with the noun, and verb modifiers with the verb, but single subjects or objects stood alone.

    (d) Clauses were set off and, if long, broken into appropriate thought units. (Klare, *et al.*, p. 42)

In the O'Shea *et al.* study, these procedures were amended as follows:

    (a) Contractions containing subject and verb were not separated.

(b) Subject and verb at the end of a sentence of dialogue were not separated, as in the phrase, *said Andy*.

The stories were typed so that spacings between phrases and sentences were constant with five spaces used to set off the thought units. The *results* of the study indicated that segmenting sentences in this manner improved the comprehension of both high and low performance readers. The authors suggested that since segmentation aids young developing readers in comprehension, its use in the classroom would seem appropriate as a supplement to basic instruction.

To make *social studies textbooks* more readable to children in the *fourth* and *seventh grades*, Weiss (1983) tested the effects of *segmenting*. One method tested was the *pausal phrase format* based on Johnson's (1970) technique of phrasing text. He segmented passages by locating the phrase points where 50 percent of an adult sample would pause when reading the passage aloud to add meaning, to add emphasis, or to catch their breath. For example:

Obtain three pieces of string
    long enough to reach from the chair to the table leg
    and pass over the baseline.

A second method of segmentation was called the *syntactic phrase format* based on Lefevre's (1964) method in which noun phrases, verb phrases and pattern completers were divided for each passage. In addition, each phrase segment was kept as short as possible, with a minimum of two words per line to allow the reader to make maximum usage of his or her *peripheral vision*. The passages were placed on single-spaced individual lines, as in the following example:

Obtain three pieces
    of string
    long enough
    to reach
    from the chair
    to the table leg
    and pass over the baseline

The *results* of the study indicated that both types of segmenting were equally effective in improving the *comprehension* of good, average and poor readers. The effect of segmenting was achieved in the absence of providing any specific *training* to the students in the use of segmentation. The author suggested that, if training had been provided, greater improvements in comprehension would have been achieved.

Underlining. A number of studies of underlining have been conducted with *college students* (Cashen and Leicht, 1970; Crouse and Idstein, 1972: Rickards and August, 1975). In the Cashen and Leicht study, statements of *principles* or *concepts* in *Scientific American* reprints were *underlined in red.* The results indicated that *recall* of the principles and concepts was significantly higher when the statements were underlined than when they were not. Also, *statements adjacent* to the underlined material were recalled significantly more often in the underlined condition. Readers given underlined text segments in the Crouse and Idstein (1972) study recalled significantly more underlined material than readers not given any underlined segments. Rickards and August found that contrary to their prediction, *subject-generated* underlining of sentences of high structural importance did not improve recall of the underlined material any more than *experimenter-provided* underlining of the same material. However, subjects who underlined their own material *recalled* more of the *nonunderlined* material than was recalled by students who read passages underlined in advance. In a passage of 2,305 words, Kulhavy (1972) found that underlining testable items within the passage, and *telling students to pay attention* to the underlined sections, led to higher scores on the post-test of both cued and non-cued material. Crouse and Idstein (1972) in a study of *undergraduate students* found that underlining those parts of a text which were later tested did not lead to better post-test scores, when the text and *reading time* were short (212 words, 2.5 or 5 minutes). But with a 6,000 word text and 25-minute reading period, underlining did lead to higher scores, especially for faster readers.

Glynn (1978) *concluded* after a review of the literature reporting on the effects upon recall of providing readers with underlined prose that, in general, underlining has little or no effect upon *recall*. However, the provision of underlined text does affect a reader's attention to certain parts of the text and underlined propositions are recalled at the expense of nonunderlined propositions. Perhaps as Meyer (1975) suggested, underlining, like signals, might best be used with propositions lower in the prose structure, as *high level propositions* are already generally well recalled. The benefits of underlining provided by the learner is discussed later in this chapter.

In a study of students in *grade eight*, Hershberger and Terry (1965) used typographic *cueing* of new and familiar *key words, key statements* and *key examples*. They employed *red capital letters, lower case red underlined*, lower case red and lower case black with red underlining. The authors concluded that simple typographic cueing significantly enhanced the ratio of important to unimportant content learned, without reducing the total amount learned. However, complex typographical cueing distinguishing five categories of lesson content did not benefit *recall* or *comprehension*. In fact, the complex combination of cues may actually have *confused* the readers.

What should be cued? Earlier studies (Dearborn, Johnson and Carmichael, 1951; Klare, Mabry and Gustafson, 1955) *cued single words*, while more recent work has cued *statements* or *sentences* (Crouse and Idstein, 1972; Fowler and Barker, 1974). If the intention is to cue the most *important sections*, one is faced with the problem of identifying the important content, which may vary from reader to reader, depending upon their familiarity with the text content. In principle, however, one should be able to cue the text for a particular group of readers. In addition, cueing should be able to assist the novice without impeding the expert. Fowler and Barker (1974) had one condition in which *college subjects* highlighted their own choice of content. The amount of highlighted material varied from 4.2 percent to 32.1 percent. Rickards and August (1975) reported that *college students*, instructed to underline sentences of high structural importance, identified sentences that were significantly lower in importance than those underlined by Rickards and August (Foster, 1979).

Texts vary in the *density of core content*, some having more elaboration of the central issues than others. In a high density text, a large portion of the content may be rated as core. In this case, the majority of the text could be cued; one might then obtain a figure-ground reversal in which the uncued material might be more visually distinctive. Crouse and Idstein (1972) found *underlining* to be ineffective, when the answers to 22 questions in a 210 word text were underlined, but beneficial when the answers to 30 questions in a 6000 word text were underlined. Their argument was that the *density of the cued material* influenced the response to the cueing. Is there an optimum proportion of text that should be cued, and is this proportion relative to the number of words or to the elements of thematic content (Foster, 1979)?

Headings. Wittrock (1974) studied the effects upon *recall* of *one or two word organizers* at the top of each paragraph in *grades five* and *six* reading materials. Below average and above average readers were given (a) one or two word headings, (b) one or two word headings plus the requirement of writing a sentence to summarize each paragraph or (c) only the requirement of writing a summarizing sentence after each paragraph. For both below and above average readers, one and two word headings improved *comprehension* and *recall* over that of students in the control group. The one and two word headings plus the *summarizing sentence* produced the greatest improvement. In fact, the above average readers receiving two word headings plus the sentences obtained scores that were twice those earned by subjects in the control group. The effects of the headings and the sentences were significantly greater for the above average readers.

Similar results were obtained in a study by Doctorow, Wittrock and Marks (1978) of readers in *grade six*. In one condition, the researchers used a *single word heading* above each paragraph. The word used was the noun that occurred most often in the paragraph, if the noun was the name of a story character. For all other nouns, however, a synonymous noun of higher frequency value than the noun in the story was used. The frequency value of each noun was determined by a table developed by Carrol, Davies and Richman (1971).

In a second condition, the same procedure was used to establish the first word in a two-word heading. The second word was selected as follows. First, the direct object of the first word—and the second most often occurring subject in the paragraph—was determined. Secondly, a synonymous word of a higher frequency than the direct object or subject, whichever occurred most often in the paragraph, was used as the second word in the heading. Interested readers are referred to the study by Doctorow *et al.* for a more detailed description of the results obtained in the study.

Questions. The effects upon comprehension and retention of questions *printed* before, during or after a prose passage are discussed in the following paragraphs. Questions posed *orally* by teachers are discussed in a later section of this chapter. In the studies described below, subjects answer a number of *test questions* after having read a passage of text. The ability to answer these questions is a function of having answered other *priming questions* about the passage; these questions are presented either before, during or following the text. The nature of the priming questions asked also influences performance on the test questions. As previously discussed, Anderson (1972) described the differential effects of *verbatim* and *paraphrase questions*. Questions of these types may occur as priming or test questions. Also, questions may simply focus the reader's attention on factual information, and require rote recall of such information. Alternatively, the questions may require integration of the material. Watts and Anderson (1971) found that *integrative priming questions* improved post-test recall. In contrast, subjects asked rote questions, such as "name the scientist associated with a particular principle," did worse on the post-test than if no priming question had been asked.

In the opinion of Watts and Anderson (1971), questions that focus on the recall of names, dates, technical terms and quantities do not adequately assess general educational goals. The authors suggested that questions should force readers to go beyond the *literal content* of instruction. Using *high school students*, Anderson and Watts tested the effect of *multiple choice questions*, where the correct choice gave an *example* that was *different* from that given in the text. For instance, in the text, when the psychological principle of displacement was discussed, the following example was given: "John failed to make the basketball squad, because he was too small, so he practiced hard to win a

cheerleader position." The multiple choice alternative corresponding to this example in the text was, "When punished for sucking
his thumb, Timmy stopped that habit, but spent hours chewing
gum." The example in the question is quite different from that
described in the text. High school students who answered priming
questions of this nature performed significantly better in the
post-test than did students who answered questions that exactly
reproduced the example described in the text. The use of
questions that required the reader to *interprete a parallel example*
not only had a beneficial effect, when the same questions were
repeated on the pretest, but also improved performance on other
questions.

Barrett (1968) developed a taxonomy of the cognitive and
affective dimensions of reading. The taxonomy describes five
major *categories of comprehension*: literal, reorganization, inferential, evaluation and appreciation. Each category has a number of
sublevels. Questions may be developed to selectively assess each
major and minor category of comprehension.

Rothkopf (1966) divided a 5,200 word chapter into seven
sections, each three pages in length. Before or after reading each
section of the chapter, groups of *adults* answered two questions
based on that section. After reading the entire chapter, subjects
were given a test that consisted of the questions answered during
reading and additional questions that had not been practiced. On
the *practiced questions*, subjects performed 40 percent better than
subjects in the control group, who did not answer questions during
the chapter. Answering questions after, but not before, reading
sections of the chapter also had a significant effect on answering
previously *unpracticed questions*. Asking questions before a
person reads a passage appears to cause the reader to search for the
answer to these questions, and to deemphasize information that
does not relate to the questions.

Yost, Avila and Vexler (1977) interspersed questions of
differing degrees of complexity every 20th frame of *programmed
instructional material* given to students in the *seventh grades*. The
groups of students that responded to the *interspersed questions*
scored significantly higher on a recall test than the students who
were not given interspersed questions to answer.

The typical finding with *adults*, that questions placed following a passage of prose facilitate recall on a later test, has not consistently emerged in studies of *children* (e.g., Fischer, 1973; Richmond, 1976; Rowls, 1976; Watts, 1973). However, the general conclusion in reviews of the literature (e.g. Anderson and Biddle, 1975) is that post-questions produce more recall than pre-questions or no questions at all. *Post-questions* appear to benefit the recall of both material directly questioned and material that was not questioned. Rickards (1979) suggested that there are four basic kinds of processing associated with post-questions. Post-questions may lead to a review of specific material directly questioned, thereby improving the recall of that material. Post-questions may also promote a general review of physically *adjacent and thematically related* material. This type of review has a broader effect upon recall. Post-questions may also have an effect upon recall of subsequently read material. Questions that ask for specific types of information may focus attention and improve the recall of information of that sort in subsequent reading. Alternatively, more general questions may increase attention to a broader range of material read in later passages.

Rothkopf and Bisbicos (1967), in a study of *high school students*, observed that treatment in which questions were asked after a passage had been read resulted in better overall retention than when the same questions were located before the text or when no questions were asked. No significant difference in recall was observed when questions came before the passage or when no questions were asked.

Marginal notes. Marginal notes appear in the margin of a page adjacent to corresponding discussion in the text and provide an *outline* and *summary* of major points. The *value* of marginal notes lies in their potential to act either as (a) a summary of text content, (b) a device facilitating selective access to various parts of a passage, (c) a summary aiding review of major points following the reading of a text or (d) a conceptual framework assisting organization and recall of major points (Duchastel and Chen, 1980). Research reports describing the value of marginal notes have not been found in a review of the literature. Figure 8.1 provides an example of marginal notes; students may also be taught to make and review their own marginal notes.

Figure 8.1

An Example of Marginal Notes in Text

HISTORICAL DEVELOPMENT OF SO-
CIAL SECURITY

*Social Security and the Original Social
Security Act.* Social security refers to
Social Security (SS) :   OASDHI : Old Age, Survivors, and Dis-
1. OASDI   ability Insurance (OASDI) and Health
   (Cash benefits)   Insurance (HI) as provided under the
2. HI   Social Security Act. OASDI is the cash
   (Service Benefits)   benefit portion of social security. Indeed,
                           payments under OASDI are commonly
                           called "social security benefits." HI is the
                           non-cash benefit portion popularly
                           known as Medicare, which has two
                           parts—hospital insurance (Part A) and
                           medical insurance (Part B). Medicare ben-
                           efits are paid on behalf of a beneficiary to
                           a person or organization that provides
                           health care services.
SSA passed in 1935   The Social Security Act was passed in
                           1935. The collection of payroll taxes for
                           old-age benefits was begun . . . (Duchastel
                           and Chen, 1980)

Advance organizers. According to Ausubel (1963), an advance
organizer is a substantive introductory statement preceding textual
material that *previews* the *principal ideas* to be described in the
text. The statement is written at a much higher level of generality,
abstraction and inclusiveness than the passage to be read. The
organizer provides a structure to which more detailed information
in the text can be related. For *elementary school pupils*, Ausubel
(1963) recommended that organizers should be presented at a
lower level of abstraction, and should also make more extensive
use of concrete, empirical props. The purpose of an organizer is to
relate the potentially meaningful materials to be learned to the
already *existing cognitive structure* of the learner (Ausubel, 1963).

The organizer is designed to provide the learner with a general overview of the more detailed material that is to follow, and provide *organizing elements* that are inclusive of the particular content of the material and relevant concepts in cognitive structure. The organizer, thereby, is designed to make use of established knowledge to increase the learnability of new material. Ausubel distinguished between *organizers and overviews or summaries* commonly found in textbooks. According to him, overviews and summaries are typically written at the same level of abstraction and generality as the learning material and accomplish their effects through repetition, selective emphasis on key words or central concepts. In contrast, organizers are written at a higher level of abstraction and generality and provide relevant subsuming concepts.

Barnes and Clawson (1974) reviewed the research literature on the effectiveness of advance organizers. They reviewed studies that examined the effect of *length of treatment* (1-10 days), different *subject populations* (low, average and high ability), various *subject areas* (social studies, science, mathematics and religion) and *grade levels* (grade three to college). They concluded that the efficacy of advance organizers had not been established. Of the 32 studies reviewed, 12 reported that advance organizers facilitated learning, while 20 reported that they did not. When each of the previously mentioned variables was analyzed separately, no clear pattern emerged regarding the facilitative effects of advance organizers. The majority of studies conducted with students of average and low ability produced nonsignificant results; however, inconsistent results were found with students of high ability. The grade level of the students was not a significant variable except at the post-secondary level.

Kosoff (1981) investigated the effects of three qualitatively different types of written introductions, presented to *grade five* children immediately prior to their reading of informational passages on social science topics. The *textually explicit* introduction consisted of sentences taken verbatim from the passage and following the original sequence. A *textually implicit* introduction provided explicit representation of information implied in the passage. This type of introduction provided explicit linkages (e.g., connective words or phrases) between propositions when such linkages were merely implied in the passage. A *scriptally implicit* introduction presented substantively new, topic-related information that was neither stated nor implied in the passage. Further, this type of introduction explicitly linked this new information to an idea in the passage. A sample passage and three types of introductions to it are shown below.

Sample Stimulus Passage

For thousands of years the Nile River has made the land around it rich. But the ancient people of Egypt could not control the huge river. Often the river overflowed too much. Then there were bad floods. At other times there was too little water from the Nile. Then the crops died, and the people went hungry. The people said these things happened because the river god was angry.

They threw dolls and gifts into the river. They hoped that these gifts would make the river god happy. Today, we know that wet seasons can make a river overflow. Dry seasons can make a river dry up.

A dam can stop the flow of a river. A dam can store water in wet seasons for use in dry seasons. Egypt began to build the Aswan Dam in 1960. This dam is 3 miles long and 350 feet high. It can control floods on the Nile River.

The Egyptians of today do not need to try to keep a river god happy. (McGraw-Hill, 1977, in Kosoff, 1981)

Sample Passage Introductions

Textually explicit introduction

For thousands of years, the Nile River has made the land around it rich. But, the ancient people of Egypt could not control the huge river. Often the river overflowed too much. At other times, there was too little water from the Nile. The people said these things happened because the river god was angry. Egypt began to build the Aswan Dam in 1960.

Textually implicit introduction

Although the Nile river made the land around it rich, it caused problems for the ancient Egyptians. When the huge river overflowed too much, it caused bad floods. At other times the crops died because the river did not overflow enough. In 1960, the people of Egypt began to build a dam for the river.

Scriptally implicit introduction

In ancient times many people believed in different kinds of gods. They believed that the gods controlled the forces of nature, such as the wind, the sun, and water. The ancient Egyptians thought that a river god made the Nile River overflow. When the river overflowed, it watered the farms and left fertile mud on the fields.

The seven passages studied, and the student's *immediate* and *delayed recall*, were segmented in propositions using a modified form of Frederiksen's (1975) system of text analysis. An example of each of the propositions in the passage and a corresponding form of recall of each passage is listed below.

Textually explicit propositions

A proposition was classified as textually explicit if its constituent concepts and/or relations were identical to, or a paraphrase of, those in a proposition derived from the passage. (Paraphrases were defined as synonymous or anaphoric referents for concepts within passage propositions.)

> Example : Passage : The river god was angry.
>   Recall :   He was mad.

Textually implicit propositions

A proposition was classified as textually implicit if it represented a proposition that was implied in the passage. Four types of text-based inferences were included within this category :

(a) concepts which were superordinates or subordinates of concepts within propositions from the passage.

> Example : Passage : They (people) threw dolls and gifts into the river.

Recall : Little children threw dolls and things into the river.

(b) recall propositions which represented presuppositions or consequences inferrable from passage propositions.

Example : Passage : Egypt began to build the Aswan Dam in 1960.
Recall : Modern Egyptians solved the river problem.

(c) recall propositions which represented a synthesis of segments from separate propositions within the passage.

Example : Passage : For thousands of years the Nile River has made the land around it rich. Then there were bad floods.
Recall : The Nile River flooded the land around it.

(d) recall propositions which represented an explicit logical relation between propositions when that relation was implied in the passage.

Example : Passage : Then the crops died and people went hungry.
Recall : The people went hungry because there wasn't enough food.

Scriptally implicit proposition

A recall proposition was classified as scriptally implicit if it was plausible and if it represented new concepts or new information which were not stated or implied in the passage.

Example : Passage : (Indicated only that the Nile River was in Egypt.)
Recall : The Nile River is in a tropical region.

The *results* of Kosoff's study indicated that all subjects, regardless of the type of introduction they received, produced a significantly greater proportion of (a) textually explicit propositions in *immediate recall* than in *delayed recall*, and (b) scriptally implicit propositions in delayed recall than in immediate recall. Students who had received the scriptally implicit introduction generated a significantly greater proportion of scriptally implicit propositions than students who had received textually implicit or explicit introductions.

Pictures and prose. The use of pictures to accompany passages of prose may serve *several purposes*. Pictures may heighten motivation and interest, summarize the content of the prose, focus attention on critical features of the message, graphically illustrate complex points, enhance imagery, and increase comprehension, review, encoding and retrieval. Studies of the motivational benefits of pictures have not been reported (Duchastel, 1980). Studies of the effects of pictures on comprehension and recall are described in the following passages.

Levin and Lesgold (1978) reviewed the research literature describing the effects of pictures on prose recall. They restricted their review to *fictional, narrative* passages presented *orally* to children where the content of the pictures *overlapped* that of the story, and where learning was demonstrated by *factual recall*. They found overwhelming support for the use of pictures. For example, Guttmann, Levin and Pressley (1977) found that across *grades K, two* and *three*, children correctly responded to 80 percent of the short-answer questions, when pictures accompanied oral narrative. Children learning the same narrative without pictures responded correctly to 57 percent of the questions. Similar results were reported by Lesgold, DeGood and Levin (1977). Their sample of children in the *first grade* recalled 68 percent with pictures, and 47 percent without pictures. A group of *educable, mentally retarded children*, ages 10-16, studied by Bender and Levin (1978), correctly responded to 64 percent of the questions, when pictures were used, compared to 34 percent when pictures were not used. When pictures are used with orally presented prose, there is generally a 40 percent improvement in recall over the condition where pictures are not used (Levine and Lesgold, 1978). *How* the *pictures* are *presented* does not seem to be relevant. Levin and Lesgold described studies in which pictures were presented: (a) simultaneously with the text, (b) following each sentence, (c) following each passage, (d) as slides on a screen and (e) as plastic laminated cutouts on a background board. In each case, the pictures improved recall. Pictures benefitted children: (a) males and females, (b) from grades 6-12, (c) from middle class white populations and from lower class black populations and (d) individuals of average intelligence or educable levels of mental retardation. The beneficial effect of pictures has been observed with 50 and 100 word passages.

Pictures do not appear to benefit certain types of passage information at the expense of others. In a study by Levin, Bender and Pressley (1979), children in *grades two and five* were asked to recall both *central, thematic information*, and *incidental details* contained in sentences. Subjects who used the *cartoon-like pictures* recalled more of each type of information in comparison to children who were not presented with pictures. Peng and Levin (1979) found that the amount of picture facilitation for children in the *second grade* tested three days after the presentation of the passages was as great as that for children tested immediately following the passages. Moreover, comparable improvements resulting from the use of pictures were observed for *verbatim* and *paraphrase questions*. Note that all of the previously mentioned studies reported by Levin and Lesgold (1978) refer to *orally* presented *narrative* passages where the picture content overlapped that of the story.

Guttmann, Levin and Pressley (1977) read stories to children in *kindergarten*, and in the *second* and *third grades*. The children were presented with sets of pictures that either *fully or partially illustrated* the content of the stories. Subjects in the partial picture condition were instructed to *form mental images*. For example, the initial sentence from one of the passages in the story is "One evening Sue's family sat down to eat a big turkey for dinner." The fully illustrated picture depicting this sentence showed a family of four seated around a table with a turkey on a platter in the center of the table. The partially illustrated picture depicted the same family in essentially the same manner except that the head of one of the persons at the table now obscured the viewers' observation of the turkey. The question relating to the content of the passage was "What did Sue's family eat for dinner one evening." The answer, *the turkey*, is not represented in the partial picture.

The *results* of the study indicated that even kindergarten children learned more when presented with pictures illustrating the story. These children, when shown a partial picture and when told to imagine the situation, did not perform better than children who had not received pictures or instructions to imagine. Similarly, there was no difference between partial picture, imagery and control conditions for children in the second grade. Thus, the fully illustrated pictures clearly facilitated recall. Similarly, grade two children who had received the complete pictures outperformed subjects in the partial picture and control conditions. However, there was no memory performance difference between children receiving fully or partially illustrated pictures. At the second grade level, partial pictures were not as facilitative as complete pictures. Children in the third grade, with partial or complete pictures, outperformed control subjects. With children in grades two and three, even partially illustrated pictures facilitated performance.

Haring and Frye (1979) conducted a study of children in the *fourth* and *sixth grade* using a *narrative* passage where picture content overlapped that of the text. Redundancy of picture and text content was specified by basing picture content on a *content analysis* of the text using *Meyer's* (1975, 1977) analytical approach to determine which details to include in the pictures. In contrast to previously reported research, the children *read* the passages. *Written recall* was tested immediately following completion of reading and again five days later. On both tests, children who had been shown pictures (line-drawings) recalled significantly more than children who were not shown pictures. In accord with Meyer's analysis of the prose content structure, some pictures contained detail only from the *top level* of the prose structure. Other pictures contained detail from both the top and *lower levels* of the prose structure. No significant difference in recall of either top or lower level information was obtained from the use of either type of picture.

Haring (1982) conducted a similar study of children in the *fourth* and *sixth grades*. A set of 13 pen-and-ink drawings depicted the 350 top and lower level idea units in the story. These idea units were derived from Meyer's prose analysis. The pictures did not affect recall of top level information; however, students who received pictures recalled detail of lower level information more consistently than children who did not receive pictures.

Levin and Berry (1980) evaluated the effects upon children in the *fourth grade* of using pictures with *non-fictional reports* of actual incidents. One of the passages studied is reported below.

The Dying Honey Bees

> The honey bee, Wisconsin's official state insect, is dying. It is dying from a poisonous spray that farmers use to destroy bugs on their crops. The farmers don't mean to kill the bees, but some spray they use gets carried through the air to the hives of neighboring beekeepers. These beekeepers want the farmers to stop spraying their crops so the bees won't die. If the farmers won't stop spraying, the beekeepers want the farmers to tell them when and where they will be spraying so the beekeepers can move their bees away from sprayed crops. (Levin and Berry, 1980, p. 14)

For each passage, a single 8 1/2 by 11 inch, colored, line-drawing was presented to illustrate the main idea of the passage. The picture used for the honey bee passage is presented in Figure 8.2. One-half of the recall questions tapped information that was specifically pictured, the remaining questions related to information that was not pictured. Recall was tested immediately and after three days.

Subjects in this study who viewed pictures recalled 80 percent of the information tested; subjects who did not view pictures recalled 65 percent. For pictured information, the average recall of subjects who viewed the pictures was 94 percent compared to 81 percent for subjects who did not view pictures. Moreover, for nonpictured information, the recall means were quite comparable for picture and control subjects, respectively, 52 and 56 percent. Thus, *text relevant pictures* facilitated recall of that information, but not at the expense of the typically less important, *unillustrated information*.

Duchastel (1980) studied the use of pictures with *expository text*. He used a 2 x 2 inch *photograph* or *line-drawing* with 14- and

*Figure 8.2. Picture Accompanying the Honey
Bee Passage. (Levin & Berry, 1980, p. 179)*

15-year-old *high school* students. Each picture provided a visual summary of the content of the text and did not add any additional information. Recall was evaluated with *written, free recall* and *short-answer tests*. The illustrations did not significantly influence retention.

Brody (1980) described a number of *problems* associated with the picture/prose comprehension and recall *research*. Reading passages and their accompanying pictorial illustrations barely resemble materials students use in the classroom. For example, Rigney and Lutz (1976) presented stimulus materials by means of a computer; such an *artificial treatment* makes accurate and meaningful synthesis of results difficult (Brody, 1980). Also, whereas texts, particularly at the high school and college level, usually contain a limited *number of pictures*, several studies have used an inordinately large number of pictures for relatively brief reading passages. In Dwyer's (1971) study, for example, *college students* viewed 37 visuals while reading a 2000 word passage, thus requiring the students to view one visual for every 54 words read. Similarly, in the Rankin and Culhane (1970) study, subjects viewed 17 visuals in a 250 word passage, or approximately one visual for every 15 words. Brody also questioned the validity of research that compares learning from passages that include pictures, while neglecting to isolate and compare different pictorial attributes. The research should determine which *attributes of pictures* affect various forms of learning for different types of learners, and identify the conditions under which the effects of the various attributes can be maximized (Brody, 1980). Brody also pointed out that in some studies with elementary school children (e.g., Haring and Frye, 1979; Ruch and Levin, 1977) conclusions were based on the use of line-drawings rather than the more replete illustrations typically found in elementary texts.

The foregoing studies appear to have assessed the effects upon prose comprehension and recall of the simple *justaposition* of pictures with the oral or written presentation of prose. These *studies* are *limited* in a number of ways that influence the nature of the conclusions that may be drawn. None of the studies appears to have verified whether, in fact, the readers actually looked at the pictures. None of the reports describes the manner in which the pictures were regarded by the readers. In oral presentations of prose, no mention is made of efforts to attract the learner's attention to particular aspects of the pictures. The studies do not report whether or not the persons reading the passages pointed to important features of the pictures before or during reading of the passages. *Teacher prompting* like this is common when passages are being presented orally to children. In written presentations of text, no mention is made of attempts to *highlight graphically critical features* of the pictures. In fact, in most of the studies, little description is provided of the exact *nature* of the *pictures*, cartoons, photographs, line-drawings and other types of graphic representations that were used. None of the studies reported attempted to assess the reader's *knowledge and skills* regarding the use of pictures before conducting the studies. No attempts were made to train the readers to (a) attend to critical aspects of the pictures, (b) relate these features to the content of the textual material or (c) use the pictures while reviewing the content of the prose. Thus, it appears that this area of study is in the early stages of development and that the potential value of the use of pictures with prose remains to be determined. Conclusions drawn at this point must be tentative.

Learner Controlled Aids to Recall

Notetaking. Ganske (1981) completed an exhaustive study of notetaking studies. The recommendations on outlining and notetaking described in 38 study manuals are summarized in Table 8.1. A common observation was the similarity of the recommendations on notetaking procedures in the absence of supporting research evidence.

Ganske (1981) reviewed a number of comparison studies in which students were told either to take notes or not to take notes. In eight of eleven studies reviewed, students who were told to take notes, when a period of *time* was *provided* for *review*, had higher recall than students did who had been told no*t* to take notes.

Several studies involving *training* notetaking were reviewed; four studies involved *high school* students, and two involved *college* students. The results indicated that training in notetaking did not lead to an improvement in performance. However, as Ganske pointed out, the very *short training* period characteristic of these studies may not have been sufficient to make a significant change. For example, Palmatier (1968) *trained high school juniors* to take notes from tape-recorded lectures. Training was provided on only two days of the eleven day program; no significant difference was produced by the notetaking. One study (Driskell, 1976) in which significant improvements were observed was with borderline *college* students who were trying to raise their grade averages to stay in school. These students were probably able to appreciate the functional benefits of the skill; in addition, a whole study skills training program was involved. According to Ganske, most of the previous work has indicated that students do little *review* of notes. In studies where notetaking only is compared with notetaking plus notes-review, in general, notes plus review

Table 8.1

*Summary of Recommendations on Outlining
and Note-Taking from Books*

Recommendation	Frequency
Have a neat and carefully thought-out system for taking notes; that is, place new topics on fresh sheets arrange statements to show the main heading by system of indentation.	29
Organize material read under headings and topics	24
Make brief outlines	21
Do not take down everything	19
Get thought units from paragraph heads, topic statements, etc.	18
Use your own words	15
Judge value of the outline	14
Use looseleaf notebook with good size paper	14
Invent and use abbreviations	13
Realize importance of notes	12
Take in full: quotes, unfamiliar material important facts	11
Understand what you are trying to organize	11
Read, then outline	10
Summarize by underlining	8
Adapt procedure to nature of book and use to be made of notes	7
Put main headings in question form	6
Take points and organize later	6
Realize notes and be accurate	6
Do not have too much detail in summary	6
Skim explanatory material	5
Review notes before filing	5
Realize that written outline is preparation for mental review	5
Use key words	5
Intend to remember	4

Laycock and Russell (1941, pp. 373-374)

produces improved recall (Ganske, 1981; Rickards and Friedman 1978).

Rickards (1980) observed that the perceived *importance* of the material presented exerted a dominating influence on the *quantity of notetaking*. A *cue*, such as "Take this down," *repeating* important points *slowly* enough for students to write them down verbatim, or simply asserting that good notes are important have produced improved quality of notes as measured by the presence of information in student notebooks. Research by Weener (1974) found that students who take *too many notes* may recall less than students who take fewer notes and perhaps concentrate on the main ideas of the material presented. Peters (1972) suggested that some students may be less able than others to *take notes*, and simultaneously *listen* to a lecture. The more efficient listeners may benefit from notetaking, while the less efficient listeners may find notetaking detrimental to their performance. Another consideration raised by Aiken, Thomas and Shennun (1975) is that depending upon the nature and complexity of the material, *notetaking* may be more effective when done *during breaks* in a lecture rather than during the lecture itself. In some of the previously described studies reviewed by Ganske (1981), student performance actually deteriorated after instruction in notetaking; perhaps, in these cases, performance may have been improved had students been instructed in a manner of notetaking that was geared to their listening skills, for example listen and then take notes. Because notetaking after a lecture period actually involves review, rehearsal and processing of the material, retention of the material may be improved merely as a matter of this activity.

Brown and Smiley (1978) conducted a study of *notetaking* with students in the *seventh* and *eighth grade*. The authors found that the pattern of notes taken was similar to that found with *underliners*, although fewer notes were taken than were underlined. *Spontaneous notetakers* recorded important elements; *induced notetakers* were not so sensitive. With respect to recall, the spontaneous notetakers were similar to college students, while induced notetakers and students who do not take notes were similar to younger children. The spontaneous notetakers showed the diagnostic adult-like pattern of increased *recall* of the important units of the texts. There was a strong relationship between notetaking and increased recall.

In a study of students in the *fifth, seventh* and *eighth grades*, Brown and Smiley (1978) found that the most proficient prose learners were those who elected spontaneously to take *notes and/or underline* while they were reading. The less proficient prose learners did not benefit from a *preinstructional suggestion* to take notes and/or underline. It should be noted, however, that in this study no explicit instructions were provided as to how to take notes or underline. In fact, the students induced to take notes, as a result of these instructions, produced notes and underlines of inferior quality.

Doctorow, Wittrock and Marks (1978) instructed students in the *sixth grade* to write a sentence *summarizing* the content of each paragraph as they read it. Control students were exposed to the passage for the same amount of time. The students who paraphrased outperformed control students in both an immediate multiple choice test and a modified cloze test given one week later. Paraphrasing increased student performance by over 50 percent on both tests.

Levin and Pressley (1981) claimed that to say that a paraphrase or note-taking strategy was employed in a particular study is not sufficient. Attention to implementation details is necessary; the *quality of the notes* must be evaluated. In addition, one must also specify how much and what *type of instruction* in notetaking and underlining was involved. How much *practice* and how many *examples* were provided? Was the training adequate?

Economical and *efficient notetaking* involves recording important features of *oral* or *written prose* that one may not otherwise recall. An effective notetaker must be aware of (a) his/her ability to recall prose; (b) strategies to enhance recall, if it falls short of a desirable level of accuracy; and (c) the structure of the passage, particularly its important and unimportant parts (Brown and Campione, 1978).

Brown and Campione presented readers in *grades 5, 7, 8, 11, 12,* and *college* with stories printed on index cards. The students were asked to select 12 out of approximately 50 units that they would like to have as *retrieval cues* when recalling the passage.

Half of each group was asked to select units before experience with the passage (the inexperienced group) while the remaining students were first given practice studying and recalling the passage (the experienced group). Inexperienced students at all levels showed a marked preference to select the most *important text elements* as retrieval cues. Following experience in reading and retrieving the stories, school children continued to select the most important text elements; however, the college students radically shifted their choices. These students after experience with the passage discovered what they could and could not recall without assistance; as a result, they no longer selected the most important parts of the passage as retrieval cues, as approximately 80 percent of this material had been readily recalled. Instead, the college students selected *information of intermediate importance* as retrieval cues, as this information had been difficult to recall. This ability to gain from previous experience was not displayed by students in grades eleven and twelve In a replication study, conducted by Brown and Campione, *grade eleven* and *twelve* students were given three opportunities to read and recall the passage. After the third reading, these students modified their selection of retrieval cues to parallel the selections made by college students. That is, they reduced selection of the most important features of the prose passage, which they were already able to recall, and increased the selection of elements of third and fourth levels of importance. These results, arising only after extended practice or experience with the materials, would seem to support the suggestions made by Ganske (1981) and by Levin and Pressley (1981) that the adequacy and duration of instruction must be evaluated.

In a related study, Brown (1981) reported research in which students in *grades 5, 7, 11,* and *college* were given a story to read and recall. Students able to recall 80 percent or more of the content of the stories were then asked to *write a summary* of the story in their own words. After they had written the summary, they were asked to write a second summary using only forty words. Grade eleven and college students included primarily level three and four (important) units in their summaries. While some lower level units (one and two) were included in the free paraphrase, these units dropped out when word restrictions were imposed.

When free to paraphrase, *grade five* students included many more level four units in their summaries than any other level, but showed no preference for level three over levels one or two. However, when constrained to forty words, the fifth graders eliminated level one units. Further limited to twenty words, they excluded level two words. Brown reported that this elimination of units as a function of their rated importance is the first evidence that fifth graders are in any way sensitive to fine differences in importance between levels one, two and three.

In a series of studies on notetaking by mature students, Brown (1981) identified a number of generic *rules for effective notetaking*. The first rule is that trivial material should be deleted. Even grade school children are quite adept at this, if the content of the material is familiar. The second rule is that redundant material should also be deleted. The third rule relates to the substitution of a superordinate term or event for a list of items or actions. For example, if a test contains a list such as *cats, dogs, gerbils*, and *parrots*, one can substitute the term *pets*. The fifth rule relates to selection of a topic sentence. The final rule involves invention of a topic sentence, if none exists in a passage.

To study the *developmental progression* associated with use of these skills, Brown and colleagues examined the ability of students from grades 5, 7, 10 and college to use the rules while summarizing. Even the youngest children deleted trivial and redundant information. The most difficult rule, that of inventing a topic sentence, was rarely used by students in the fifth grade, was used on only a third of the appropriate occasions by tenth graders, and on only half of the occasions where it was appropriate by college students. Fifth and seventh graders, reportedly tend to treat the task of summarizing as one of deciding whether to delete or include elements of the surface structure of the paragraph. The strategy is as follows: (a) read text elements sequentially; (b) decide for each element on inclusion or deletion; (c) if inclusion is the verdict, copy it more or less verbatim from the text (Brown, 1981).

Day (1980) *trained junior college* students to *summarize* text.

Students were assigned to one of four conditions. In the *self-management* condition, students were given general encouragement to write a good summary, but they were not told the rules for achieving this end. In the *rule* group, students were given explicit instructions and modeling in the use of the previously mentioned rules. For example, they were given various colored pencils, and were shown how to delete redundant information with red, delete trivial information with blue, write in subordinates for any lists, underline topic sentences, if provided, and write a topic sentence, if required. In the third group, *rules plus self-management*, students were given both the general self-management instruction and the rules, but they were left to interpret the two sets of information for themselves. In the *control plus monitoring group*, students were given explicit training in application and monitoring of the rules. For *monitoring*, the students were shown how to check if they had a topic sentence for each paragraph (either underlined or written-in), and to check that all redundances were deleted, etc. It took very explicit training, rules plus monitoring, before the performance of remedial students reached that set by four-year college students. The remedial readers with the most serious problems also showed improvement following training. Selection of the topic sentence remained difficult, and poor readers experienced major difficulty before, during and after training with inventing a topic sentence when none was present. The best performance was obtained by the *rules plus monitoring* condition; the next best was the rules plus self-management group; the third best was the rules alone training; insignificant gains were made by the self-management alone group (Brown, 1981).

In most situations, students have a *limited amount of time*. Obviously, taking notes requires more time than simply reading the text. The time that note-takers use to record some information is time subtracted from processing other information. In the absence of knowledge of the criterion task, students take notes what they think will be tested. Probably students select the *main idea* or *most important* information as the focus of the note-taking efforts; they may not have *time to process* less important information. Research has shown, however, that people tend to remember the *most important* information anyway. Therefore, notetakers may be learning *main ideas* very well, but at the expense of learning other information. On the other hand, subjects who use less time-consuming studying techniques (e.g., *read-reread*, and *underline*) are able to distribute their attention and effort more evenly over the passage. Therefore, a read-reread group, for example, might have an advantage over a notetaking group when the criterion task taps information of lesser importance, or when the criterion task is free recall (in which case the score reflects the number of idea units recalled without respect to importance). The second possibility for the apparent ineffectiveness of notetaking is that subjects may not be taking notes in a way that entails deep processing. For example, subjects may choose to record information *verbatim* from the text rather than recording a reworked, *paraphrased* representation of text meaning (Anderson and Armbruster, 1982).

Saski, Swicegood and Carter (1983) have designed two formats to assist *secondary level students* in note-taking from *lectures* or *textbooks*. These formats are designed to facilitate study for future tests. The formats are shown in Figures 8.3 and 8.4. A line is drawn across the top of the page for the topic title. Each page initially contains only one topic or idea to prevent an overload of information that might be confusing to the student.

The *new information* in Figure 8.3 is completed with current facts, figures, dates and discussion notes—information germane to present class studies or the page topic. This is the basic notetaking column in which the majority of information is recorded.

The *old information* column is completed with notes concerning facts or ideas a student has previously learned or studied. It may be used as a *connections* section, linking previously covered material to present facts and ideas. This step is designed to reinforce the relevance of current studies and highlight the idea that content-area information is not a series of isolated events but an interrelated body of knowledge.

Questions is an especially important column. Here the student marks information that needs to be clarified, notes possible test information, and checks to insure that all needed information is listed. Gaps in notes are also indicated in this column, as are

Figure 8.3. Notetaking Format 1.

OLD INFORMATION	NEW INFORMATION	QUESTIONS
2" (Previously studied information: connections between old and new information)	5" (Basic notetaking column)	I" (Comments about notes that need to be elaborated on or which are important for future assignments)

Figure 8.4. Notetaking Format 2.

TOPIC SENTENCE : _____		
BASIC IDEAS	BACKGROUND INFORMATION	QUESTIONS
5" (Basic notetaking column, stress on information for tests, reports, etc.)	2" (Related or interesting information)	I" (Comments about notes that need to be elaborated on or which are important for future assignments)

questions relevant to future use of the information on tests, reports, etc.

In Figure 8.4, the top of the page contains the topic sentence for the particular material to be covered. The *basic ideas* column contains facts, figures, dates, important people and places—material that will be needed on future tests or reports. *Background* includes ideas, topics and facts that are interesting to the student. This column also includes pertinent background information. *Questions* includes markings regarding unclear information or information in need of elaboration. The authors have provided the following guidelines for teaching use of these note-taking formats.

(a) Teachers supply students with completed note-taking formats; students copy the notes onto blank formats and follow their copied notes in a lecture or textbook activity.

(b) Teachers direct specific note-taking, pausing during lecture or textbook activities to tell students what to write down in their notes.

(c) Students identify relevant and irrelevant information from lecture or textbook activities, either during lectures or from completed notes supplied by the teacher.

(d) Students use *format 2*, with topic sentence supplied by the teacher, to complete their own notes from lecture or textbook activities. Teacher cues students on relevant and important information to be included in their notes.

(e) Students use *format 2*, with topic sentence supplied by the teacher, to complete their own notes from lecture or textbook activities without cues from the teacher.

(f) Students use *format 2* to select two to four topics during a lecture or textbook activity but do not fill in notes.

(g) Students use *format 2* to select topics and complete their own notes from lecture or textbook activities.

(h) Students use *format 1 or 2* to complete the basic note-taking column, then rewrite notes according to specific topics and complete the remaining columns with teacher assistance.

(i) Students use *format 1 or 2* to complete all three columns. Afterwards the teacher checks their notes.

(j) Students use *format 1 or 2* to engage in independent note-taking.

Learner-generated underlining. Glynn (1978) conducted a review of the literature on the topic of learner-generated underlining; his observations are described below. Several studies of *college students* (e.g., Fowler and Baker, 1974; Idstein and Jenkins, 1972) found that subjects who underlined any information they wished experienced no overall increase in learning relative to subjects that did not underline. Likewise, Rickards and August (1975) in a study of *college students* found no overall differences in favor of subjects who underlined sentences of high structural importance compared to control subjects who only read the text. Fowler and Barker noted, however, that propositions that readers chose to underline were recalled better than propositions that they decided not to underline. Interestingly, Rickards and August (1975) found that subjects who generated underlining of any *one sentence per paragraph*, had greater overall recall than subjects who only read the text. Rickards (1980) recommended that it seems reasonable to conclude that students should be urged to restrict themselves to a small amount of underlining; also, students should not be told exactly what to underline. The optimal number of sentences to underline per page probably depends upon the *information density* of the material and the number of words per page. Also, the degree to which underlining of key phrases is effective may depend in part on the *difficulty level* of the material (Rickards, 1980).

Glynn's *summary conclusions* were that learner-generated underlining appeared to function in much the same fashion as experimenter-provided underlining. When processing times were controlled, there was no *overall* increment in learning achieved relative to a no-underlining group. However, available evidence suggested that the requirement to generate underlining encouraged learners to interact with the instructional material longer. As a consequence of this extended interaction, more information was acquired.

Brown and Smiley (1978) conducted several studies of underlining with students in *grades five, seven* and *eight*. The results of these studies are similar to those reported by the authors for note-taking. In grade five, *induced underliners, spontaneous underliners* and *nonunderliners* did not differ significantly in their recall of material at lower levels of the content structure; however, spontaneous underliners recalled significantly more of the higher level material. Children in the fifth grade who underlined spontaneously, underlined more high level units, and subsequently recalled more of this material. The induced underliners did not underline effectively and, as a result, their recall was not improved. In the seventh and eighth grades, students were much more selective than were students in the fifth grade, and tended primarily to underline material high in the content structure. Unlike the children in the fifth grade, who underlined only after prompting, students in the eighth grade, who were similarily induced to underline, did show increased sensitivity to the importance of the content, but they were not nearly as effective as those students who chose to underline on their own volition. Note, once again, that the authors merely directed the students to take notes or use underlining; no instruction was provided on *how* to take notes or underline, or how to use those study aids once they had been completed. As a result, the study does not indicate what benefits may be derived from making optimal notes or underlining.

Brown and Smiley noted in their study of grades five, eight, eleven and twelve that the number of students who spontaneously elected to take notes increased with age; .28 of the young students and .41 of the median group, while .76 of the older group used either one or both of underlining and note-taking. Brown and Smiley concluded that a general *summary* of the literature indicates that underlining and note-taking are less helpful than one might predict on intuitive grounds; only a few studies find a clear advantage for the use of underlining or note-taking, and these studies may be methodologically flawed. An important factor in prior studies has been that *subjects* have been *randomly assigned* to treatment groups, that is, *forced* to adopt one or another strategy. Thus, spontaneous and induced subjects are randomly combined, a procedure Brown and Smiley have shown to mask the effectiveness of these strategies. This routine practice might explain the common failure to find improved study scores.

In a study of children in the *fifth grade*, conducted by Rickards and Denner (1979), underlining was found to be quite ineffective. The children underlined sentences of low structural importance even when restricted to one sentence per paragraph, and they recalled less information than the children who only read the material. Rickards (1980) remarked that it would be interesting to ascertain when *comprehension* skills are *sufficient* for underlining to be an effective study strategy. Rickards and Denner (1979) suggested that *extreme caution* be exercised in recommending underlining for children at the *fifth grade* level. Only if they spontaneously underline on their own is it an effective strategy; when induced, it appears to be ineffective at this level of schooling. Recall that in Brown's previously reported study of underlining (1981), children in the fifth grade were able to detect trivial and redundant information in text, and they were sensitive to fine differences in the relative level of importance of the textual material. These studies, like those of Brown and Smiley, do not assess the benefits of teaching students effective underlining strategies and effective use of underlining once it has been completed.

Reading strategies: SQ3R. Readers may be taught to employ generic reading strategies to enhance their comprehension and recall. The SQ3R method (Robinson, 1961) describes a five stage survey, *q*uestion, *r*ead *r*ecite and *r*eview strategy. The *survey* stage involves an overview of the content of a passage, and provides a prereading *warm-up*. The reader skims the passage, reads titles, advance organizers and summaries, and examines pictures and graphs. The purpose of the survey is to provide a framework to facilitate organization and comprehension of the material to be read. The survey also assists recall of related information that the reader already knows. The *question* stage involves a second skimming of the passage during which the chapter title, subheadings and unfamiliar terms are converted into questions. These questions are designed to give the reader purpose and interest in the material as she/he reads to find answers to the questions. A reader may also attempt to answer the questions before reading, and may, while reading, pose additional questions. The *reading* phase involves purposeful reading. Attention is focussed on main points, and an attempt is made to group supporting details with main ideas. The reader also attempts to locate answers to the previously posed questions. The *recite* phase is designed to supply the reader with feedback about what has been recalled and forgotten. *Recitation* requires the reader to translate the information read into his own words, develop retrieval skills and enhance retention. During this phase, the reader attempts to recall main and supporting points and answers to previously posed questions. The *review* phase provides the opportunity for the reader to survey the passage again, noting what could not be recalled during the recite phase. The review may involve a rereading of the entire passage immediately after the recite phase or after some delay. A delayed review may be assisted by the use of an outline or summary of the passage, or a list of questions prepared during an earlier phase.

Petros and Hoving (1980) compared the effects upon prose recall of an *imposed post-reading review* versus a *subject-generated, post-reading review*. The *eight year old children* in the study *listened* to two passages. Subjects in various experimental groups either: (a) recalled the passage immediately after hearing it, (b) recalled the passage without assistance one week after initially hearing it or (c) listened to both stories again one week after initially hearing them. For all subjects, delayed retention was assessed two weeks after the passages were initially presented. The results indicated that two weeks after initially hearing the passages, no significant differences existed between subjects in group "a," who had recalled the passage immediately after initial presentation, and subjects in group "c," who heard the passages again one week after initial presentations. Both of these groups recalled significantly more than subjects in the control group, who did not review the passage. Also, subjects in group "a," who recalled the passage immediately after hearing it, reproduced significantly more idea units during the review two weeks later, than subjects in group "b," who recalled the story one week after initially hearing it.

Andre and Anderson (1978-79) developed *self-questioning*, study techniques in which *high school* students were taught to locate sections of texts containing important points and to *generate questions* about them. The authors found that the questions facilitated learning more than was achieved by simply reading and rereading texts or making up questions without regard to important points. The training was effective for students of lower ability.

Singer's (1978) conception of *active comprehension* involved reacting to a text with *questions* and *seeking answers* during subsequent reading. He found that *student-generated* questions were more effective in promoting comprehension than *teacher-generated questions*, even for children in *elementary school*. Collins, Brown and Larkin (1980) suggested that many deficiencies of comprehension are in fact due to a failure to ask the right questions. A study by Nash and Torrance (1974) has shown that participation in a program designed to sensitize children in the *first grade* to gaps in their knowledge led to a significant improvement in the kinds of questions they asked about their reading material (Brown, 1981).

Anderson and Armbruster (1982) in an extensive review of the literature found only seven studies that had evaluated the use of the SQ3R method. The authors concluded that because of the uneven quality of these *dissertation studies* and the mixed results, no *conclusions* are possible about the effectiveness of the SQ3R method as a whole. In sum, *empirical evidence* in favor of the method, either for SQ3R compared to other methods or for the component steps of SQ3R is lacking (Anderson and Armbruster, 1982).

When using the SQ3R method, students are making *best guesses* about criterion test items on the basis of chapter headings; this approach has several obvious pitfalls. A second questionable assumption is that authors choose *headings* that capture the important information or main ideas of the content. According to Anderson and Armbruster, the usual topic heading fails to indicate much about the information to be included, and how information about the topic will be organized. A third questionable assumption is that an instructor's *criterion test questions* will test information cued by the author's headings. This assumption may be reasonable, if the headings reflect main ideas and if the instructor tests main ideas of individual sections of the textbook. In many cases, however, these conditions are not met.

Another questionable assumption is that students are able to *transform headings into questions* that capture main ideas. The default option for transforming headings into questions may be simply placing "What is. . .?" in front of the heading. Such a question may tap only a small portion of the content of a particular section. For example, consider the topic label heading "The Louisiana Purchase." In reading the answer to the question according to the SQ3R prescriptions, the student might stop processing the text after discovering in the first few sentences that the Louisiana Purchase was a purchase of the Louisiana Territory from France. This information answers the "What is. . .?" question. The section goes on, however, to explain President Jefferson's reasons for making the Louisiana Purchase, France's reasons for selling it and the effects of the purchase on the discovery and settlement of the West. Therefore, the student's question would fail to promote attention focussing and encoding of most of the content communicated in that section (Anderson and Armbruster, 1982).

Teacher Controlled Aids to Recall

Table 8.2 displays a five-phase *generic reading strategy* developed by Brezin (1980). The phases: *planning, attending, encoding, reviewing* and *evaluating* are reminiscent of those described in Robinson's (1961) SQ3R method. Brezin's schema describes two levels of instructional techniques that teachers can employ to assist readers to adopt the five phase approach to reading. The teacher begins instruction with the *secondary format* designed for *younger* or relatively *inexperienced readers* of prose. In this format the teacher takes the major responsibility and presents purpose statements, overviews or pictures; directs the student to skim, or provides embedded questions, etc. In this manner the teacher assists the student through each phase of reading, and models the appropriate procedures at each phase. In the *primary phase* for *older* or *more experienced* prose readers, the teacher merely gives direction and instruction, and the responsibility for employing appropriate procedures shifts to the reader. Brezin's schema describes the type of instruction that should be provided at each phase.

Table 8.2

*Brezin's Instructional Techniques for
Teaching Five Phases of Reading*

Cognitive Operation/ Monitoring Strategy	Primary format	Secondary format
PLANNING Select	Give directions to preview the text and to identify purpose objectives	Preview purpose statements, overviews or objectives
Prepare	Present questions on how this topic relates to previous instruction or to the student's word knowledge	Present picture or statement that relates the material to previously learned information
Gauge	Give directions to compare objectives and background knowledge to determine whether to read critically, skim, etc.	Give directions to skim, read critically, etc.
Estimate	Give directions to determine task difficulty on basis of answers in the first three strategies	Provide a brief description of the amount of new information, the complexity of the ideas, etc.
ATTENDING focus	Give directions to be alert for information directly related to the objectives	Provide embedded questions or pictures before text paragraphs
search contrast validate	Provide process questions, e.g., What is being said? Is it as you thought it would be? If not, how is it different?	Same as Primary Format

(Continued)

Table 8.2 (Continued)

Cognitive Operation/ Monitoring Strategy	Primary format	Secondary format
ENCODING elaborate	Give directions to visualize the information, create an analogy, generate a summary sentence; suggest a mnemonic strategy	Provide organizing words for summary-sentence generation, pictures or partial pictures for student completion, or a mnemonic (e.g., loci)
qualitatively relate	Direct students to provide titles for pictures in the text, headings for sections or paragraphs, and alternative solutions to problems raised by the text; also direct student to suggest possible applications to other contexts	Direct the student to provide titles for pictures in the text, headings for sections or paragraphs, or alternative solutions to problems raised in the text
REVIEWING confirm	Direct students to relate text to complete text-provided content questions, and to generate their own questions	Direct students to complete embedded questions or to complete partial pictures or pictures following completion of the text or a section of the text
repeat	Direct students to recall the elaborations devised while reading the text	Same as the Primary Format

(Continued)

Table 8.2 (Continued)

Cognitive Operation/ Monitoring Strategy	Primary format	Secondary format
revise	Direct students to modify the recalled elaborations on the basis of new information or thoughts that have come to mind	Same as the Primary Format
EVALUATING test	Direct students to question themselves: Did the text make sense? Are there inconsistencies in the text? What questions do I have about the information in the text? Are there parts I should reread?	Provide questions that require students to compare the new information to previously held contradictory understandings; questions to identify inconsistencies in the text; questions that require students to estimate a result that would be obtained by using the information in the text
judge	Direct students to write, draw, or act out brief emotional reactions to the text (Brezin, 1980, p. 237).	Same as Primary Format

Brezin does not provide *evidence* for the efficacy of these procedures used in combination but does report research supporting some of the separate and specific techniques that are recommended. Some of this evidence, for example, that relating to the use of imbedded questions, has been incorporated into various parts of this text. Additional related information and evidence derived from a variety of sources is discussed in the following paragraphs.

In the conventional approach to teaching *comprehension*, a teacher (a) relates the content of the passage to the reader's background, (b) introduces potentially troublesome vocabulary, (c) sets purpose and poses questions and (d) asks questions after the passage has been read. Consistent use of this approach to reading, in which the teacher does most of the pre- and post-reading activity, may lead students to become *passive* rather than *active readers* (Johnson and Barrett, 1981). A number of authors (Smith, 1975; Goodman and Goodman, 1977; Stauffer, 1975), are in agreement with this idea—that a student's role in reading should be active. They argue that the reading-thinking process must begin with the reader. Readers must be responsible for developing questions, making conjectures, predicting and proving. The teacher's job is to keep the process active and alive. In this respect, these authors concur with Brezin's idea of moving from a secondary to a primary format in reading instruction, where the reader becomes progressively more involved in implementing various procedures before, during and after reading a passage.

Prior knowledge. Many passages that students read require preexisting knowledge to which new information can be related. Prior knowledge is used to clarify situations, fill in the gaps, draw inferences and interpret new concepts. A number of studies, described in the following paragraphs, have demonstrated the importance of insuring that readers, before beginning reading, possess sufficient prior knowledge of the basic concepts described in a passage.

Gordon, Hansen and Pearson (1978) found that children in the *second grade* who had prior knowledge about spiders learned more from those portions of a passage about spiders, where that prior knowledge could be applied, than children did who had little or no prior knowledge about spiders.

Brown, Smiley, Day, Townsend and Lawton (1977) asked *second, fourth*, and *sixth grade* students to listen to a passage about a fictitious *Targa* tribe. One week before the passage was actually presented, various subgroups of the children were given different preinformation about the Targas. One group was informed that the Targa were peaceful Eskimos. Pictorial and verbal detail, such as depictions of snow and polar wildlife, were provided. A second group of children were told that the Targa were a warring Indian group. These children were given pictures and descriptions of burning deserts and water shortages. These two groups of children *recalled* 25 percent more passage content than control students whose preinformation about a Spanish group was unrelated to the Targa passage. In addition, the nature of the preinformation influenced the manner in which the children processed the passage. In particular, the *recall errors* that were made were consistent with the preinformation provided. That is, students who had received information related to Eskimos, *recalled* associated information that, in fact, was not mentioned in the passage.

Davidson (1976) gave *The Mat Maker* chapter from Melville's *Moby Dick* to a group of *college freshmen*. This difficult passage describes a number of abstract concepts such as fate, chance and free-will. These concepts are metaphorically related to various parts of a loom, for example, the warp, the woof and the shuttle. One group of students was given preinformation as to the nature of looms and their working parts. Both pictures and verbal descriptions were used. Students who had received preinformation about looms *recalled* 50 percent more on a true-false recall test than did two control groups of students. In addition, it was observed that preinformed students were much more likely to abstract concepts from the passage to concrete loom parts than were control subjects, who tended to maintain separate abstract and concrete concept clusters.

Imagery instructions. Levin and Pressley (1981) reported that although there is good reason to believe that reader-generated visual imagery produces prose *comprehension* gains in children *eight years* of age *and older* (Levin, 1976; Pressley, 1977), on the basis of other research (Dunham and Levin, 1979), the same cannot be concluded for children younger than this. The few attempts that have been made to provide children with extended instruction in the use of visual imagery have not yielded very impressive returns (Pressley, 1976) especially when the children are transferred to slightly different contexts (Lesgold, McCormick and Golinkoff, 1975; Triplett, 1980).

Gambrell, Koskinen and Cole (1981) point out that caution should be exercised when interpreting the results of the research on prose recall, comprehension and imagery. In general, when mental imagery is used, increases in learning from *written text* are small relative to the results of learning from *orally presented prose* (Pressley, 1977). However, Gambrell *et al.* found conflicting results in a study of the effects of imagery on the prose recall of above and below average readers in the *sixth grade*. Subjects given imagery instructions were told to "Make pictures in your head to help you remember." The results of the study suggested that instructions to use mental imagery were equally effective under *listening and reading* conditions. An interview conducted immediately after the passage was presented indicated that 17 percent (listening) and 21 percent (reading) of the below average readers reported that they were *unable to induce mental imagery*. Only three percent (listening) and six percent (reading) of the above average readers reported similar difficulty. Note that the study did not examine the effects of *teaching* students to make appropriate mental imagery. Subjects were merely directed to produce mental images. As the data indicates, a number of subjects experienced difficulty generating images. As a result, the study does not assess the effectiveness of creating visual imagery while listening or reading.

Teacher questions. Questions can be presented to students in an *oral or written form*. Rothkopf and Bloom (1970) and Rothkopf (1972), in studies of *high school* students, found that orally asked questions were superior in facilitating learning. Many of the points discussed earlier in this chapter in relation to printed questions, for example, whether they require factual or rote recall, application, interpretation, evaluation, generalization or inferences, also apply to oral questions. Table 8.3 displays a number of question-

Table 8.3

Teacher Questioning Strategy

Questioning Strategy		
Type	**Purpose**	**Question**
Focussing	Initiate discussion or refocus on the issue.	What did you like about the story? What was the question we started to answer?
Controlling	Direct or dominate the discussion.	First, would you review the plot?
Ignoring or rejecting	Maintain current trend in discussion. Disregard a student's interest.	Would you mind if we don't go into that now?
Extending	Obtain more information at a particular level of discussion.	What other information do we have about the hero?
Clarifying	Obtain a more adequate explanation. Draw out a student.	Would you explain what you mean?
Raising	Have discussion move from factual to interpretive, inferential, or abstraction and generalization level.	We now have enough examples. What do they have in common? (Abstract) Was it always true for his level of behavior (Generalization).

Student Response Level

Factual or literal (What the author said)
Interpretive (Integration of ideas of inference)
Applied (Transfer of ideas or judgment that idea is
  subsumed under broader generalization)
Evaluative (Using cognitive or affective criteria for judging issue)

(Singer, 1978, p. 903).

ing strategies that teachers can employ, and describes the purpose of each type of question. The type of question posed influences the material in a passage that a reader focusses on, and the manner in which the materials are processed, comprehended and recalled.

Several studies have demonstrated the role of *questions* in improving retention. For example, Van Wagenen and Travers (1963) taught German vocabulary in a lecture format to groups of children in *grades four, five and six.* The teacher held up large cards on which German words and two English alternatives appeared. For each card, one child was called upon to guess the correct English associate. Only four of the eight children in each group actively participated in answering the questions. The other four children merely observed. On the post-test, the children who answered the questions performed better than the children who simply observed.

Michael and Maccoby (1961) showed classes of *high school juniors* and *seniors* a film on civil defense in an atomic war. Some classes only saw the film, and no *questions* were posed. For other classes, the film stopped three times, during which the teacher read questions covering some of the points presented in the previous section of the film. On post-test questions that had been asked and answered during the film, classes that had been asked the questions did substantially better than the classes that had merely viewed the film. There was no difference between the groups on additional post-test questions that had not been asked during the film.

Manipulation of objects. Wellman, Rysberg and Sattler (1979) studied young readers' awareness and use of concrete objects (e.g., farmhouse, barnyard and animals) while they read short stories. Several of the sentences in the story used abstract relational words, such as *on, across, between, under, around* and *over.* The storyboard presentation accompanying each child's reading enhanced comprehension of the terms. As a child completed a sentence, she/he manipulated the arrangement of objects on the board. For example, after reading the sentence "The cow jumped over the fence and crossed the river," a reader would enact the scene. This activity improved the child's learning of the story and provided a visual check of his/her comprehension.

Chapter Nine

Generalization and Maintenance

Stimulus Generalization

Most teaching involves three phases: acquisition, generalization and maintenance. Briefly described, *acquisition* occurs during the initial phase of instruction, and refers to the newly learned ability of an individual to perform a response without assistance, at criterion level, within the instructional context. *Generalization* refers to performance of a response without assistance, under *stimulus conditions* that are different from, but usually similar to, the conditions that existed when the response was initially acquired. "Stimulus conditions" in this context is a generic term that may refer to a stimulus object, characteristic, event or setting. *Maintenance* refers to the durability of the acquired response, and the learner's performance of the response without assistance, after a period of time, following the termination of instruction, under conditions that are the same as, or different from, those that existed during initial acquisition of the skill.

Because of the *potentially* large number of *conditions* in which the response being taught may be appropriate, it is frequently not possible during instruction to provide a learner with examples of each and every condition under which she/he may eventually be expected to perform. An alternative approach is to teach the learner to perform the response under a limited number and type of conditions (*instructional conditions*) specially selected to represent the range of conditions (*generalization conditions*) under which she/he may be required to perform. The expectation is that, if the learner is taught to perform the response under the instructional conditions, because of the similarity between the instructional and the generalization conditions, the learner's acquired response will generalize, and she/he will be able to perform the skill under both instructional and generalization conditions within the range represented.

For *example*, suppose that the purpose of a particular instructional sequence is to teach a learner to perform a given mnemonic strategy in the presence of a broad range of conditions alphabetically labelled from *a* to *l*. Suppose, too, that analysis of the common characteristics of these conditions shows that they can be grouped in the following manner: (*a, b, c*), (*d, e, f, g, h*) and (*i, j, k, l*). During the acquisition phase, the learner may be taught to make the mnemonic response in the presence of the instructional conditions *b, e, h* and *j* selected to represent each group of conditions having common characteristics within the full range of conditions from *a* to *l*. Then, once the instructional conditions have gained *stimulus control* over the mnemonic response, if generalization of learning is successful, stimulus control will generalize to the conditions within each group that share common characteristics with the instructional conditions, and the learner will make the mnemonic response to all of the conditions *a* to *l*. Then, if both maintenance and generalization have been achieved, the learner will continue to make the mnemonic response to all of the conditions *a* to *l* for a continuing period following the termination of instruction. The ultimate *goal* of most *instruction* is to achieve maintenance of an acquired response(s) under both the instructional and the generalization conditions so that the learner makes the learned response in the presence of the full range of appropriate conditions within the set, and does not make the response to conditions outside the set.

Thus, it is apparent that in the above example, *stimulus generalization* involves the *generalization of stimulus control*. *Response generalization* occurs when instruction directed at a particular response produces a corresponding effect upon one or more other responses that are related in some manner to the response being instructed. Generalization *across subjects* refers to a change in behavior of persons to whom training had not been directed. Stimulus generalization and maintenance of behavior of the individual on whom training has been directed is the focus of the following discussion. Drabman, Hammer and Rosenbaum (1979) offer a review of various types of generalization not included in the present discussion.

One fact that has been repeatedly demonstrated throughout the research literature in various areas of study is that *generalization rarely occurs automatically* with the acquisition of a new response. One dramatic example of a failure to achieve automatic generalization is provided by a study conducted by Ericsson, Chase and Faloon (1980). The authors worked with a *college student* of average intelligence and memory ability. After more than 230 hours of practice in the laboratory, the subject had *increased* his *memory span* from 7 to 79 digits to equal the performance of memory experts with lifelong training. In one experimental session, the subject was switched from digits to letters of the alphabet after three months of training, and exhibited no generalization. The subject's memory span dropped back to about six consonants.

There is a need to *systematically program generalization and maintenance* (Brown, 1977; Kazdin, 1975; Stokes and Baer, 1977). According to Borkowski and Cavanaugh (1979), the failure of many research studies to obtain generalization and maintenance of trained mnemonic strategies is frequently not a function of a deficiency in the learner, but is the result of an *instructional deficiency* resulting from inadequate instruction.

In the present context, *stimulus generalization* may be described as the performance of an acquired behavior, without assistance, under conditions that are different from, but usually similar to, the conditions that existed during training, and where special prompts and contingencies used in training are absent. As was described in the previously cited example, stimulus generalization may be explained in terms of the transfer of stimulus control from the conditions used in training (e.g., *e* and *h*) to other conditions that are similar to the training conditions (e.g., *d, e, f, g* and *h*).

During acquisition training, several procedures may be used to increase the probability of generalization. One of the procedures, *sequential modification* (Stokes and Baer, 1977) involves directly teaching a learner to make the desired response in every condition in which generalization of the response is desired. Fortunately, there are more instructionally economical approaches available to enhance generalization. For example, Becker and Engelmann (1978), and Horner, Sprague and Wilcox (1982) have successfully employed a procedure called *general case programming*. Elements of this procedure synthesized with ideas expressed by Baine (1982), Becker, Engelmann and Carnine (1982), Horner *et al.* (1982), and Wehman, Abramson and Norman (1977) are described below.

a. Decide on the conditions or situations in which the particular mnemonic response being trained is eventually expected to be performed (e.g., *a* to *l*).

b. Conduct a *stimulus analysis* of the conditions to identify the discriminative and nondiscriminative features. The *discriminative features* of a set of conditions or situations in which a particular mnemonic response is appropriate are those that characterize, or are possessed by, all of the conditions in the set. It is these discriminative features that must eventually gain *stimulus control* over the mnemonic response being taught. Although each of the situations in the set possesses the same discriminative features, the value of a particular feature may vary in different situations. Also, situations outside of the set may possess some, but not all, of these same features. *Nondiscriminative features* found in various values in some, but not all, of the situations within the set in which a particular mnemonic response is appropriate, and also found in situations outside the set, do not indicate when the mnemonic response is appropriate. Instruction must insure that these features do not gain stimulus control over the mnemonic response.

c. Group together those conditions that share common discriminative features and that may have a variety of nondiscriminative features (e.g., *d, e, f, g* and *h*).

d. Select one or more conditions from this set to use in training (e.g., *e,* and *h*). Select a sufficient number and type of conditions

to represent all of the conditions in the set (e.g., condition *e* may
have been selected because it represented a range of values of
discriminative features found in conditions *d, e* and *f*. Similarly,
condition *h* may represent variations in the discriminative features
of *g, h* and *d*). Horner, Sprague and Wilcox provide a more
detailed discussion of the steps to follow in selecting suitable
training conditions. These procedures provide a systematic means
of operationalizing the technique referred to by Stokes and Baer
(1977) as *training sufficient exemplars*. It is optimistic to note
that frequently a sufficient number of exemplars is a small
number, frequently no more than two (Stokes and Baer).

e. Establish stimulus control with the training conditions *e* and
h; that is, teach the learner to make the desired response in the
presence of the training stimuli.

f. *Teach* the learner *concurrently* to make the mnemonic
response to several different types of conditions. The usual
approach of teaching a learner to respond to criterion with
condition one, before proceeding to instruction of condition two,
does not lead to generalization as effectively as teaching the
learner concurrently to respond appropriately to conditions one
and two.

g. Suppose that conditions *a, d* and *e* have been selected as
training examples to represent the set of conditions *a, b, c, d, e, f*
and *g*. The training examples each possess variations of the
discriminative features and a variety of different nondiscriminative
features. During initial instruction the learner may be unable to
identify which features are discriminative. If the learner's performance is brought to criterion with *a*, before being introduced to *b*,
the student may learn to respond to nondiscriminative features of
a that will have to be unlearned with the introduction of *b*. Only
by the *concurrent teaching* of several different examples will the
student learn to attend to the set of discriminative characteristics
that is common to all examples. Research literature indicates that
concurrent instruction of this nature leads to greater generalization and maintenance (Hiew, 1977; Horner and McDonald, 1982;
Panyan and Hall, 1978; Schroeder and Baer, 1972; Shea and
Morgan, 1979).

h. *Probe* to determine if stimulus control, acquired by the training conditions, has transferred to the generalization conditions in the set represented by the training conditions.

i. If stimulus control has not been achieved—*undergeneralization*—use one or more additional conditions in the set as training conditions, and continue to probe for generalization.

j. *Overgeneralization* occurs when the learner makes the acquired response to stimulus conditions outside of the set *a* to *l*. To avoid overgeneralization, include in the initial acquisition phase of instruction, a number of conditions that are similar to, and likely to be confused with, the set of conditions from *a* to *l*. These confusing conditions possess some, but not all, of the discriminative features, as well as some of the same nondiscriminative features as those possessed by conditions *a* to *l*. The learner must be taught to *discriminate* these conditions so that the learned response is made only in the presence of conditions *a* to *l*.

k. To avoid teaching the learner to respond to nondiscriminative features of the training conditions as if they were discriminative (a situation that occurs when the student is inadvertently taught to make a response when a nondiscriminative feature is consistently present) ensure that the conditions selected for training provide a wide variation in their nondiscriminative features. No nondiscriminative feature should be contained in all conditions.

l. Also, to avoid inadvertently bringing a learner's behavior under the control of the nondiscriminative features of the *instructional environment* in which training is conducted so that the response is performed only in the presence of these nondiscriminative features, vary the nondiscriminative features of the instructional environment and/or provide instruction in several environments having a variety of nondiscriminative features. Stokes and Baer report that consistent optimism should follow examination of the studies showing generalization after training in only a few settings.

Steps *k* and *l*, above, provide a means of operationalizing a procedure that Stokes and Baer described as *training loosely*. These procedures are described more fully in the following paragraphs. Unfortunately, the *highly structured training environment* that is most conductive to initial acquisition of a response may be least conducive to generalization of the response. In the training environment, the removal of distracting stimuli and the consistent use of instructional procedures, such as cues, instructions, reinforcement and feedback, provide a contrived simplicity and continuity of stimulation that are not found in the natural environment. The greater the difference between the training environment and the natural environment, the less likely it is that generalization will occur.

To overcome these difficulties, the *training environment* may be systematically transformed to approximate the characteristics of the natural environment. This process should be preceded by a thorough study of the natural environment to determine the variety of ways the response being trained is usually prompted, performed and reinforced in various contexts and circumstances. When stimulus conditions change, sufficient transition time must be scheduled to allow for adaptation. *Changes in stimulus conditions* should be gradual. When changes in stimulus conditions are made, there are likely to be some initial increases in inappropriate behavior or decreases in appropriate behavior. *Change agents* must be prepared for these events and continue the program until behavior again comes under control in the new setting (Wehman, Abramson and Norman, 1977).

The *training situation* should provide the learner with experience within the *range of stimulus variations* found in the natural environment. Thus, as training proceeds, more *nonessential stimuli*, distractions, interruptions, variations in materials, sequence changes and different types and schedules of reinforcement may be progressively introduced as the training environment approximates the variation and complexity of the natural environment. An additional way to introduce variation and enhance generalization is to use more than one teacher, if the purpose of instruction is to generalize stimulus control to various people in whose presence a particular response should be performed (Garcia, 1974; Langone and Westling, 1979; Schworm and Abelseth, 1978; Stokes, Baer and Jackson, 1974). Borkowski and Cavanaugh (1979) suggested that as instructional prompts and cues are reduced in their degree of explicitness near the end of instruction designed to teach a mnemonic strategy, the increased similarity between the training and the generalization environments generally facilitates a child's discrimination of when to use, and when not to use, a trained strategy. Another consequence of a *fading strategy* of this nature is that it forces the child to become an *active participant* in using the strategy. Procedural inconsistencies during mnemonic strategy training are facilitative rather than inhibitive of both generalization and maintenance (Borkowski *et al.*). Thus, in the instructional environment in which stimulus control is initially acquired by the discriminative features of the instructional stimuli, the environment should be simple and nondistracting to focus learner attention on the discriminative features. However, when stimulus control has been established, the environment may become more complex and variable to approximate the range and variation of the different environments into which it is desirable to generalize the stimulus control.

Conway and Bucher (1974) point out that a frequently encountered *difficulty* in a treatment program occurs when children make inadequate use of discriminative cues that exist in the environment indicating when a particular response is appropriate. This difficulty may arise in the training situation and/or in the natural environment. The problem may be corrected by *highlighting* or increasing the *saliency* of the discriminative features that are common to both the training and the natural environments. These features may be emphasized by directly *embellishing* the stimuli or through the introduction of *artificial prompts* that draw attention to the discriminative features. Of course, these prompts must be *faded* from use as the learner is taught to respond in the presence of the *naturally occurring stimuli*. Also, when there is a similarity between stimuli that signal when a response is appropriate, and stimuli that signal when the response is inappropriate, or stimuli that should not have any controlling power over the response, the learner should be taught to *discriminate* these stimuli.

In some cases, it may be desirable to *modify temporarily* the environment into which the response is to be generalized. In some environments there may be few opportunities to practice a newly acquired response; discriminative stimuli indicating when it would be appropriate to perform a particular response may be at a relatively low intensity; and/or reinforcement for correctly responding may be infrequent and of an unfamiliar nature. In these situations, *temporary adjustments* may have to be made to compensate for these environmental shortcomings and to provide support for the generalization of the behavior until it becomes a well established response in the generalization environment. For example, Goetz and Baer (1973) reported an increase among preschool children in generalization by reinforcing its occurrence. Of course, as the response comes to be established, the temporary changes made to the environment should be *systematically faded* from use (Baine, 1982).

If generalization will occur only if there are sufficient common stimuli in both the training and the generalization settings, then a reasonably practical technique is to *program control stimuli* in both environments (Stokes and Baer, 1977). As was previously mentioned, stimuli from the natural environment may be introduced into the training environment and their salience may be enhanced. In addition, *contrived stimuli* may be introduced into both environments to cue generalization. If these stimuli are *repeatedly paired* with natural stimuli, as the contrived stimuli are faded, stimulus control will be transferred to the natural stimuli (Wehman, Abramson and Norman, 1977).

A number of studies reviewed by Borkowski and Cavanaugh (1979) have indicated the importance of providing the performer with *feedback* concerning the accuracy of performance and the efficacy of the strategy used. Feedback generally leads to a significant improvement in acquisition, maintenance and generalization of mnemonic strategies. For example, a study by Belmont, Butterfield and Borkowski (1978) demonstrated that generalization of a cumulative rehearsal strategy may be enhanced by training individuals to use two slightly different variants of a strategy (rather than one) and by providing them with feedback concerning the relationship between input (rehearsal) and output (recall) requirements.

Brown (1978) has provided a number of *suggestions* to *improve generalization* of mnemonic strategies. According to Brown, children often follow a *blind-rule* procedure in which they learn the mnemonic strategy taught, but fail to appreciate the value of the strategy and the problem-solving contexts in which it might prove helpful. Brown also suggested that the act of *generalization* should be *taught* as a basic skill in its own right. For example, she suggested, one could tell the child that the trained behavior could help him/her on a variety of similar tasks and that the trick is to know which ones. The child could then be exposed to a variety of *prototypic tasks* in which the utility of the strategy in such situations would be demonstrated. Also, tasks for which the strategy was inappropriate could be presented along with a demonstration and discussion as to why the strategies were inappropriate.

Borkowski and Cavanaugh recommended the use of *self-instructional procedures* to improve generalization. These authors suggested that children should be taught self-generating *search routines* for analyzing tasks, scanning the available strategic repertoire and matching the demands of the task with an appropriate study and retrieval plan. It may be necessary to directly reinforce successful *executive functioning* for the process to come under the control of *natural environmental contingencies*, such as a child's good feelings about solving a difficult problem (Borkowski and Cavanaugh, 1978).

In a study conducted by Wanschura and Borkowski (1975), children were told to *manipulate* the paired associate objects on the first trial of each training session. Substantial strategy *maintenance* resulted. Maintenance was perfect for children who were active during strategy training and who spontaneously manipulated the objects on the first study trial of the maintenance text. The authors suggested that *manipulation prior to the transfer test* served to evoke the entire strategy. *Passivity at transfer*, even for actively trained children, was associated with poor recall and minimal transfer of strategic behaviors. Similar improvements in maintenance as a result of active manipulation of stimuli were observed by Wolff, Levin and Longobardi (1974), who worked with kindergarten children. Children who produced interactions between pairs of toys could re-pair more items at maintenance than children who merely observed such interactions. The implication of these and other studies with *preschool and school age children* is that activity during training of a mnemonic strategy enhances strategy maintenance.

Borkowski and Cavanaugh (1978) have described a number of

steps that must be followed *to achieve generalization* of executive functioning.

> First, we need to identify several strategies each of which are operative in different learning situations. Second, we need to train children on several strategies, making sure that they know when and how to apply them. Third, we need to train the instructional package so that common elements between training and generalization contexts are evident, and distractors minimal. Fourth, we need to develop child-generated search routines, probably through the use of self-instructional procedures, that encourage the child to analyze a task, scan his or her available strategic repertoire, and match the demands of the task with an appropriate strategy and retrieval plan. Fifth, we need to instruct children in such a way that we utilize whatever skills they possess, in order to bring each child to an awareness of the advantage of executive monitoring and decision-making in solving problems. Finally, we may need to reinforce, in a very explicit way, successful executive functioning in order for it to come under the control of natural environmental contingencies, such as a child's good feelings about solving a difficult problem (p. 54).

Bringing a behavior under control of the *natural community of reinforcement* in the environment to which a response has been generalized will improve both maintenance and generalization (Stokes and Baer). Ferster (1972) suggested that generalization of a treatment program is doomed unless there is a viable plan for natural reinforcers to take on and maintain a new response. This success of bringing a behavior under control of natural reinforcers is predicated on a *thorough inventory* of the natural environment to determine the type of reinforcement usually available to a response of the type being taught. The inventory should record the characteristic variety of both intrinsic and extrinsic reinforcers, their frequency of occurrence, the delay that occurs between performance of the response and availability of the reinforcer, the manner in which reinforcers are dispensed and the range of behaviors that are and are not reinforced. Extrinsic reinforcers dispensed for satisfactory mnemonic performance during training may include money, privileges, tangibles, verbal praise, social rewards such as a smile or pat on the back, and points or tokens that can be redeemed for a variety of reinforcers.

In the natural environment following training, rewards of this nature may be uncommon for mnemonic performance. In fact, rewards may be of a more intangible nature and may be intrinsic to the task. The intrinsic rewards of using a particular mnemonic strategy may include the ability to recall a useful piece of information, improved recall of particular types of information, improved achievement, avoidance of embarrassment for failure to recall information, increased efficiency with rapid recall of required facts and increased social skills.

During training, the learner's behavior may be brought under *control* of the *natural community of reinforcers* in several different ways.

    (a) In some cases, where the reinforcing consequences of a behavior are subtle, unfamiliar or delayed, the learner may have to be taught to identify the reinforcers and to see the relationship between their occurrence and his/her behavior.

    (b) Some reinforcers, such as improvements in various areas of performance or avoidance of previously occurring difficulties, may not be readily apparent without the collection of data to demonstrate the incremental effects of changes that occur over time. In this case, performers may have to be taught to monitor, record and chart their performance gains.

    (c) Related to b, above, it may be necessary, not merely to teach a learner to use a particular mnemonic strategy, but also to teach him/her the functional value of the strategy, where and when it can and cannot be used, and the benefits derived from its proper application.

    (d) The usual consequences of a behavior in the natural environment may not have reinforcing value to a particular learner. To establish a reinforcing value, these natural consequences may be repeatedly paired with extrinsic reinforcement in the treatment environment. Through repeated association of this manner, the reinforcing value may transfer to the natural consequences.

Stokes and Baer suggested that because *reinforcement* in the natural environment is frequently unpredictable, during training reinforcement should be dispensed on an *intermittent schedule* approximating the frequency and delay of the natural environment. Similarly, because a response may be performed in a setting in which it may or may not be reinforced, training should be conducted in various settings in which the learner cannot discriminate whether or not a response will be reinforced. Thus, although a *continuous schedule* of reinforcement, in which all or most responses are rewarded, may promote acquisition of a response, intermittent or variable and delayed schedules of reinforcement may foster both generalization and maintenance.

When a reinforcement program is begun, it is essential to *provide consequences immediately* after the desired behavior occurs. The more immediate the reinforcer, the better the effects. After behavior develops and is performed consistently, presentation of the reinforcer can be *delayed*. Initially, the delay can be relatively brief, and over time the interval can be gradually extended until the person is able to perform in the absence of direct reinforcement (Kazdin and Esveldt-Dawson, 1981).

Maintenance

As defined earlier, maintenance refers to the durability of an acquired response, and the learner's performance of the response without assistance, after a period of time, following the termination of instruction, under conditions that are the same as those that existed during initial acquisition of the skill (instructional conditions), or under conditions that are different from, but similar to, the instructional conditions (generalization). The usual goal of instruction is to achieve maintenance under generalization conditions.

Horner, Bellamy and Colvin (1982) have described several *reasons* why *maintenance* of a response may *not* be *achieved*. They suggest that behavior that is under *weak stimulus control* is unlikely to be performed at a sufficient rate to produce enough reinforcement from the natural environment to maintain the response. Weakly controlled behaviors are also unlikely to endure, if there exist powerful *competing stimuli* that occasion or reinforce the occurrence of other, perhaps previously established, behaviors that replace the newly taught response. Unless training procedures establish strong stimulus control, neither generalization nor maintenance should be expected (Horner *et al.*).

When an individual is being trained to use a particular mnemonic strategy in the presence of a specific class of stimuli, the strategy is often designed to replace the response that the individual has habitually made to those stimuli in the past. If the new response is to be maintained, a stronger *relationship* must be established between the *stimulus* and the new *response* than existed between the stimulus and the old response. Otherwise, the learner will rapidly return to a habitual mode of responding, particularly if that response has a rich history of reinforcement. Thus, as previously described, one method of enhancing maintenance is to ensure that the response has become attached to a rich source of naturally occurring reinforcers. A second and related method of promoting maintenance is to insure that training provides *sufficient opportunities to practice* the response to establish a relatively *strong habit*. The habit strength or *fluency* of a response may be defined in terms of its rapidity, consistency and accuracy of performance in various situations with infrequent reinforcement. These variables should be considered when the *criteria* are being established to indicate when training is complete. Premature termination of instruction may result in a lack of maintenance. White and Haring (1980) and Baer (1981) suggested that fluency facilitates the maintenance and generalization of behavior because it increases the possibility of the subject contacting natural communities of reinforcement.

A wide variety of experimental and applied research has documented that learned responses are maintained best if the exaggerated *cues* and *consequences* used during training are *removed gradually* rather than abruptly. Learned skills are more likely to be maintained if the subject is unable to discriminate when she/he is in a training versus a nontraining situation. The extensive research on *fading* of prompts and the gradual reduction of reinforcement confirm that if training variables are modified gradually to approximate those in the performance setting, there is a higher likelihood that the behavior will be maintained (Horner *et al.*, 1982).

Kazdin and Esveldt-Dawson (1981) have described a method of *fading* a program through *several levels*. At the first level, contingencies specify the exact behaviors to be performed before rewards will be dispensed. Rewards are provided frequently and immediately. At the second level, the connection between the behavior and the reward is reduced. The rewards are made available, but the behavior is checked only once in a while. At the third level, there may be little connection between specific behaviors and rewards. The rewards are available and the child continues to perform at a high level, while assuming more responsibility for his/her behavior. By the time persons are at the final level, they should be performing the desired behaviors largely on their own without immediate consequences.

Rhode, Morgan and Young (1983) achieved successful generalization and maintenance of the effects of a behavioral treatment program using a *seven stage* treatment *fading* procedure. In this study six behaviorally handicapped students were taught a *self-evaluation* procedure. Part of the training, conducted in a resource room, required students to compare their self-ratings with ratings made of the student by the teacher; *feedback* on the accuracy of self-evaluation was provided, as was *reinforcement* for accuracy of self-rating. Generalization to the classroom and maintenance of behavioral changes in that environment were achieved by initially introducing self-evaluation, occasional matching and reinforcement activities into the classroom and then *fading* each of the procedures from use over seven stages.

Kestner and Borkowski (1979) used an *interrogative strategy* with children in the *first grade* to achieve maintenance of recall in a paired associates task. The children were instructed for four days in the use of an interrogative strategy; experimenter assistance was gradually *faded* during training. An example of the strategy used by a child at the end of training to learn the pair *nurse-toaster* might be: "The nurse is holding the toaster" (the first step of the strategy was to think about how the two items were related); "Why is the nurse holding the toaster?" (the second step was to ask a *why* question about the relationship); "A nurse works with doctors and helps sick people. A toaster toasts bread for breakfast" (the third step was to tell what was known about the items): "The nurse is holding the toaster because she's making breakfast for sick people" (the fourth step was to use knowledge about the items to make up a reason why they go together). Several days after training was completed, a nonprompted maintenance test was given by a new experimenter. *Recall* after a single study trial for the children trained to invoke the interrogative strategy was about 60 percent versus 9 percent for labelling control children. Of 16 instructed children, 14 showed excellent strategy maintenance; the two who did not retain the strategy recalled only 25 percent on the maintenance test. Complete use of the interrogative strategy for a given item (e.g., when all four steps of the strategy were given during a final probe test) was associated with almost perfect recall (90 percent) (Borkowski and Cavanaugh). These positive results were successfully replicated with *educable mentally handicapped children* (MA 6-8) by Kendall, Borkowski and Cavanaugh (1978).

Silbert, Carnine and Stein (1981) have described two methods of peer and teacher drill for teaching *maintenance of arithmetic facts*. Variations of these methods may be used with a variety of different tasks. According to the authors, a program to facilitate *basic fact memorization* should have the following components, each of which is described more fully below.

(a) A specific performance criterion for introducing new facts.
(b) Intensive practice on newly introduced facts.
(c) Systematic practice on previously introduced facts.
(d) A record-keeping system.
(e) A motivation system.
(f) Adequate time allotment.

Mastery of a basic fact is considered to be achieved when a student can respond instantaneously to the fact question. It is recommended that an acceptable *criterion* of performance for a verbal exercise, assuming students say an entire statement, such as 4 + 3 = 7, would be a rate of one fact each two seconds. The authors also discuss a method for establishing a rate criterion for written responses to fact questions.

Instruction should provide *intensive practice* and *systematic review* of other facts. Memorization exercises should be *cumul-*

ative in that newly introduced facts receive intensive practice, while previously introduced facts receive less intensive but still systematic practice. The authors suggested that the *time allotted* to fact *practice* should total 15 to 20 minutes per day.

A *record system* should be established to assess student progress for purposes of dispensing reinforcement and determining when to progress to successive phases of instruction. Students should be rewarded for improvement despite the level of the current worksheet or slow rate of progress.

The *peer drill procedure* described by the authors is discussed below. Students working near the same level work in pairs. Both students are given worksheets. The problems and answers are written on the sheet given to the student who first acts as the tutor. The other child is given a worksheet with questions but without answers. Each worksheet contains two parts. The top half includes 36 recently introduced facts. The bottom half includes 30 previously introduced facts.

The *drill* commences when the student without the answer sheet reads each question in full while providing the answer. The student/tutor with the answer sheet follows along, and if the pupil makes an error, the tutor reads the problem and provides the correct answer; the pupil repeats the correct answer. Each practice session is timed. A minute and one-half is allowed for practice of the top half of the sheet; one minute is allotted to practice the bottom half. After the allotted time, the students switch question and answer sheets. This procedure is repeated until each student has responded twice to the facts on both the bottom and the top of the sheet. Following the drill session, each student administers a one minute *test* to the other student and records the number of errors made. The teacher makes an occasional check of the *reliability* of the *error recording* procedure. The same drill procedure is repeated each successive day until a student is able to correctly answer all but at least two of the facts correctly, at which point the next worksheet is introduced.

The *worksheets* are constructed in the following manner. The top half of the worksheet should provide practice on new facts, including facts from the currently introduced set and from the two preceding sets. More specifically, if a new set consists of four facts, each of the four facts from the currently introduced set would appear four times. Each of the four facts from the preceding set would appear twice. This pattern would result in 36 facts on the top of the worksheet; 16 new facts, 12 facts from the previously learned set and eight facts from the set before that. The bottom half of the worksheet should include about 30 problems. Each of the facts from the currently introduced set would appear twice. The remaining facts would be taken from previously introduced sets. All previously introduced facts would appear once.

The drill may also be used with *homogeneous groups*. The teacher gives each student a worksheet. The students point to the first problem. When the teacher signals, the students read the problem *in unison*. For each fact, the teacher pauses a second, says, "Get ready" and then claps. The students are to say the complete fact. The teacher repeats this *signaling* procedure with each fact in the first line. The line is then repeated until all of the students are able to answer each fact correctly within one second. This drill may require four to five *repetitions* of each.

The drill may also be conducted with *flashcards*, having the answer on one side and the question and answer on the other. Each child is *pretested*. The teacher presents each fact question to each individual child. If a student answers a fact within two seconds, a plus is recorded. If the students either answers incorrectly or takes longer than a second to respond, a minus is recorded. Before beginning instruction, the teacher prepares a pile of 15 flash cards. The pile includes 12 cards of facts the student knew instantly on the test and three facts that the student did not respond to correctly on the test. The three unknown facts are put at the top of the pile. During daily instruction, the teacher provides a 10-15 minute *intensive drill*. The teacher presents a card and the student is to read the problem and then provide the answer. If the student responds correctly within two seconds, the teacher puts the card at the back of the pile. If the student responds correctly, but takes longer than two seconds, the card is placed two or three cards from the top of the pile. Likewise, if the student responds incorrectly, the student is told the correct answer which she/he is required to repeat, and the card is placed two or three cards from the top of the pile. In this manner, cards at the top of the pile, with which a student is having difficulty, receive intensive practice. When a student is able to respond correctly to each of the cards in the deck, two cards in the deck are replaced by two cards that the student had difficulty with on the pretest (Silbert, Carnine and Stein, 1981).

Massed and distributed practice. *Massed* practice refers to instruction in which two or more trials of a task are closely sequenced, with each trial directly following completion of the previous. For example, five successive trials of task "x" would be sequenced in the following manner: *xxxxx*, with no other activity between trials. In *distributed practice*, two or more trials of a task are interspersed with other activities, such as trials from another program. For example, trials of task *x* may be interspersed with one or more trials of *y* in the following manner: *xyxyyxyyyxyx*. Experimental laboratory studies of the effects of massed and distributed practice on the acquisition and maintenance of tasks such as paired associate learning of pictures, words, nonsense words, and syllables have generally demonstrated the superiority of distributed practice. The general implication to be drawn from a large number of studies reviewed by Borkowski and Cavanaugh (1979) is that strategy training over multiple sessions separated by days or weeks is more likely to lead to significant maintenance than is training on a single session or multiple tasks given on a single day. The following discussion reviews the results of these studies, compares the nature of tasks found in experimental and natural environments, reviews the procedures employed by educational programs, identifies a number of critical variables influencing both acquisition and maintenance, and recommends a number of procedures for scheduling practice.

Mulligan, Guess, Holvoet and Brown (1980) reviewed the *research literature* on the scheduling of practice, and discussed the implications for educational programming. Their observations are reported in an abbreviated form in the following paragraphs. The evidence seems to indicate that skills taught using distributed practice are learned better than skills taught when massed practice is used. These results have been observed with both cognitive and motor learning, with both handicapped and nonhandicapped individuals. The spacing of trials primarily affects the middle portion of the learning curve. The first several trials in a distributed schedule are indistinguishable from those sequenced on a massed schedule. After initial learning, performance tends to decline with longer rest periods or more trials. The *general conclusion* is that the overall effect of massing trials is a depression in performance during the high point of the learning curve. But whether this decrease in performance actually represents a critical difference in the amount of actual learning is not clearly demonstrated. Recall has been used to compare the amount learned under the different trial schedules. Performance during the acquisition of *motor skills* tends to be depressed by the massing of trials. The performance of *cognitive skills* is depressed both in acquisition and retention when practice trials are massed. Some separation of trials appears to be superior for both cognitive and motor tasks. The evidence seems to indicate that the more unfamiliar or demanding a task, the more a distributed trials strategy assists performance (Mulligan *et al.* 1980).

Mulligan, Lacy and Guess (1982) observed that most of the studies of the effects of massed and distributed practice on cognitive learning used *nonfunctional tasks* such as paired associate responding, free recall, serial recall and rote learning. Because of the difficulty of generalizing from these artificial tasks to tasks that are typical of curricula for *severely handicapped children*, the authors conducted a study of the effects of massed and distributed practice of cognitive and motor tasks on severely retarded children, ages five to ninteen. There were four training programs including table-setting, picture/object matching, folding washcloths and communication. In the massed practice condition, all ten trials of one program were completed before the ten trials for the following program were begun; there was a total of forty trials. Sessions with distributed trials had a cluster of four trials, one from each of the four training programs. This procedure resulted in two trials from the same program separated by one trial from each of the other three programs. This procedure was repeated ten times for a total of forty trials. In contrast to the results of most other studies reported in the literature, the *results* of this study indicated no difference in the results obtained by distributed and massed trial sequencing. There was no significant difference in the number of correct or error responses, or the number of refusals to respond; however, distributed trial sequencing did generally produce higher mean levels of responding.

Kryzanowski and Carnine (1980) studied the effects of massed and distributed practice in *teaching sound-symbol correspondences* to children in the *first grade*. Consistent with previous research on paired-associate learning (Greeno, 1964; Peterson, Wampler, Kirkpatrick and Saltzman, 1964; Shaughnessy, Zimmerman and Underwood, 1974), this study found that compared to the massed format, correct responses in the distributed format were more frequent on the posttest (72 percent versus 38 percent), though less frequent during training (56 percent versus 74 percent). Given the results of this study, a question arises, is there a *combination of massed and distributed practice* that would maintain the low error rate during training associated with massed practice and the high accuracy rate on the posttest associated with distributed practice?

In previous studies, Carnine (1976, 1980) found that separating structurally and acoustically similar paired associates (letter-sound correspondences) and *cumulatively introducing* new stimuli (introducing stimuli one at a time with a new stimulus being introduced only after the learner had reached mastery on the previously introduced stimuli) reduced training errors. The results of the present study using a paired associates format to teach sound-symbol correspondences indicates that a distributed format should be followed in which previously introduced stimuli are interpolated between appearances of the new stimulus. Thus, according to the authors, the present and previous studies indicate *three procedures to improve paired-associates teaching*. First, stimuli and responses should be analyzed in terms of relative discriminability and organized so that *similar stimuli and/or responses* are *separated* from each other in the order of introduction. Second, stimuli should be *introduced cumulatively*. Third, all training trials should follow a *distributed format*. The authors note that the generalizability of these recommendations to other populations and other types of stimuli needs to be investigated. One possibly significant difference between this study and the previous one by Mulligan *et al.* is that in the Kryzanowski and Carnine study training trials were interspersed with previously introduced stimuli, whereas in the Mulligan *et al.* study, training was being conducted on all trials including the interspersal tasks.

Neef, Iwata and Page (1980) studied the effect of interspersing known items during *spelling instruction* on new words with trainable mentally retarded individuals, ages 19-24. Each *interspersal training* session consisted of twenty trials: ten training words and ten known words, presented in alternating order. Known words were initially derived from the pool of words spelled correctly on the pretest. However, these were later replaced by mastered training words; as a student met criterion for a training word, that word was then placed in the known item pool and a new training word was then added to the list. Compared to students who received high density reinforcement for task related behaviors rather than interspersal training, the students who received interspersal training mastered and retained more words during and following interspersal training.

Bloom and Shuell (1981) studied the effect of massed and distributed practice on *second language* learning of French on students in *grades 9 to 12*. Students were presented with twenty pairs of French vocabulary words and their English equivalents. A series of three, ten minute written exercises were used by all students: multiple-choice, fill-in-the-blank, and given an English word, write the equivalent French word. The students in the distributed practice group studied the material for ten minute periods on each of three consecutive days. The massed practice group worked on the same three exercises during three successive ten minute periods. At the end of instruction, students were given a vocabulary test; an unannounced test was also administered four days later. The results of the study revealed no significant difference on the initial test. However, as in most other studies, the students who used a distributed schedule remembered substantially more words than those students who had employed a massed practice schedule (performance was 35 percent better with distributed practice). The relatively long (24 hour) distribution interval used in this study is more characteristic of distribution in the average classroom environment than is the interval used in most laboratory studies. The authors suggested that one possible explanation of the benefits of distributed practice is that it provides an opportunity to practice the recall of the material after the lapse of a period of time. Thus, in successive periods of practice, the learner not only is practicing the vocabulary words but also is practicing their recall. Perhaps if the interval between successive practice and recall were systematically lengthened, the recall interval would come to approximate the recall interval that commonly occurs in the natural environment. In this manner, recall training might become *ecologically valid*.

A study by Butterfield and Belmont (1972) of the maintenance of *mnemonic strategy* learning by *educable, mentally retarded adolescents*, and a study by Borkowski Cavanaugh and Reichhart (1978) of the maintenance of children's rehearsal strategies suggested that the *number of training sessions* is only superficially related to the degree of mnemonic strategy maintenance. The key variable is the *mastery* of the strategy by the learner during training and its success in aiding recall (Borkowski and Cavanaugh, 1979). Thus, it is important during training to establish a *suitable criterion* based on the *fluency* of responding (e.g., the rate, accuracy and consistency of response) and the history of reinforcement of the response in the instructional context so as to determine when to terminate instruction and maximize the likelihood of maintenance.

Mulligan, Guess, Holvoet and Brown (1980) identified a number of *problems* with the *traditional research* in this area of study. As previously mentioned, the artificial nature of the tasks studied makes it difficult to generalize to tasks more traditionally associated with school curricula. In studies of distributed practice, the intertrial interval ranges from five seconds to seven days. In one study (Blake, 1976), there were three weeks between two trials of the same program. Strategies structured to compare periods of work with periods of rest often contained periods of work having five to 20 massed trials alternated with differing lengths of rest. Some combinations reported one minute of work and thirty seconds of rest, or thirty seconds work and sixty to one hundred seconds of rest. In some cases, the time periods between trials representing massing in one study were used as spacing in another. The majority of research studies scheduled an inactive rest period rather than an alternative activity during the intertrial interval. An educator cannot afford the luxury of scheduling rest periods in place of training sessions. In studies in which a task was used during the intertrial interval, the tasks were usually ones that the learner could already perform. Thus, the *question remains* whether the effect of distributed trials is maintained when two or three *acquisition trials* from different programs are systematically alternated.

Mulligan, Guess, Holvoet and Brown (1980), while reviewing a large number of studies, observed confusion over the definition of a trial, the distinction between distributed and spaced trials, and *controversy about the actual superiority of separated versus massed trials*. Researchers have not been consistent in their definitions and interpretations of massed and distributed practice.

Mulligan *et al.* suggested that benefit may be derived from *combining* the use of *massed and distributed trial schedules*. Massed trials could be used initially for acquisition or correction, with distributed trials being used for maintenance and generalization. A similar recommendation was made by Bloom and Shuell (1981) in their previously described study of second language learning among high school students. These researchers suggested that during early phases of instruction, when one is initially teaching new material, immediate feedback or massed practice may be most appropriate; later in the instructional sequence, when acquisition of the material has been established at some reasonable level, delayed feedback or distributed practice may be most appropriate to guarantee maximum retention.

Even though distributed practice of a response requires fewer trails to criterion and less total time on the task, the *span of time* covering the entire *training period* is greater than that required for massed practice. If rapid acquisition over a short period of time is required before another program can be initiated, then massed practice may be appropriate (Mulligan *et al.*, 1980). Mulligan, Lacy and Guess (1982) stated that the experimental literature (Dore and Hilgard, 1938; Ericksen, 1942; Kimble, 1949; Reynolds and Adams, 1953) indicated that some combination of massed and distributed practice may produce the best learning and retention.

The actual logistics of utilizing the two strategies still needs to be determined.

Listed below are some of the variables that are, or may be, critical to the *successful combination of massed and distributed practice*.

    a. The optimum number of trials in a massed practice interval may be a function of:

- the time and/or number of steps required to complete any one task. If a lengthy chain of responses is being taught, each rehearsal of the chain may take considerable time, thereby reducing the number of trials that may be conducted in a given time interval.

- the amount of mental and/or cognitive effort required to perform each task. Closely sequenced trials of a difficult task may be aversive to the learner. Difficult motor tasks may produce fatigue, and a suitable period for recovery may be required following each practice trial. Some cognitive tasks may require simple memorization of a foreign word and its English equivalent, such as livre = book. Alternatively, a cognitive task requiring few steps may be difficult because of the relatively high level of complexity or abstraction of the task. The difficulty of each trial will also depend upon whether familiar material is being reviewed, or unfamiliar material is being learned.

- the number of trials performed correctly and/or the frequency, amount and type of reinforcement received during practice. Engelmann and Carnine (1982) suggest that the learner should receive reinforcement on at least 70 percent of the trials. Stimulus materials may have to be temporarily modified and/or temporary assistance may have to be introduced to maintain and shape a sufficiently high rate of correct responding.

- whether successive trials involve identical or similar (equivalent) tasks. Practice may involve identical repetitions of the same thing, such as repeating a rule, e.g., "round things roll," or "5 x 7 = 35." Alternatively, practice of a rule may be quite varied, e.g., "What do round things do?"; "If its round it will . . .?"; "Rolling things are . . .?"; "It's not round, will it roll?" Similarly, practice on multiplication facts may involve repetition of one or more facts from the five-times table, facts from several different times-tables, or variations on a single fact, e.g., "5 x ... = 35;" "... x 7 = 35," and "5 x 7 = ..."

Given these and other considerations, including those related to individual learner characteristics, it is impossible to specify the optimum number of massed repetitions. Given a particular task and learner, the best index of good instruction is a positive acceleration or maintenance of a satisfactory rate, consistency and accuracy of a learner's response.

b. The optimum length of intervening intervals may be a function of:

- the number and type of intervening activities. A large number of activities or a small number of difficult activities may not provide sufficient recovery following massed practice. In addition, if alternating periods of practice involve similar stimulus materials, but require different responses to those materials, retroactive or proactive inhibition may result. In *retroactive inhibition*, learning subsequent to original learning affects recall of the original material. In *proactive inhibition*, prior learning influences the acquisition of subsequently presented materials. Variations in stimulus and response modalities, subject material and response types between adjacent intervals of massed and distributed practice may reduce the likelihood of inhibition, may provide an appropriate recovery interval and may also provide variety in instruction having a positive effect on motivation.

- whether familiar tasks are being practiced or new materials are being learned. If new and/or difficult tasks are being learned during the massed interval, perhaps tasks during the distributed interval should be familiar and/or relatively simple to perform. Alternatively, if familiar and/or easy tasks are being practiced during the massed interval, more difficult tasks may be presented during the intervening interval. The intervals between massed practice may include review of previously learned skills. Carnine (1979) suggested that the following priority should be assigned to review to enhance maintenance. First, review troublesome responses with a high error rate; second, review recently learned responses that may not be well established; and, third, review responses that may not have been recently reviewed.

The following recommendations relate to the duration and alternation of massed and distributed intervals.

a. During massed practice, continue to evaluate the learner's fluency of response and continue to practice as long as a satisfactory rate, consistency and accuracy, or improvement of response is being made. Do not continue practice until the point where performance begins to deteriorate. Terminating practice at this time may reinforce deterioration. In addition, practice continued to the point of deterioration may make the task aversive and reduce the likelihood of maintenance. As the learner acquires fluency of response, less practice will be required and the duration of the massed interval may be reduced.

b. Make the intervening interval between successive episodes of massed practice as short as is necessary to insure maintenance of the response at a reasonable level. For some learners and some tasks, to insure maintenance of a response from trial to trial, the intervening interval may have to be very short, for example, of less than an hour in length. For other tasks or different learners, the interval may extend for one or more days.

c. Make the intervening interval between successive episodes of massed practice as long as possible, while maintaining a satisfactory level of response. Also, progressively lengthen the intervening interval. Both of these procedures will shape the learner's ability to recall the response after successively longer periods of time to approximate the demands that may occur in the natural environment. Given the above considerations, a combined schedule of massed and distributed practice may look somewhat as illustrated in Figure 9.1, where *m* indicates massed practice and *i* indicates

Figure 9.1

A Sequence of Massed and Distributed Practice

---

mmmmiimmmmiimmmiiiiimmiiiiiiimmiiiiiiiiiimiiiiiiiiiim.....

---

the intervening interval during which one or more activities are practiced that are different from those in the massed interval.

Chapter Ten

Instructional Models and Methods

As was mentioned in the previous chapter, the failure of many research studies to obtain generalization and maintenance of trained mnemonic strategies is frequently not a function of a deficiency in the learner but the result of an *instructional deficiency* resulting from inadequate instruction (Borkowski and Cavanaugh, 1979). Generally speaking, research in the area of memory has been rigorous in its research design but imprecise in its instructional design. The following discussion provides a review of (a) a number of instructional techniques, (b) generic models of instruction and (c) exemplary instructional sequences incorporating many of the previously described instructional procedures. The methods that are described may be employed to (a) teach the use of specific mnemonic techniques or (b) enhance the memorability of any instructional content.

Prompting and Fading

A *prompt* is a supplementary stimulus temporarily introduced during instruction to *assist* a learner to respond in a desired manner. Prompts may be used to aid a learner (a) to acquire a new response and (b) to perform an established response in the presence of particular stimuli. Prompts in the form of verbal, modeling, gestural and physical assistance may be used to occasion a response ("cause" a response to occur). *Stimulus modification* may be used to increase the *salience* of *discriminative stimuli* so as to assist a learner to make a desired response in the presence of those stimuli. For example, the salience of discriminative features may be increased by (a) *embellishing* the discriminative features, (b) *diminishing* the *intensity* of *nondiscriminative features* and (c) introducing an extra stimulus to focus attention on the discriminative features.

A prompt is a stimulus that has *control* over a response. When a response does not automatically occur in the presence of a particular stimulus x, a *supplementary stimulus*, a prompt, having control over the response, is *temporarily introduced* to get the response to occur in the presence of stimulus x. Eventually, however, the discriminative features of stimulus x must take control over the response. The *transfer of control* from the prompt to stimulus x is achieved through the process of fading. *Fading* involves the systematic and gradual withdrawal of a prompt following repeated performance of a response in the presence of a discriminative stimulus. The purpose of fading is to *transfer control* of a response from a prompt to a discriminative stimulus. Prompts are faded from use as quickly as possible to avoid overdependence upon them; they are also faded as slowly as is necessary to maintain a high rate of correct responding. The *fluency* of a response, its rate, accuracy and consistency of performance, provides an indication of when fading should commence and how rapidly it should proceed (Baine, 1982). Engelmann and Carnine (1982, p. 226) provided an excellent example of a simple prompt used to help students remember which arithmetic operations to perform on fractions. In the fractions shown below, the addition sign has one arrow indicating that the student is to perform only one operation—on the top of the fraction. The multiplication sign has two arrows, indicating that two operations are to be performed—one on the top and one on the bottom of the fraction.

$$\frac{4}{3} + \frac{3}{3} = \qquad\qquad \frac{4}{3} \times \frac{3}{3} =$$

These prompts are referred to as *within stimulus prompts* because the modification is made directly to an intrinsic, distinctive feature of the stimulus. By attending to the prompt, the learner must also attend simultaneously to the discriminative feature of the stimulus. Because the prompt and the discriminative feature have been integrated, as the prompt is faded from use, the distinctive feature to which the learner was attending remains to cue the same response.

In contrast, *extra stimulus prompts* are an extra rather than integral part of a stimulus. As a result, a learner may be taught to make the correct response by attending only to the prompt rather than to both the prompt and the discriminative part of the stimulus. Thus, when the prompt is faded from use, because the student has not learned to attend to the discriminative feature, she/he is not left with anything to guide the response. For example, a macron over the *a* in the word *made*, indicating that the long *a* is to be used in pronouncing the word, is an extra stimulus prompt. Thus, a student may attend only to the diacritical mark rather than to the nature of the word to determine whether the vowel should be long or short. As a result, when the mark is faded from use, if the student has not learned to attend to the nature of words to determine whether vowels should be long or short, she/he will not be left with anything to guide pronunciation. For this reason, within stimulus prompts are preferable to extra stimulus prompts. Although, within stimulus prompts are *progressively faded* from use, it is recommended that extra stimulus prompts, when required, should be *abruptly removed* after the desired response has been established to avoid over-dependence upon the prompt.

In *printed material*, critical details of the text may be *prompted* through the use of underlining, spacing, brackets and italic, boldface or colored type. Students may *be taught* to focus particular attention on material prompted in this manner in an effort to enhance understanding and recall of the material. For example, if a student has been taught to use a particular mnemonic strategy while reading prose, during initial instruction, the text may be prompted at the points where application of the strategy is appropriate. Subsequently, the prompts may be faded and the student may be required to preview the text while underlining material to which the strategy is applicable. After the student has indicated the ability to identify appropriate applications, she/he may be required to reread the material while applying the strategy where prompted. A post-test may be used to assess retention of the prompted material and correct application of the strategy.

Similarly, a teacher may enhance recall of particular types of material presented in a *lecture format* by training the students to respond in a particular manner to prompts embedded in the presentation. For example, the teacher may draw attention to selected content by stating some words more loudly than others, by pausing for a moment before and/or after delivery of relevant material, by repeating the material either consecutively or at several points throughout the presentation, or by using direct verbal instructions, such as "This will be on the exam." As students learn to identify particular types of material in verbal presentations, the teacher may fade the prompts. In a manner similar to that used in reading, student ability to identify particular types of material in a verbal presentation may be monitored by having students raise their hands each time items of the specified nature are presented. Subsequently, processing comprehension and recall of this material may be evaluated. Additional examples of prompting and fading are discussed in the following paragraphs. Further discussions of prompting and fading are available in Baine (1982) and Engelmann and Carnine (1982).

Chaining

A chain is comprised of a series of *stimulus and response links* joined together and performed in a relatively fixed order. Many common verbal, motor and/or cognitive sequences involve chains. For example, the *keyword mnemonic* strategy (Atkinson and Raugh, 1975), described in Chapter Two, is a chain. As previously described, the keyword strategy has been used to store and retrieve information such as foreign language vocabulary and its English counterpart, the names of U.S. states and capitals, and faces and names. The stimulus response links of this chain are described below.

  (a) The chain is initiated when information that has been presented (a stimulus S) is identified by an observer (a response R) as being only temporarily available.

(b) A characteristic of the information *S* leads to the recognition *R* that the information is important, and that it may have to be recalled later following its removal.

(c) A second characteristic of the information *S* leads to the decision *R* that the information is of the type that requires use of a mnemonic strategy to assist storage and retrieval.

(d) A third characteristic of the information *S* leads to the recognition *R* that the information is an example of the class of information to which the keyword mnemonic strategy is applicable.

(e) Thus, given the Latin word *hocopus* meaning *hard work* *S*, stimulates the first step in the actual keyword mnemonic, forming the acoustic link *octopus R*.

(f) Completion of step (e), acts as a stimulus for the response, making an interactive image to link the acoustic link to the meaning of the word. Thus, the octopus may be visualized with sweat on its brow and with all of its many arms involved in a particular type of hard work.

In the future, given either the word *hocopus* or the words *hard work*, the corresponding term may be retrieved by recalling the image of the keyword *the hardworking octopus*. Each of the essential steps in the keyword chain has been identified through a process called *task analysis*; this procedure is described below. To effectively employ the keyword mnemonic strategy, a learner must master each of the steps in the sequence, and perform each of them in a consistent order. All of the steps must be performed in a consistent order so that completion of each step begins to stimulate performance of the successive step in the sequence. When the chain is performed in this manner, no essential step will be inadvertently eliminated in future application of the strategy.

Prompts may be *introduced* to facilitate acquisition of each of the steps. For example, several researchers have used *pictures* to teach students how to develop acoustic links (step e) and interactive images (step f) (e.g., Levin, Shriberg, Miller, McCormick and Levin, 1980). As the learner acquires the ability to form appropriate links and images, the pictures may be *faded* from use by using pictures that provide successively less information and that require increasingly more learner participation. Prompts may also be used to assist the learner to identify information that is within the class to which the keyword method is applicable. For example, the teacher may identify three characteristics that all examples within the class possess. Then, following presentation of a variety of examples of information that are either in or outside of the class, the teacher may present *questions as prompts*, e.g., "Does this example have characteristic x, and y and z"? The questions may be faded after several presentations. The teacher may ask fewer questions as the learner assumes successively more responsibility. The teacher may begin fading by asking only the initial portion of each question as the student learns to ask successively more of each particular type of question.

Chains may be *taught* in several different ways.

a. One or more of the steps in the chain may be taught in isolation before they are linked together. This approach is sometimes adopted if particular steps in the chain are especially difficult to learn. Also, if several of the steps require a common skill, this skill may be pretaught before the chain is linked.

b. Alternatively, where each of the steps is readily learned, the steps in the chain may be taught and linked at the same time.

c. Each step in the program may be linked in a reverse order called *reverse chaining*. In this procedure, if a chain is comprised of steps a, b, c and d, the teacher may demonstrate each step in order, and then teach the learner to perform the last step to complete the task. When the learner has mastered the last step, the teacher may *demonstrate* steps a and b, *teach* the learner to perform c, and have the learner *practice* step d to complete the task. In this manner, the student learns the skills in the order d, c, b and a; however, the chain is always performed in the order a, b, c and d. The advantages of this approach are that the teacher's repeated demonstrations define the nature of the task and lead to acquisition of skills through modeling. In addition, from the very first step, the learner has the satisfaction of performing the step that completes the task. Depending upon the skills of the learner, this step may be analyzed into smaller steps, and/or prompts may be introduced to insure that the learner's response is successful.

d. *Forward chaining* involves teaching the learner the skills in the order *a, b, c*, then *d*. The learner must first *master* step *a* before step *b* is *taught and linked* to *a*.

e. In *total task chaining*, the learner is simultaneously taught to perform steps *a* to *d*. In this approach, prompts are introduced at each stage of instruction. As prompts are faded from use at any one step in the chain, the learner performs more of that particular step without assistance. For example, the learner may be prompted to perform steps *a, b* and *d* while performing *c* independently. The last step in the chain that the student learns to perform independently may be step *b*.

Rules for teaching chains

a. When linking steps in a chain, always practice the steps in the order in which they must eventually be performed. Thus, if step *a* is consistently performed before step *b*, completion of step *a* will begin to stimulate commencement of step *b*. If the steps are not repeatedly practiced in a consistent order, step *a* will not be strongly linked to step *b*. As a result, step *b* may be replaced by another step, with which step *a* has become associated. Consequently, step *b* may be resequenced or eliminated from the chain.

b. For the same reason, adjacent steps in a chain should be practiced in rapid succession in the absence of any intervening activity.

c. When a particular step in a chain (e.g., *b*) is being learned and a time consuming number of steps precede *b*, during the acquisition phase of instruction, it may not be necessary to rehearse each of the preceding steps from *a* to *g* each time that step *b* is being instructed. However, to maintain steps *a* to *g* at an acceptable level of fluency, they should be practiced intermittently.

d. When one or more parts of a chain have been difficult to learn, or when parts of the chain have been infrequently practiced, use *overlearning* and continue to practice the entire chain rapidly, consistently and accurately after the chain has reached criterion. Overlearning should increase the *associative link* between each step in the chain, provided that repeated practice is rewarding rather than aversive.

Task Analysis

Task analysis is a procedure used to identify the *minimum essential steps* involved in performing a task. The analysis is prerequisite to effective teaching in which the learner is taught to perform the minimum essential steps required to perform a task in the simplest manner, to an acceptable standard, under the range of conditions that commonly occur in the natural environment. Instruction that incorporates these considerations is likely to enhance both generalization and maintenance of learning. Task analysis actually involves *three* separate but related *analyses* that are conducted at the same time: performance analysis, conditions analysis and standards analysis.

The procedure begins with a *conditions analysis* designed to identify the range of stimulus conditions that commonly occur in the *natural environment* in which the learner may be required to perform. The *performance analysis* that follows involves an analysis of the performance of a variety of accomplished and naive individuals performing the task under the range of commonly occurring conditions identified in the conditions analysis. *Accomplished performers* are studied to identify various ways in which a task may be successfully performed. The simplest method of performing the task under the commonly occurring range of conditions is then identified; this is the method that is taught during subsequent instruction. *Novice performers* are studied to identify common errors that occur during performance of the task. During later instruction, learners may be directly instructed to avoid these errors. Alternatively, instruction may be designed to avoid the occurrence of such errors. Study is also made of the manner in which changing conditions affect changes in performance; learners are taught to make these accommodations and thereby to improve generalization. The *standards analysis* is used to identify the *minimum essential standards* of performance under each of the commonly occurring conditions. Failure to achieve these standards of performance during instruction precludes maintenance and generalization (Baine, 1982).

Structuring Instruction

Sequencing instructional events within a lesson. Each lesson may be divided into four phases of instruction, as described below (Baine, 1982).

a. **Phase one:**
- *Rehearsal*: review of previously learned skills that are components of or prerequisite to the skill to be taught in the acquisition or generalization phases of instruction. This phase of instruction acts as a transition from previous activity, establishes readiness skills, and functions as a refresher bringing skills up to an acceptable level of fluency.
- *Pretraining*: phase one may also include or be comprised of pretraining of difficult steps in a chain to be taught during the acquisition phase. Pretraining may facilitate rapid and relatively errorless linking of steps in the chain during later instruction.

b. **Phase two:**
- *Acquisition*: teaching a new skill. Involves incorporation of previously learned skills and removal of instructional assistance as fluency is attained.
- *Generalization*: phase two may also include or be comprised of generalization training of a previously acquired skill. Learner is taught to perform the skill under the commonly found range of conditions.

c. **Phase three:**
- *Maintenance*: one or more skills taught in the previous lessons are reviewed.

d. **Phase four:**
- *Review*: skills taught earlier in the lesson are maintained and reevaluated through review.

The instructional process may be further structured through the application of a well designed instructional format used for the presentation of each skill being taught during *individual or group instruction*. The following *generic instructional format* (Baine, 1982) is a derivation and modification of instructional methods described by Becker, Engelmann and Thomas (1971), Williams, Coyne, DeSpain, Johnson, Scheverman, Stengert, Swetlik and York (1978) and Williams and York (1978). The format is comprised of four parts.

Part one:

Orientation: involves presentation of a *readiness signal* indicating who is to respond and in what manner. The signal may be directed to the group or to a particular individual, for example: "Everyone, listen to this" or "Harry, watch my hand"; or, after several repetitions of the same task, a less specific signal may be used, such as "Ready." An optional *focussing prompt* may be included in the orientation. This prompt may be in the form of additional verbal, gestural, modeling or physical assistance to focus learner attention on the discriminative features of the instructional material. The focussing prompt may also include the use of *stimulus modification* to increase the salience of the discriminative features.

Part two:

Instruction. A *task command* is used to begin the instructional phase. The task command indicates who is to respond and what response they are to make. For example, during the early stages of instruction, the teacher may be modeling the task that the learner is eventually to perform. For example, "Now, *I'm* going to make an acoustic link for the word *hocopus*" or "Make an acoustic link for the word *livre* (*you* is implicit in the command). The task command may be followed by an optional *task confirmation* during the early stages of instruction, when it is desirable, before continuing, to confirm that the learner understands what she/he is to do. For example, the *task query* may take the form of, "O.K. What are you going to do?" while the confirmation may be in the form of "Yes, that's right, you're going to . . . ." This statement offers positive confirmation and restates the task command. Alternatively, if the response following the query is incorrect, the response may be disconfirmed, for example, "No, you're going to . . . ," followed by another task query.

Part three:

Responding. During this phase, either the teacher responds with the model previously described in the task command (makes an acoustic link), an individual learner responds as commanded or the group responds. If a group response is to be made by all of the group members *at the same time* so that slower learners are formulating their own response rather than simply imitating the response of learner who responded earlier, then a *response signal*, such as a hand signal, may be employed to indicate when the group is to respond. Prompts may also be included during this stage: (a) to assist the learner(s) to make the desired response or (b) to focus learner attention on critical aspects of the model.

Part four:

Repetition. This stage involves either providing the learner with a number of demonstrations of the task before asking him/her to imitate the model or giving the learner a sufficient number of practice trials to achieve a degree of fluency. An integral part of this stage of instruction is *consequation*: providing the learner with feedback, reinforcement or correction following his/her response.

Since most of the *errors* that occur during instruction are predictable, effective *correction procedures* can be planned in advance. Some of the errors and their corresponding correction procedures are described below. The procedures described below have been adapted from Baine (1982) and Engelmann and Osborne (1976).

Response errors.

(a) Failure to respond: increase the salience of the readiness signal and/or the focussing prompt and/or the instructional material. Alternatively, delay instruction, and introduce *orientation training*, teaching the learner to respond in the desired manner to the readiness signal. Or use prompts to assist the response.

(b) Resists orienting (has previously, frequently and recently demonstrated the appropriate response to the same stimulus): evaluate instructional variables, such as the duration of instruction, the number of consecutive trials, the pace of instruction, distracting stimuli, task difficulty, reinforcement, previous activity in the schedule; correct the instructional variables as required. Alternatively, use *time-out* and temporarily remove all instruction, reinforcement and attention; recommence instruction after a period of waiting. Where this procedure does not produce the desired results, *compliance training* in the form of *paced-practice* (Baine, 1982) and *mandating* (Baine, 1982, Haring, 1977-1978) may be required; these extraordinary procedures are beyond the limits of the present text.

(c) Orients to wrong part of stimulus: use teacher prompts or stimulus modification (within or extra stimulus prompts). Temporarily remove distracting stimuli, or use *interception* to prevent completion of the incorrect response; for example, "No!" Prevent completion of the response, and introduce a prompt to facilitate the correct response: "Look *carefully* at *both* of them." Alternatively, *precorrection* may be used. When an error is anticipated, rather than letting it happen, precorrect the error before beginning the instructional sequence in which the error is expected to occur. For example, if a learner is likely to fail to notice that a randomly presented group of stimulus words to be memorized has been selected from a number of *categories*, preteach attention to categories by first presenting groups of words in which attention to the categories is obvious, and to which attention is highly reinforced.

(d) Becomes distracted during instruction: temporarily reduce distracting stimuli and slowly reintroduce as attention become better focussed. Examine instructional variables as in (b) above. Use interception, as above.

Latency errors (responds too quickly or slowly to the task command).

When the same task has been presented repeatedly in an attempt to increase the fluency of the response, a learner will sometimes fail to wait for the task command and will respond prematurely. In this situation, the instructional context rather than a discriminative feature of the stimulus may have gained *stimulus control*, and the response may be made before the task command and without attending to the stimulus material. This error may be corrected by randomly introducing minor changes in the stimulus to which attention must be directed to avoid errors. Alternatively, the premature response may be intercepted with, "No! Wait for the task command." Alternatively, if the response is made too slowly, a particular problem during group instruction where a *unison response* is required, precorrection may be required in which the subject's rate of response is increased in successive approximations of the desired rate.

Right type of response but wrong response of that type. (for example, points to [correct response] wrong object).

Respond with, "No!" (repeat the task command) e.g., "Point to *x*," and model or physically prompt the correct response. If a discrimination is required, increase the discriminative feature of the stimulus and/or decrease the nondiscriminative features; increase the differences between the stimuli being selected. If it is anticipated that the learner, when presented with a complex stimulus, will have difficulty attending to a particular discriminative feature of the stimulus, use *precorrection*. Before presenting the task, have the learner respond to a simple stimulus in which the discriminative features is salient. Several trials with this stimulus may establish a *set* to attend to discriminative features of the nature presented. *Overcorrection* may be used. Once an error is committed, the probability is high that the error will be made again. If the error is corrected only once, on the next trial there may be little difference between the probability of making the correct response and that of recommitting the error. However, if the error is corrected repeatedly and the learner is provided with *massed practice* making the correct response, the probability is increased of making the correct response on successive trials.

Wrong type of response (touches rather than picks-up).

Respond with "No!" repeat the task command and model or physically prompt the correct response. Precorrection and overcorrection may also be used as in the previous example.

Response bias errors: in a discrimination task repeatedly and consistently makes a wrong choice on the basis of a nondiscriminative feature such as color or location.

Consistently require the learner to respond to a stimulus in another location or of another color, as appropriate. As the learner modifies his response bias to respond to the new stimulus configuration, begin to randomize the color and/or location. The correct response may also be modeled and/or physically prompted. As in any correction procedure, one must avoid the *teacher trap*. In that trap, the more errors a student makes, the more a teacher sees that she/he is needed; and the more attention the student receives contingent on making errors, the more errors the student will make.

Modeling

Modeling involves teaching by demonstration. The model provides a demonstration of verbal, cognitive or motor behavior that the observer is expected to *imitate*. The imitation may be *immediate or delayed*, and the behavior displayed may be *identical* or merely *similar* to the behavior modeled. Modeling may be used to teach a variety of skills, such as the application of mnemonic strategies, various methods of recalling stored information, self-directing verbal statements used in cognitive behavior modification, and the steps involved in solving mathematics problems, as well as athletic, dramatic, artistic, social and other forms of behavior. Zimmerman and Rosenthal (1974) have reviewed a number of studies in which modeling was used to teach a variety of generalized language rules, abstract concepts or principles, problem solving strategies and creative responses. In fact, most human behavior is learned observationally through modeling (Bandura, 1977). The technique is particularly useful with *young children* or *developmentally delayed* individuals who, because of limited language development, may be unable to learn from verbal or written explanations. Also, even with higher functioning learners, a demonstration, like a picture, may be worth a thousand words. Modeling affects the acquisition, generalization and maintenance of a skill. If the skill demonstrated illustrates a simple and efficient method of performance that is adaptive to a variety of common environmental demands, then imitation of the skill is likely to be both generalized and maintained.

An *abstract, generalizable rule* can be taught by varying *nondiscriminative* aspects of a demonstration (those not pertaining to the concept or rule being learned) while holding the rule constant across presentations. In this situation, the learner does not imitate the exact nature of the behavior modeled but abstracts a rule or common feature from the modeling sequence and then generalizes this rule to new and different stimulus circumstances. By randomly varying nondiscriminative features of the model across trials (e.g., the model's words in a syntactic rule learning study), it is possible to minimize the exact mimicry of those nonessential details (Zimmerman and Rosenthal, 1974). In this case, an *exact imitation* of the behavior modeled is *not desirable*. Instead, the nondiscriminative features of the behavior are expected to vary while the *discriminative features* of the behavior are either held constant or are modified, within an acceptable range, to accommodate circumstances to which the behaviors are appropriate. Zimmerman and Rosenthal (1974) have described several studies in which these procedures have been successfully used in *language training with children* (Bandura and Harris, 1966; Carroll, Rosenthal and Brysh, 1972; Harris and Hassemer 1972; Odom, Liebert and Hill, 1968). Rosenthal and White (1972) concluded that typically observers appear to acquire patterned rules for conduct and then judiciously select from their repertoires specific components congruent with situational, social and task demands. In the following paragraphs, a number of *variables* are reviewed that *influence the effectiveness of modeling*.

Modeling may be used in conjunction with *shaping* and *fading*. Clark, Sharman and Kelley (1971) taught *verb tenses* to *retarded and disadvantaged children* using these procedures. The model demonstrated each word of the answer and reinforced the learner when all of the model's words were imitated. Once the child could reliably perform single words, larger phrases were introduced (*shaping*) until the child could successfully reproduce them completely. Then, the experimenter began to fade his model of the correct response by speaking the last words of each sentence more softly. The sentences were *successfully faded* in this manner until the child could give correct verbs without modeling. This approach led to substantial generalization to new verbs as each tense was successively trained (Zimmerman and Rosenthal, 1974).

Modeling may be used in conjunction with various types of *orienting instructions* introduced before presentation of a model. In a study of children in the *third grade* conducted by Rosenthal and Zimmerman (1972), *four types* of instructions were given: (a) implicit instructions merely telling the child to watch the model, (b) explicit instructions telling the child to emulate the model, (c) pattern instructions alerting the child to look for a rule in the model's response and (d) mapping instructions which provided the rule guiding the model's behavior. Informative instructions enhanced *acquisition* more than implicit instructions, especially for the mapping group. However, these differences were not *maintained* on the *generalization* task. Yussen (1974) found that with *preschoolers* and children in the *second grade*, it helped to pinpoint the children's attention to task relevant behaviors by giving the children explicit instructions to watch the demonstration so that they could remember and report the model's actions.

Modeling may be used in conjunction with *verbal labels* or *statements*. Rosenthal, Alford and Rasp (1972) conducted a study of the acquisition, generalization and maintenance of a *clustering concept* by *children* (average C.A. 7.6 years). Modeling was accompanied by either (a) no verbalization, (b) a low information verbal code, (c) a high information code or (d) a high information code, plus a statement of the rule governing the concept. In each condition, the concept was acquired, generalized and maintained several weeks after the end of instruction. The strength of acquisition and generalization was related to the amount of information provided by the model.

In a study of students ranging in *age from 7.5 to 10.5 years*, modeling, when accompanied by a *verbal rule*, produced the highest level of acquisition and generalization. Simple provision of the rule or the observation of a silent model provided significant but intermediate levels of acquisition and generalization, when compared to an untreated control group. After a seven week delay, each child was retested on the initial training and transfer tasks and on new generalization items. *Retention testing* was conducted by a new experimenter, who was a complete stranger to the children. The pattern of *results* found in acquisition and generalization was maintained with the retention data. Significant transfer to new items was found despite the lengthy delay. Thus, the evidence indicates that modeled instruction of concepts, in the absence of verbal rules, can be retained over extended periods; also, that verbal instructions and rules provided during the model can further enhance acquisition, maintenance and generalization.

During modeling, the *observer* may become *actively involved* in *describing* or *labelling* the activity to improve the organization and retention of his/her observations. Bandura (1977) claimed that observers who code modeled activities into either words, concise labels or vivid imagery learn and retain behavior better than those who simply observe or are mentally preoccupied with other matters while watching. However, Zimmerman and Rosenthal (1974) concluded from their review of several studies that *overt responding*, particularly if it is temporally coincident with the model's performance, can interfere with an observer's ability to attend to the modeled display. Second, an observer's spontaneous description of the model's behavior need not assist organization and retention, and may interfere, especially with older subjects. Instructions to spontaneously describe observations do not necessarily establish a more parsimonious, simpler organization of information. The facilitating or impeding effects of *labelling or description* depend on the adequacy of the verbalization in summarizing and retrieving information. If a verbal description enables the observer to classify or summarize salient aspects of the modeled display, learning should improve. However, it is not the active response alone that improves performance. Unless overt responding leads to a *concise summary* of the observations, it may interfere with observational learning. If children are at an age where they do not automatically mentally organize and label their observations, or if the task is of such a nature that it is not readily mentally processed in a similar manner by older subjects, then providing or eliciting verbalizations about the model's behavior may augment learning (Zimmerman and Rosenthal). For example, Cullinan (1976) found that requiring *mildly retarded children* to describe the motoric behaviors of a model during the demonstration facilitated imitation. If, because of the nature of the task or the learner, the learner does not have cognitive representations of all of the components of the task in his/her repertoire, any additional rehearsal or verbalization that instates representation of task components may be expected to aid performance. In contrast, when the model displays activities in which the constituents are already present in the observer's repertoire, additional activity during acquisition may interfere (Zimmerman and Rosenthal, 1974).

Denney (1975) studied the effects on *6-, 8- and 10-year-old children* of *self-verbalization* made during modeling of a 20-question task. In this task the subjects guessed which picture out of an array of pictures the experimenter was thinking of by asking questions that could be answered by either "yes" or "no." Three statement conditions were employed in this study: (a) exemplary modeling, (b) strategy modeling and (c) strategy modeling with self-instruction. In the exemplary modeling condition, the experimenter used but did not explain his strategy while playing the 20-questions game. In the strategy modeling condition, the experimenter verbalized the strategy that he used as he performed. In the strategy modeling with self-instruction condition, the subject received the same information from the experimenter as in the strategy modeling condition, but he was also required to overtly verbalize the strategy that the experimenter had used. The results of this study indicated that for the 8- and 10-year-old children, all three of the modeling procedures facilitated performance. However, only the strategy modeling procedure facilitated the performance of 6-year-old children. Since the strategy modeling was the same in both the strategy modeling group and in the strategy modeling with self-instruction group, Denney concluded that the overt self-instruction must have interfered with the information processing of the 6-year-old children.

In a later study, Denney and Turner (1979) examined the effects of self-verbalization during modeling on children *3-, 4-, 5-, 6-* and *10 years of age*. Four tasks were used: signal, match-to-standard, paired-associate and 20 questions. Two modeling conditions were employed: strategy modeling and strategy modeling with self-verbalization. The results indicated that both strategy modeling and strategy modeling with overt self-verbalization were effective training techniques for facilitating performance on all of the cognitive tasks included in the present study. The two modeling procedures were also equally effective across all age groups studied. The only interaction between age and treatment conditions indicated that on the two more complex tasks, paired-associates and 20-questions, neither training technique was effective in facilitating performance in the three younger age groups. Thus, there appears to be no support for the position that children between the ages of three and ten need overt self-verbalization in order to facilitate their performance on the type of tasks included in the present study. Also, it appears that, if the demands of the overt self-verbalization do not obviously interfere with adequate performance on a task, the effects of the overt self-verbalization will neither interfere with nor facilitate performance in normal children. Strategy modeling without overt self-verbalization thus appears to be the more practical and efficient method for facilitating cognitive performance among normal children. It is possible, however, that overt self-verbalizations will benefit children whose performance is typically somehow deficient (Denney and Turner, 1979).

Imitation may follow a *partial model*, one *complete model* or *several demonstrations* of the same skill. In a study conducted by Goldschmid and Bentler (1968), it was found that with *four-year-old children*, the usual training procedure of having the model provide six successive demonstrations of a response before requiring the child to imitate the model was unsatisfactory. The children were either unable or unwilling to pay sustained attention during the series of models. Therefore, an *alternation format* was adopted in which the model performed, then the child imitated the response, followed by additional alternations of modeling and imitation. This procedure was effective in creating imitation and transfer of a Piagetian conservation task by four-year-old children. Rosenthal (1979) also recommended use of the alternating format with *preschool children*. He suggested that although children often erred in their early attempts, the alternation format kept the attention and involvement of the children who would be otherwise distracted during lengthy and repetitive demonstrations. Also, after the first few trials, the adult can supply corrective feedback to rectify the child's mistakes. Alternatively, Rosenthal suggested, with adult models, *older children* often gain most, if they first observe 8 to 20 demonstrations of correct responding before getting their turn to perform.

When a demonstration is lengthy or involves a large number of steps, the task may be divided into a *series of segments* that are presented individually. The learner may be required to master each segment before successive segments are presented. As each new segment is presented, previously learned parts may be *integrated*. This procedure is similar to the previously described process of *chaining*, and the same instructional techniques are applicable. According to Litrownik, Franzini and Turner (1976), for *moderately retarded* persons, *distributed modeling* in which the model performs before each trial resulted in better matching on complex tasks than *mass modeling* in which the behavior is modeled once then the observer performs numerous trials.

People cannot learn much by observation unless they attend to and accurately perceive the significant features of the modeled behavior (Bandura, 1977). *Focussing* of *attention* on *critical details* is important to all learners and is particularly important to *mentally retarded individuals*. For example, studies have shown that there is a marked tendency among children to fixate on a detail of a picture that is often of irrelevant significance (Travers and Alvarado, 1970). Children under *five years of age* are distracted easily and tend to focus on as many task-irrelevant as task-relevant model cues (Yando, Seitz and Zigler, 1978). The ability to selectively attend to the appropriate cues necessary for successful performance and to ignore irrelevant cues does not stabilize until about *11 years of age* (Weiss, 1982). Westling and Koorland (1979) reported that when learning attention and discrimination skills, *mentally retarded individuals* were not as competent as normal individuals of equivalent mental age. *Autistic, mentally retarded and learning disabled children* exhibit difficulties selectively attending to the relevant cues available in a learning task (Brown, 1975; Lovaas, Schreibman, Koegel and Rehm, 1971: Ross, 1975; Wilhelm and Lovaas, 1976). Mentally retarded children attend to a limited number of the features of a stimulus and may respond to those that are not critical to discrimination (Wolfe and Cuvo, 1978; Zeaman and House, 1963). However, once a mentally retarded or learning disabled child attends to task-relevant dimensions, their performance approximates that of normal subjects (Berlyne, 1970; Ross, 1975; Wolfe and Cuvo, 1978).

Thus, it is necessary to insure that observers focus their attention on critical features of a model. *Attention* may be *focussed* in several different ways. The nondiscriminative features of the model may be decreased both in terms of *number and salience*, while the salience of the discriminative features is increased. For example, if a *verbal rule* is being modeled, extraneous verbiage should be removed, and while the rule is being stated, critical terms might be stated with greater intensity. Similarly, when *motor responses* are being modeled, critical features of the model may be emphasized by use of a verbal prompt labelling and drawing attention to a particular feature. The nondiscriminative features of a model can be minimized by using a careful *task analysis* to identify the essential and nonessential features. The model that is derived should be as simple as possible, eliminating unnecessary detail, while insuring the inclusion of all essential detail. In addition, as described in the previous discussion of correction procedures, attention to particular, discriminative aspects of a demonstration may be increased through the use of *preteaching*. Before presentation of a model, a premodeling task may be presented in which the learner is required to respond to salient stimulus characteristics identical to those to be presented during a later demonstration. In this manner, the learner may acquire a *set* to attend to the discriminative stimulus characteristics of the model. Later, when the model is presented, the learner's attention to the discriminative features may be verified by preinstructing the learner to point to the features each time that they occur.

Zimmerman and Jaffe (1977) have provided a dramatic demonstration of the positive effects of *focussing attention* on the critical features of a demonstration. In their study, *six- and eight-year-old* students were presented with one of three types of modeling of a novel *clustering rule*. In one condition, twelve stimulus cards were presented to the children already sorted into three piles according to a conceptual categorizing rule. Each child was allowed to examine the cards and to infer the sorting rule that had been used. In a second type of modeling, the teacher looked at each picture and then placed it in one of the three category piles. In the third condition, the teacher looked at each picture, pointed to the critical feature, and then placed it in the proper group. For pictures depicting things that roll, the teacher made a circular gesture (prompt) around the rolling surface. For pictures depicting pointed things, the teacher's finger traced the stimulus to its point. For pictures depicting rectangular things, the teacher traced one right angle corner of the shape. The *results* indicated that modeling in which the children's attention was directed to critical features of the demonstration was significantly more effective than modeling of the other two types that did not produce significantly different results from each other. Six-year-old children learned relatively less than eight-year-old children, when the cards were presented in preorganized piles and when modeling involved unprompted sorting. However, when prompted sorting was used, these age differences disappeared.

When people *mentally rehearse* or actually *perform* modeled response patterns, they are less likely to forget them than if they either think about them or practice what they have seen. Mental rehearsal, in which individuals visualize themselves performing the appropriate behavior, increases proficiency and retention (Bandura and Jeffery, 1973; Michael and Maccoby, 1961).

Learning is not perfected through observation alone. In most everyday learning, people usually achieve a close approximation of the new behavior by imitation and then *refine* their *response through self-corrective adjustments* on the basis of informative *feedback* from performance and from focused demonstrations of segments of the model that have been only partially learned. Imitation in the absence of *corrective feedback*, however, may not result in improved performance. For example, in a study conducted by Zimmerman and Jaffe (1977) *six-* and *eight-year-old children* were taught a rule learning task. One half of the children were required to imitate the teacher's model directly following the demonstration. *Overt imitation* in the absence of corrective feedback had no beneficial effect on either age group. Litrownik (1972) demonstrated that educable mentally retarded children and normal functioning children of equivalent mental age performed better, when allowed to respond to observed tasks immediately after viewing them, rather than performing after some delay.

A modeled behavior is more likely to be adopted, if it results in outcomes that are *rewarding* then if the behavior is unrewarded or punished. Bandura (1977) wrote that behaviors that seem to be effective for other people were favored over behaviors that did not appear to serve a beneficial purpose. Knowing that a given model's behavior was effective in producing valued outcomes or in averting punishing ones can improve observational learning. Moreover, *anticipated benefits* can strengthen retention of what has been learned observationally by motivating people to code and rehearse modeled behavior that they value highly. Observational learning can be achieved more effectively by *informing observers*, in advance, about the *benefits* of adopting modeled behavior than by waiting until the observers happen to imitate a model and then reward them for it. According to social learning theory, reinforcement is considered a facilitative rather than a necessary condition because factors other than response consequences can influence what people attend to. Whether or not people choose to perform what they have learned observationally is strongly influenced by the consequences of such actions; however, according to social learning theory, reinforcement must include *external, vicarious and self-generated consequences* (Bandura, 1977). Ross (1970) found that with *mildly retarded* individuals, association of a model with rewards prior to being observed tended to facilitate observational learning. Similar results were observed by Talkington and Hall (1975), who found that rewarding or punishing a model affected imitation.

Demonstrations may be presented using *live models, videotape, film, pictures* or *photographic slides*. Engle and Nagle (1979) used videotape to teach categorization, semantic coding and repetition to *educable, mentally handicapped* students in grades five and six. The videotape depicted a woman experimenter and a subject receiving two trials on the tasks, using the strategy appropriate for that particular condition. The subject in the film was a college-age woman chosen to look and talk in a manner similar to the students in the study. The model exhibited perfect recall and clustering on each task. Each tape was 10-12 minutes in length. Before the film, the experimenter explained that she was going to teach each child how to remember better, and then explained the strategy used for that particular condition. The child was then shown the film and told to try to learn the words in the same manner as the model in the film. As each picture was presented, the experimenter prompted the child as to the strategy to be used, and asked the child questions relevant to the item condition. The technique was successful in teaching the subjects each of the mnemonic strategies. Mercer and Algozzine (1977) suggested that teachers of trainable mentally retarded children may increase appropriate behaviors by selecting films or videotaped programs that offer adequate models of the desired behaviors.

The *characteristics of the model* may affect the results of a demonstration. Becker and Glidden (1979) studied the observational learning of *educable mentally handicapped* children (mean CA 12.2; mean IQ 61) who were presented with either an adult model or a peer model, represented as either competent or incompetent with respect to the task being modeled. All modeling was presented on *videotape*. The task modeled was a *vertical aspiration board* that the learner was required to manipulate as a ball rolled on the surface. The models demonstrated where to stand and where to hold the board. The scores of the models were systematically manipulated by control of a magnet in the board. The models differed in a number of nontask (social) behaviors they exhibited. The relative competence of the models was represented by the scores they obtained by rolling the ball on the board. Highly competent models obtained high scores that improved over the ten trials. Low competency models obtained low scores that did not improve. The observers were told which ranges of scores were considered to be either poor or good.

The results of this study indicated that the subjects imitated the off-task behavior of high scoring subjects more than those of low scoring subjects. Also, the behavior of peers was imitated more than that of adults. The results also indicated that there was a significant change in behavior from the pretest to the post-test regardless of the nature of the model; both types of modeling had a strong positive effect. The boys imitated the on-task behavior of the high scoring models, where they stood and how they held the board, more than they imitated the on-task behavior of the low scoring models, regardless of the age of the models. Boys who showed greater imitation of on-task behavior tended to also show greater imitation of off-task behavior. These results are in agreement with Bandura (1968), who suggested that peers were more powerful social models than were adults. Barry and Overmann (1977), in contrast, found that adult models were more effective than were peer models. However, because they used a concept formation task in which it would be assumed that adults would be more competent, and because the experimenters did not manipulate competency directly, the present results are not really in disagreement with previous results. Similar results were obtained by Strichart (1974), who found that the competence level of the model was a crucial variable with educable mentally handicapped individuals. However, the nurturance of the model (whether or not the observer liked the model) was not a significant influence (Strichart). Holt, Richard and Ellis (1972) found that with mildly retarded students, the sex of the model did not differentially affect observational learning.

Chapter Eleven

Instructional Sequences

The previous discussion has provided a review of various instructional procedures, such as prompting, fading, chaining, modeling and the use of generic instructional formats incorporating readiness signals, task commands, response signals, review, reinforcement and correction. In this chapter, several examples are provided of exemplary instructional sequences illustrating application of many of the previously introduced instructional procedures. The first instructional sequence reviewed has been taken from Dixon and Engelmann's program, *Morphographic Spelling* (1976), designed for children in grades four to twelve. In the discussion that follows, the morphographic instructional sequence has been divided into segments, each of which is followed by interpretive comments describing the *inferred* purpose of the instructional procedures. Note that instructions to the teacher are printed within parentheses (e.g., Repeat step d.); statements made by the teacher are printed in capital letters, and responses made by the learner are printed in lower case letters between quotation marks. Letters within parentheses, e.g., (*a*) have been inserted into the lesson to assist the interpretive discussion. The lessons are designed to teach recall, comprehension and application of rules relating to morphographs and spelling.

LESSON 1: Exercise 1

Word Rule

1. LISTEN.(a) ALL WORDS ARE MADE UP OF MORPHO-
GRAPHS. (b) SOME WORDS ARE MADE UP OF ONE
MORPHOGRAPH. (c) SOME WORDS ARE MADE UP OF
MORE THAN ONE MORPHOGRAPH.

REMEMBER: ALL WORDS ARE MADE UP OF MORPHO-
GRAPHS.

Interpretation: the word LISTEN is a *readiness signal* indicating
who is to respond (the entire group) and in what manner (listen).
Statement (a) provides a concise rule that is applicable to all cases.
Because the word morphographs is plural, statements (b) and (c)
clarify rule (a): there may be *one or more* morphographs. The
word REMEMBER is an *attention signal* designed to focus the
learner's attention. Following the explanation (b) and (c), the
essential information, rule (a) is restated.

2. IF IT IS A WORD, WHAT DO YOU KNOW ABOUT IT?
(Signal.) "It is made up of morphographs."

To correct:
a. IT IS MADE UP OF MORPHOGRAPHS.
b. (Repeat step 2 until firm.)

Interpretation: this step evaluates simple *recall* of the rule. Unless
the rule is remembered, there is no value in proceeding with
instruction. Thus, if the learner fails to recall the rule, a *correction
procedure* is provided in which the teacher *models* the rule, "It is
made up of morphographs." Step 2.b. is designed to insure that
retention of the rule will not be transient. After the correct answer
has been modeled, instruction returns to the original question.
Sufficient *practice* is provided answering this question to achieve a
firm (rapid, accurate and consistent) response before proceeding
to the next stage of instruction.

3. IF IT IS NOT A WORD, WHAT DO YOU KNOW ABOUT IT?
(Signal.) "It is not made up of morphographs."
(Repeat until firm.)

Interpretation: step number three involves more than simple recall of the rule, the learner must exhibit *comprehension* of the converse of the rule that "word = morphographs," therefore, "*not* word = *not* morphographs." Once again, this step is repeated until firm before proceeding. The *signal* indicated in each of the previous steps refers to a hand signal provided by the teacher indicating when a group of learners should respond in unison. Thus, the sequence may be used for group or individual instruction. When each member of the group responds in unison, a student who did not initially know the correct response cannot merely copy the example of students who responded first. During choral responding, when a student answers incorrectly, the group response is not well orchestrated and the error is apparent, thereby, signalling that a correction procedure is required.

4. (Write *orn* on the board. Point to *orn*.)
READ THIS. (signal) "orn."
IS *ORN* A WORD? (signal.) "No."

To correct:
a. *ORN* IS NOT A WORD.
b. (Repeat step 4.)

ORN IS NOT A WORD, SO WHAT DO YOU KNOW ABOUT IT?
(Signal.) "It is not made up of morphographs."

To correct:
a. IT IS NOT MADE UP OF MORPHOGRAPHS.
b. (Repeat step 4.)

Interpretation: step 4. begins with a negative instance requiring the rule "word = morphographs" to be applied in its converse form "not word = not morphographs." When *application* of the rule begins with a negative rather than a positive example, the learner cannot simply respond automatically by restating the rule in its positive form as she/he had been doing in the previous recall phase of instruction. Instead, the learner must select his/her response based on an analysis of the nature of the word being presented. Thus, the learner must attend to *orn* and determine whether it is word or a non-word to which either the rule or its converse is applicable. This instructional step involves (a) recall of the rule, (b) simple comprehension of the rule requiring its translation into the converse form and (c) application of the rule in either its positive or negative form depending upon the nature of the word presented.

5. In this step, a second non-word is presented when *orn* is changed to *gorn*. The significance of the step is discussed below.

6. (Change *gorn* to *born*. Point to *born*.)
   READ THIS. (Signal.) "born."
   IS BORN A WORD? (Signal.) "Yes."
   BORN IS A WORD, SO WHAT DO WE KNOW ABOUT IT?
   (Signal.) "It is made up of morphographs."

Interpretation: in this step a minor change has again been made to a non-word; this time, the result is to produce a word. This is the first occasion in this instructional sequence where the rule "word = morphographs" has been applicable. Pointing to the word under study as in this and other steps in the program is a *focusing prompt* designed to insure that the learner attends to the visual stimulus of the word rather than simply attending to the auditory stimulus presented during the teacher dialogue.

7. (Change *born* to *reborn*. Point to *reborn*.)
   READ THIS. (Signal.) "reborn."
   IS *REBORN* A WORD? (Signal.) "Yes."
   REBORN IS A WORD, SO WHAT DO YOU KNOW ABOUT IT?
   (Signal.) 'It is made up of morphographs."

Interpretation: in this step, and in steps eight and nine, letters are added to or subtracted from words to make either new words or non-words to which the rule is correspondingly applicable or not. Thus, the learner is given additional practice analyzing the words/non-words presented, and responding accordingly. In addition, the learner is being prepared for Exercise 2, where she/he is taught a second rule that *all morphographs have meaning*. In Exercise 3, this rule is applied when the word *repack* is presented. The morphograph *re*, meaning *again*, is added to the word *pack* to make a new word. In this lesson, and in those that follow the learner is taught that morphographs *having meaning* can be added to and subtracted from words to make new words. In successive steps of instruction, the learner is taught that the morphograph *re* means *again*, and is given practice attaching this morphograph to the words *color* and *born*.

In each stage of instruction, the program systematically introduces rules and/or morphographs, then tests for recall, comprehension and application of the material. Sufficient practice is provided at each stage to insure that a fluent response is acquired. In addition, maintenance and generalization of learning are systematically programmed through the use of *cumulative practice*. The sequences are designed so that there is a continual review of every morphograph and rule taught in the program. The intermittent review of a particular morphograph may also function as an application exercise, since the familiar morphograph is now presented in the context of a word that has never before been spelled by the student. For example, the morphograph *port* may be presented in the word *purported* or *portage*. These words not only serve as a review of the morphograph *port*, but also demonstrate an application of the generalizable nature of what the student has learned (Dixon and Engelmann, 1976).

Bain (1983) used *direct instructional methods* to teach the *spelling* of phonetically irregular words to children, *ages 8, 9 and 10*, who were two years or more behind in spelling achievement. These children, of normal intelligence, were described as hyperactive, distractible and in need of individual instruction. The instructional format, described below, was successfully used in a teacher administered presentation and in an individual format in which each child administered the program to himself. Considering the nature of the group, their history of spelling difficulties and their usual instructional requirements, it is interesting to note that both the teacher- and the self-administered methods of instruction produced a significant improvement in spelling that was maintained over a two week period following the end of instruction. There was no significant difference between the two approaches with respect to either acquisition or maintenance.

The instructional sequence used in the study was based on *forward behavioral chaining*. Spelling an irregular word that was not constructed on the basis of phonics rules was viewed as a behavioral chain where each letter in the sequence functions as a stimulus to spell the next letter in the sequence. Thus, each student was given repeated practice successively linking the letters in each word. The student received *immediate feedback* regarding the correctness of each letter that he spelled, so that, if a letter was incorrectly linked, the learner was required to return to the beginning of the chain, rehearse the letters that he had previously spelled correctly and then attach this sequence to the correct letter before proceeding.

During instruction each word that was being learned was printed in one-half-inch high, red letters on a strip of card 1.5 inches wide. The strip of card could be moved in and out of a cardboard sleeve to reveal one or more letters or the entire word at one time. In the description that follows, instructions to the teacher are printed within parentheses, teacher dialogue is printed within quotation marks, and instructional techniques are described in capital letters.

Teacher administered spelling instruction

1. (Pull the word from the sleeve).
2. "Look at this word:" TASK COMMAND. (Point to the base of the first letter: FOCUSSING PROMPT).
3. "This word is .....:" MODEL. (Slide finger along base of word while reading the word: FOCUSSING PROMPT).
4. "Say it with me: LEADING, when my finger moves along.

Ready: READINESS SIGNAL, ..." (Slide finger along base of word).

5.   "What word? ....: LEADING HAS BEEN DROPPED. (Slide finger along base of word).

6.   "I can look at the letters and spell this word outloud. My turn:" MODEL. (Successively touch the base of each letter as the letter name is spelled: FOCUSSING PROMPT).

7.   "Spell it with me when I touch each letter, ...:" LEADING. (Successively touch the base of each letter while spelling the letters with the child).

8.   "What word?" .... .

9.   "When I touch the letters you spell ....:" LEADING HAS BEEN DROPPED.

10.   "What word?" .... .

11.   "Now you are going to write the word .... ." (Put the word into the cover).

12.   "Write the first letter in .... ."

13.   (Slide the first letter from the cover). "Look at the first red letter: WITHIN STIMULUS PROMPT FOCUSSING THE CHILD'S ATTENTION ON THE MODEL RATHER THAN ON THE PARTICULAR LETTER THAT HE HAS PRINTED. (Touch the first red letter: CONFIRMS THAT CHILD IS ATTENDING TO THE CORRECT LETTER). "What is the first red letter?" .... . "What is the letter you wrote?

14.   "Are they the same?" ....: FEEDBACK.

***   (If the letters are the *same*: pull the whole word out). ADVANCE TO NEXT STAGE OF INSTRUCTION.

a.   "When I touch the letters you spell .... ." (Touch base of letters).

b.   (Put word back into cover).

c.   "Turn to a clean page."

d.   "What word are you spelling?" .... .

e.   "Print the first *2, 3,...* letters in .... .

f.   (Slide the letters out of the cover one at a time).

g.   "Say the red letter." .... .

h.   "Say the letter you wrote." .... .

i.   "Are they the same?" .... . (If the letters are the same return to ***, above).

***** (If the letters are *different*, pull the whole word out).
       CORRECTION PROCEDURE.
a.   "Look at this word. What is the word?"
b.   "When I touch the letters you spell them .... ."
       (Touch the base of each successive letter).
c.   "What word?" .... .
d.   (Repeat steps b. and c. two times: OVER CORRECTION).
e.   "What word? .... .
f.   "Turn to a clean page."
g.   "Print the letters you got right before, and add the correct
       letter."
h.   (Slide the letters out one at a time).
i.   "Say the red letter." .... .
j.   "Say the letter you wrote." .... .
k.   "Are they the same?" (If they are the same, return to ***,
       above: if they are different, return to *****, above).

The instructional techniques employed in both of the spelling programs described above are referred to as *direct instruction*. These techniques have been very successfully used in several other programs designed by Engelmann and his colleagues, for example: *Reading Mastery* (Engelmann, and Bruner, 1983), *Spelling Mastery* (Dixon, Engelmann and Olen, 1981), *Corrective Mathematics* (Engelmann and Carnine, 1982) and *Corrective Reading* (Engelmann, Becker and Carnine, 1976). Techniques of direct instruction are discussed more fully in Baine (1982), Carnine and Silbert (1979), Engelmann (1980), Engelmann and Carnine (1982) and Silbert, Carnine and Stein (1981).

Kendall, Borkowski and Cavanaugh (1980) successfully used a training sequence to teach a *mnemonic interrogative strategy to educable mentally retarded children* (CA: 10.2; MA: 6.9). This same training strategy, described below, was also successfully used to teach the interrogative strategy to normal functioning children in the first grade. In both cases, maintenance and generalization of the strategy was achieved. The authors described the essential features of the training procedures as: (a) active participation by the student, (b) extended training of the strategy over several training days, (c) semantic processing of the paired-associate items being taught, (d) feedback as to the value of the strategy, (e) extensive use of experimenter examples detailing components of the strategy and (f) fading of experimenter involvement as training progressed.

The interrogative strategy used in the paired associates task involved four components: (a) thinking about what the two items could be doing together and saying this relationship aloud (e.g., "The *nurse* is holding the *toaster*"), (b) asking a *why* question about the relationship (e.g., "Why is the nurse holding the toaster?"), (c) analyzing the items semantically or telling what is known about them (e.g., "A nurse works with doctors, and helps sick people; A toaster is used to toast bread, and is used at breakfast time") and (d) using what is known about the items to make up a reason why they go together (e.g., "The nurse is holding the toaster because she wants to make breakfast for a patient"). The components of the strategy were gradually introduced over three successive days, with the experimenter systematically fading the prompts.

Training Session: 1

    (a) The value of the interrogative strategy for learning paired-associates was explained. The children were told that people who ask questions about items before trying to associate them generally learn more rapidly and easily.

    (b) The experimenter demonstrated how to use the interrogative strategy with *three* pairs of pictures.

    (c) Each child was given *three* opportunities to describe a relationship between the two items in each picture pair.

    (d) Each child was requested to ask a "why" question about each relationship described in step (c), above.

    (e) If a child failed to respond in steps (c) and (d), the experimenter prompted the child to form a relationship between the words and to ask a question about the relationship.

    (f) For each pair, the experimenter performed the semantic analysis of the items (described what was known about each of the items) and answered the three questions posed by the child in step (d) (given three pairs of pictures).

Training Session: 2

(a) The explanation of the benefits of the interrogative strategy was repeated.

(b) The experimenter demonstrated how to use the strategy with *one* pair of pictures.

(c) The child was given *four* opportunities to describe a relationship between the two items in each picture pair.

(d) Each child was requested to ask a "why" question about each relationship described in step (c).

(e) For each word pair, the experimenter performed the semantic analysis of the items and answered each of the questions posed by the child in step (d).

Changes from Session: 1

(f) The child was presented with *five* additional picture pairs and was given the opportunity to form the relationship between the two items in each pair.

(g) The child was requested to ask a "why" question about the relationship between each of the five picture pairs presented in step (f).

(h) The child was requested to perform the semantic analysis of each of the five picture pairs presented in step (f).

(i) The experimenter answered each of the "why" questions posed by the child in step (g).

Training Session: 3

(a) The explanation of the value of the interrogative strategy was repeated.

(b) The experimenter demonstrated how to use the strategy with *one* pair of pictures.

(c) The child was given *one* opportunity to describe a relationship between the two items in each picture pair.

(d) The child was requested to ask a *why* question about the relationship.

(e) The experimenter performed the semantic analysis of the picture pair presented in step (c).

(f) The experimenter answered the *why* question posed by the child in step (c).

(g) The child then stated a relationship between the next items.

(h) The child asked a *why* question about the relationship.

(i) The child performed the semantic analysis for an additional *three* pairs of pictures.

(j) The experimenter answered the questions based on the child's semantic analysis of the three picture pairs.

(k) Finally, the child was presented with *five* picture pairs and was required to perform all stages of the interrogative strategy.

Training Session: 4

(a) The explanation of the value of the interrogative strategy was repeated.

(b) The experimenter demonstrated how to use the strategy with *one* pair of pictures.

(c) *Eighteen* pairs of pictures were presented and the child was required to perform *all* phases of the interrogative strategy; all experimenter assistance had been faded.

Chapter Twelve

Pictures and Mnemonics

Pictures have been used successfully with children, adolescents and adults to enhance recall of various types of information, including pairs of words, word lists, foreign language vocabulary and word definitions, as well as prose passages. The following discussion reviews various applications of pictures to enhance recall, the nature of the pictures used and implications for further research on the use of pictures to improve children's memory storage and retrieval.

The ability to correctly recognize previously seen pictures is nearly perfect in adults. Standing, Conezio and Haber (1970), for example, reported 90 percent *recognition* for more than 2,500 pictures even with delays of three days between presentation and testing. Picture recognition is also well developed in *preschool* children. In a study by Brown and Scott (1971), four-year-old children on an immediate test recognized 98 percent of the 100 previously presented, colored pictures cut from children's books. In long-term retention tests, 1, 2, 7 and 28 pictures, initially seen twice, were recognized 94 percent of the time after a single day, and 75 percent of the time after one month. Pictures seen only once were recognized 84 percent after one day, 75 percent after one week and 56 percent after one month. Nelson (1971) tested recognition memory of children in *grades 1, 4 and 7*. A *recognition* test followed immediately and after two weeks. At both sessions, *realistic paintings* were recognized more accurately than *abstract* paintings. Kail (1979) pointed out that realistic and abstract paintings may differ in terms of familiarity, complexity, meaningfulness and the availability of a verbal label. It is not clear which of these characteristics may influence retention.

There is some evidence that recognition memory in retarded individuals may also be extremely efficient. Martin (1970) studied the recognition memory of *moderately retarded children*. His subjects viewed a series of 100 pictures, followed by 100 test pairs, each consisting of one old and one new picture. The retarded subjects were able to correctly identify 97 percent of the old pictures. Of interest is the fact that retarded children who are inferior to adults in memory tasks requiring deliberate strategies, such as rehearsal, can perform like adults in recognition memory tasks (Brown, 1974).

A number of studies of young children and adults have indicated that pictures of objects are more memorable than spoken or printed names of objects (Higbee, 1979; Pressley, 1977). Perlmutter and Myers (1976) found that *children between 2.5 and 5 years* of age performed significantly better on a recognition memory task with picture lists than with word lists. The same effect was observed by Corsini, Jacobus and Leonard (1969) with *children 4.5-6 years*, and by Bird and Bennett (1974) with children *4-10 years* of age.

Although it is generally true that students recall pictures better than they recall words, significant *individual differences* between children exist in their ability to learn from pictures and words. Levin, Divine-Hawkins, Kerst and Guttman (1974) designed a *test* to discriminate among various types of learners. The test involved a group-administered, paired-associates learning task of both pictures and words. Two parallel forms of the test were administered 24 hours apart to children in grade four. Parallel form reliability was .76. Comparing forms A and B, 75 percent of the students classified as high picture/high word learners on one test were classified in the same manner on the other test. Similar agreement in classification occurred with high picture/low word (78 percent), and low picture/low word (70 percent) subjects.

Thus, *three types of learners* were identified. A second study by Levin *et al.* showed that when students in the sixth grade were presented with word pairs, both high picture/low word and low picture/low word subjects performed poorly. However, when presented with pairs of pictures, the performance of high picture/low word subjects improved, while the performance of low picture/low word subjects was not significantly affected.

In general, the research literature indicates that by *eight years of age*, children can successfully use *visual imagery* to increase recall (Lesgold, McCormick and Golinkoff, 1975; Pressley, 1976). For children eight years of age and older, pairs or lists of words are usually better recalled if children produce their own visual images (Higbee, 1979). However, the recall of *children five years of age or younger* is not improved by instructing them to generate their own mental images. For children at this age, and for *older mentally retarded* children (Campione and Brown, 1977), recall is improved by providing *interactive* pictorial representations (Rohwer, Ammon and Levin, 1971; Paivio, 1980). Visual images and pictures in which the objects depicted are interacting produce greater recall than when the objects are depicted separately. Some studies have shown that when two objects were illustrated in some type of interaction rather than side-by-side, recall was more than double (Wollen, 1969; Paivio, 1971).

The period from *six* to *seven years* of age appears to be one of *transition* during which children acquire the ability to generate visual imagery to improve recall. These age levels act as general guidelines for making instructional decisions. However, variation in research findings suggest that the efficacy of visual imagery or pictures for particular children depends upon the nature of the task, the manner of its presentation and the type of instruction or training that is provided. In addition, various types of learners have been identified for whom instructions to visualize has a differential effect. Levin, Divine-Hawkins, Kerst and Guttman (1974) administered their previously described test to a group of students in the *fourth grade* to identify *three categories of learners*. Each category of learner was then given a short prose passage to read and instructions to create *visual images* of the people and events in each story. Following the stories, *comprehen-*

sion questions revealed that high picture/high word and high picture/low word learners improved following instructions to create images, whereas the performance of low picture learners declined.

Danner and Taylor (1973) used a series of pictures to *train* children in *grades one, three* and *six* to use *interactive imagery*. Three objects were depicted interacting in each picture. Taylor, Josberger and Prentice (1970) used pictures in which four objects interacted to train children in grade six. Thus, with younger children pictures may be used in place of visual imagery where children are unable to generate their own visual images. Alternatively, pictures may be used to train children to use visual imagery, and in particular to use interactive visual imagery to improve retention.

Pictures have been used with *prose* passages to (a) summarize the content, (b) add details of facts in addition to those provided in the text, (c) focus on important features of the text, (d) illustrate complex ideas, (e) enhance imagery, (f) depict relationships, (g) introduce a passage, (h) assist review and (i) heighten interest. Pictures have been used to enhance *narrative prose recall* with children in *grades k, 2 and 3* (Guttmann, Levin and Pressley, 1977) and with *educable, mentally handicapped children ages 10 to 16* (Bender and Levin, 1978). Levin and Berry (1980) examined the effect of *cartoon-type line-drawings* on the immediate and delayed (three day) recall of non-fictional prose by children in *grade four*. The pictures enhanced the recall of the information that was depicted and reduced the recall of unillustrated information. Bender and Pressley (1979) found that with children in *grades two* and *three*, cartoon-like pictures enhanced the recall of both central, thematic information and incidental details.

Haring and Fry (1979) and Haring (1982) used *Meyer's* (1975) method of *analyzing* the structural organization of *expository prose* to determine superordinate and subordinate relations. The results of this analysis were used to develop *pen and ink pictures* to depict various levels of superordinate and subordinate information in the text. The pictures produced a significant improvement in the immediate and delayed (five day) recall of children in *grades four* and *six*. Duchastel (1980) used *photographs* (2 x 2) to provide a visual summary of the content of *expository* prose. The photographs did not significantly influence the recall of *14* and *15 year old* students. Levin and Lesgold (1978) reviewed a number of studies of children in *grades six to twelve* in which pictures were presented (a) simultaneously with the text, (b) following each sentence or (c) following each passage. In each case recall was improved with the use of pictures.

Fleming (1979), when referring to Levin and Lesgold's (1978) review of the literature, pointed out two things: (a) that the *pictures* used in the studies completely *overlapped* the content of the story, a condition that may not be typical of natural conditions, and (b) that the *stories* were *presented orally*. When stories are presented orally and pictures are presented visually, each message can be received simultaneously through separate channels. However, where words and pictures are both visual, as in children's books, pictures and words may compete for the child's limited visual attention. Where both pictures and words provide important information, they may justify the extra time either by providing repetition, or by providing additional information.

A number of authors have criticized the use of *pictures in print* (Concannon, 1975; Rankin and Culhane, 1970; Samuals, 1970), especially with young readers. The competition between pictures and text can reduce learning (Levine and Divine-Hawkins, 1974). Interesting color pictures may be distracting to young readers; on the other hand, since the act of reading is a multidimensional process, the pictures may have several benefits. Pictures help to make story books more attractive to children (Samuals, Biesbrock and Terry, 1974) make abstract or confusing objects, events or relations more concrete, and enhance visual imagery and retention, especially among young children. Thus, a multidimensional analysis must be made of the value of pictures in prose, and in particular following the use of instruction designed to improve the use of pictures in prose. The majority of studies reported do not describe any procedures used to *train children* to *use* effectively *pictures* in prose.

Guttmann, Levin and Pressley (1977), in their study of children in *grades k, 2 and 3*, successfully employed *line-drawings* with a minimum of non-essential *detail*. There was no deliberate distortion in proportion, nor was there an attempt to accurately represent each object, but rather to simplify and depict the objects with a few simple lines. All shapes were represented by continuous contour lines with a minimum of essential internal detail. For example, the human face was represented by a single, smoothly curved line. The usual bulges and indentations were not drawn. The hair was drawn with a continuous wriggly contour line; no internal detail or color were provided. The mouth was represented by a single curved line. No shading was used. Levin and Berry (1980) used *colored, cartoon-like line-drawings* of 8.5 x 11 inches. These pictures were similar to those used by Guttmann, with the exception of the addition of a small amount of cartoon-like distortion. For example, in one picture the mouth of an angry man was disproportionately large, showing a fearsome row of sharp teeth. Each of the figures had a disproportionately large nose.

The *keyword mnemonic* developed by Atkinson and Raugh (1975) has been used to teach foreign language vocabulary and word definitions. The procedure has been employed in the following manner. As noted earlier, the French word *livre*, meaning book, is associated with a similar sounding, high imagery keyword *leave*. An *interactive visual image* of *leaves* pressed in a *book* joins the keyword to the definition of the French word. Thus, to recall the French word meaning *book*, one would recall the image of *leaves* pressed in a book and, through *acoustic association*, the word *livre* is recalled. Several studies of children and of adults have shown that, when pictures are provided that depict the interaction between the keyword and the word representing the meaning of the foreign word, higher recall has been achieved then when subjects generated their own images (Pressley, Levin and Miller, in press).

McCormick, Miller, Berry and Pressley (1982) used *cartoon-like line-drawings*, similar to those previously described, to teach *keyword mnemonics*. The authors added an additional feature to the pictures, that of *dialogue balloons* in which the utterance of one character contained the keyword, while the dialogue of the other character contained the vocabulary word. Levin, Shriberg, Miller, McCormick and Levin (1980) used cartoon-like line-drawings and the keyword mnemonic to teach the names of U.S. states and capital cities to students in *grades four* and *five*. One picture, for example (see Figure 4.2, page 92), showed two apples (Annapolis) being married (Maryland). Similarly, Levin, McCormick and Dretzke (1981) used cartoon-like drawings in conjunction with pegword and loci mnemonics to teach students in the eighth grade the chronological order of 20 U.S. Presidents.

Several of these latter studies have published examples of the nature of the pictures employed (Haring and Fry, 1979; Guttmann, Levin and Pressley, 1977; Levin and Berry, 1980; Levin *et al.*, 1980, and 1981; McCormick, Miller, Berry and Pressley, 1982). Many authors, however, have not provided an explicit description of the type of pictures used. As a result, it is impossible to determine which characteristics of pictures are most or least suitable for various applications and age groups? The characteristics of various types of pictorial representations are described in Table 12.1.

Photographs and pictures may vary in a number of other ways that may influence perception and retention. These variations, introduced in this paragraph, are discussed more fully in the remainder of the chapter. Pictures may depict *static situations* or *dynamic events*. Young children are sometimes unfamiliar with the methods conventionally employed in pictures to represent motion. Each object in a picture may be fully or partially displayed. *Partial representations* occur when a portion of an object extends beyond the boundaries of the picture. Research has indicated that whether or not an object is fully represented influences the interpretation of the picture by young children. Other research has indicated that recall of objects in pictures is influenced by their *relationship* to the dominant *theme*. Obviously, too, the *complexity* of a picture, determined by the number of objects or details, may influence recall.

Travers and Alvarado (1970) claimed that it was doubtful that children could recognize the *dynamic* aspects of pictures prior to the third grade. This problem is particularly important, as many pictures found in school textbooks are designed to depict movement or action. Movement is generally depicted in a static picture in several symbolic ways. A moving object may be

Table 12.1

Characteristics of Various Pictorial Representations

Photographs: high fidelity color photographs designed to accurately represent reality.
  —natural intensity, angle and color of lighting to reproduce surface qualities; influences features such as shadows, colors, details, and the figure-ground relationship.
  —natural angle and span of viewer's (camera's) regard of the objects and events observed; influences familiar appearance of size, proportion, depth perception and salience of features.
  —natural colors with respect to brightness, hue and saturation.
  —natural representation of surface qualities such as reflectance and texture.
     High fidelity photographs may include some minor variations from the original scene. For example, the span of regard may be truncated to a degree without distorting the natural appearance of the object or event pictured. Artistically rendered photographs may contain considerable variation in any one or more of the foregoing features. As a result, the appearance of the original object or event may be significantly modified.

Realistic drawings: in color or black-and-white may provide a close approximation to high fidelity photographs in their ability to accurately represent pictured objects or events.

Simple line-drawings: are usually characterized by an attempt to represent reality, without distortion, by selecting the least amount of detail to portray each of the major elements in a scene, for example, shadows are either removed or minimized; lines are usually simplified by *smoothing-out* small indentations or expansions; internal details representing the surface qualities (design or texture of objects) are frequently removed or are replaced by a solid color to contrast it with surfaces having different textures or material. Subtle variations in color, shading and blending are often replaced with a low saturation wash.

Cartoon-like drawings: similar to simple line-drawings in most respects, cartoons are usually characterized by varying degrees of exaggeration or distortion of parts or features. The distortion may be minimal and be used either to emphasize a detail, represent stylistic variations, increase interest or provide amusement or humor. Cartoons may also include dialogue enclosed within balloons flowing from the mouth of one or more of the characters.

Stylized pictures: are not designed to provide an accurate representation of reality, but to permit an artist creative interpretation. For example, an artist may use distortion, obvious brush strokes and/or color contrasts to evoke an emotional rather than a perceptual representation.

represented as a blurred image, the rear contour of the object may be repeatedly traced along the path of movement to simulate successive impressions of the object, or a wake may be drawn that is similar to that shown behind a moving boat. Movement of an object may also be represented by depicting the object in a state of disequilibrium. To perceive movement in pictures, children must learn to interpret these conventions.

Several studies in which *action concepts* were taught to *mentally handicapped children* through the use of still pictures apparently have not resulted in the difficulties described by Travers and Alvarado. DeGraaf (1972) designed a successful program to teach action concepts to institutionalized mentally retarded children (mean IQ: 51; mean MA: 7.5). He used photographic slides with four line-drawings on each. Stephens and Ludy (1975) compared the effectiveness of teaching 20 action concepts using photographic slides, motion pictures and live demonstrations by teachers. The subjects in the study had an average IQ of 48 and an average MA of 4.7. The results of this study showed that the motion pictures produced greater gain scores than were achieved with the use of slides or live demonstrations. The authors found that the live demonstrations were less systematic and more complex than the slides and that the demonstrations were not as effective in holding the children's attention.

Perhaps the difference between the results of these studies and the observations made by Travers and Alvarado arises from small but significant variations in the type of still pictures or line-drawings used. For example, Travers and Alvarado found that *color* enhanced the perception of dynamic features. Important differences may also have occurred in the manner in which the pictures were displayed. The topic is sufficiently important to warrant caution, further study and more detailed description of the pictures used in instruction (Baine, 1982).

Higgins (1980) conducted several studies in which dogs shown in either line-drawings or photographs were *truncated* by the border. Either only the front or rear section of the animals were visible. Alternatively, a portion of some of the animals was obscured by other objects in the picture. Higgins studied the picture perception of *children aged four, five, six* and *seven* years. Whether or not these children interpreted the pictures literally was established by asking questions regarding various capabilities of the animals or persons partially represented. A picture was considered to have been interpreted literally if a child reported that she/he thought that a partially represented animal had fewer capabilities than a fully represented animal. The results of the study indicated that literalism varied across the age levels studied. Four-year-olds displayed the least literalism, five-year-olds the most. Six-year-olds were significantly less literal than the five-year-olds. There was no significant difference in the four- and seven-year-olds. Higgins conducted a second study of *five-year-olds* in which obscured or truncated pictures of either people or dogs were depicted. The results of this study indicated that 75 percent of the subjects responded literally to both canine and human pictures. The human pictures were interpreted less literally than those of the dogs. In these and other studies, Higgins observed that literalism was found to occur as an *all* or *none* phenomena. It was exhibited with a high degree of consistency across pictures of different kinds (e.g., line-drawings or photographs). The incidence of literalism did not appear to be significantly related to differences in the way depicted characters were made to look incomplete. It was also found that whether the objects depicted were dogs or humans made no substantial difference in the nature and extent of the literalism. In *summary*, many children in the four to seven year age range derive from pictures information that is significantly different from the information the picture was designed to communicate (Higgins, 1980).

Goodman (1980) conducted a number of studies of pictures in which a main character was involved in a *salient activity* (e.g., sitting at a desk reading). Each picture contained a number of items that were closely related to the theme (relevant items), such as books, bookcase, lamp, etc., that had a logical or associative relationship to the activity being performed. A number of items of low relevance to the activity were also in each picture. Relevant and irrelevant items were located in both the foreground, lower-half of the picture, and the background, upper-half of the picture. Items in the foreground are frequently considered to be more important. Goodman's study was designed to determine whether recall of items in the pictures was based on a semantic (relevant or irrelevant) or perceptual (foreground or background) basis. The results of the study are most interesting. On an immediate *recognition* test of recall, there was no significant difference between the number of foreground and background items recalled. On a test delayed by one hour, background items were less likely to be recalled. Nine-year-old children had greater *recognition* than seven-year-old children. Items of low relevance and foreground items were recognized with greater accuracy than highly relevant background items. These findings are consistent with Goodman's hypothesis. Goodman postulated that because high relevance items were expected, little attention would be paid to them; thus, little specific detail about them would be stored. Therefore, when highly similar distractor items were presented, subjects would not be able to recognize (discriminate) which item had actually been previously seen. Alternatively, Goodman suggested that, because low relevance items were not anticipated, subjects were expected to spend more time examining them while attempting to relate them to the theme. Thus, a more detailed representation of low relevance items would be stored.

Opposite results were obtained on *recall* tests. Highly relevant items were recalled more than were low relevance items. Background items were recalled more frequently than foreground items. Low relevance, background items were recalled with greater frequency than low relevance foreground items. Highly relevant, foreground items were recalled with greater frequency than highly relevant background items. All ages recalled more high relevance items than low relevance items.

Goodman has identified a number of *variables* that should be considered in *developing pictures* and in assessing what children remember about the content of the pictures. First, it is apparent that, as in other areas of memory research, *recognition* and *recall tests* produce quite different, and in the previously described case, opposite results. The relevance of items in a picture to the salient activity that is depicted influence the durability and the detail of the stored image, and thereby produce different results on recognition and recall tests. Also, the location of objects in a picture, foreground or background, influences the perceived importance of the item. The location and relevance of an item influences the durability and detail of the stored image.

The foregoing research reveals that many common variations in pictures can significantly influence the manner in which the pictures are perceived and remembered by children. These observations indicate the need to carefully control the nature of pictures presented to children and to describe carefully the exact nature of pictures used to produce particular results.

Is there a differential effect upon memory resulting from either the use of *objects, photographs* or *drawings*? Swanson (1977) studied *learning disabled* (mean IQ: 100) and *educable mentally retarded* (mean IQ: 73) children on a serial recognition task. The results indicated that: (a) both groups recognized objects better than pictures; (b) the learning disabled children recognized objects significantly better than did the retarded children; and (c) there was no significant difference between learning disabled and retarded children on their ability to recognize pictures. Studies of children with various types of learning problems have consistently found a greater effectiveness of objects over pictures (Swanson, 1977).

The following studies comparing the effects of *objects, photographs* and *line-drawings* have produced inconsistent results. Evertson and Wicker (1974) found that objects and color photographs were more effective than line-drawings for children in *nursery school* and the first grade on a paired-associates learning task. Holyoak, Hogeterp and Yuille (1972) found that the performance of children in *kindergarten* and the *third grade* on a paired-associate learning task was better when line-drawings rather than photographs were used. In a study by Yuille and Catchpole (1973), color photographs were as effective as objects for students in the *first and second grades*. In one of Emmerich and Akerman's studies (1976), line-drawings were as effective as colored drawings for *preschool and kindergarten* children. Differences in the results of these studies may have been produced by subtle but significant differences in the nature of the objects, pictures and photographs used, as well as, differences in the experimental tasks involved.

O'Connor and Hermelin (1961), in a study of picture perception, found that *trainable mentally retarded* subjects were able to correctly identify *outline figures*. Hull, Barry and Clark (1976) conducted a study of the learning of *vocational concepts* by *adolescent, learning disabled, educable mentally handicapped* and *culturally deprived* students. These researchers found no statistically significant difference in learning concepts with the use of line-drawings, detailed drawings, photograms, photographs, 35mm color slides or actual objects. However, they did find trends favoring line-drawings and color slides as the most effective means of teaching concepts. In a second study, they found no significant difference in concept learning when line-drawings or actual objects were used. Devore and Stern (1970) found that for boys, there was no significant difference in gain scores which favored the use of concrete objects over pictures for teaching the names of common household articles.

Does the use of real objects and events lead to more rapid *acquisition, generalization* and *retention of concepts*? Becker, Tosner and Nelson (1979) studied the *performance of preschool children* randomly assigned to groups in which concepts were taught by pictures or objects. Neither the rate of acquisition nor the amount of retention was affected by the use of either pictures or objects. However, generalization of learning was influenced significantly. Generalization was assessed by having the children who had learned concepts through the use of objects, identify new examples of the concepts (not presented during instruction), when the examples were displayed in either an object or a pictorial form. Similarly, children taught concepts through the use of pictures were asked to identify new examples of the concept presented in either an object or picture form. Generalization in the object-object condition was lower than that in the picture-object or in the picture-picture condition. The items used to assess generalization ranged over four levels of elaboration. At level one, the objects used were white, two-dimensional forms depicting the basic outline; all extra features had been omitted. Objects at the fourth level of elaboration had as much detail as the training examples. The results of the study showed that generalization to items differing in level of elaboration from the training items was significantly better for children who had received concept instruction with pictures rather than with real objects. The authors hypothesized that picture training may have established a more abstract mental representation of the concepts that facilitated identification of unelaborated items. According to Becker *et al.*, object training may lead to greater reluctance to identify ambiguous items as concept examples.

Developmental factors and experiences may also influence the differential effects upon memory of objects, pictures and line-drawings. It is unlikely that many *preschool children* have had experience with the types of line-drawings and black-and-white photographs that experimenters frequently use. With the beginning of *kindergarten*, they receive practice with a variety of different types of pictures. Thus, the increase in the ability of children to learn from pictures with the onset of schooling would be expected on the basis of increased experience. But why is there not an additional improvement derived from the use of pictures following the onset of schooling? Possibly, very little experience is necessary to learn the rules relevant to interpreting pictures (Pressley, 1977). According to Sigel (1978), *picture literacy* is analogous to *reading comprehension*. In both cases, one must learn to interpret symbolic information according to a set of rules. Children must learn that pictures represent a flat, miniaturized form of a referent. Pictorial comprehension is a cultural convention. Some cultures do not have pictures, nor do they comprehend the notion that an object or person can be represented in pictorial form (Miller, 1973; Serpell, 1976). Cross-cultural studies have demonstrated that responses to pictures are not automatic, and that they are the product of learning. According to Sigel (1978) the *concept of equivalence* is prerequisite to picture comprehension. The concept of equivalence states that instances (pictures and objects) that may appear different can be judged as members of the same class, if they share the same defining attributes of that class. The awareness that instances can be similar and different at the same time is an achievement that evolves gradually. Equivalence resides in the mind of the respondent, not in the ostensive reality, because the respondent extracts the *meaning from* the stimuli (Sigel, 1978).

According to the *eye-scan* data of Vurpillot (1968) and

Mackworth and Bruner (1970), children *read* pictures inefficiently. For example, five-year-old children spend far less time than adults do looking at the informative part of pictures. Furthermore, children's attention becomes so attached to detail that their visual tracking averages only two-thirds that of adults. The children studied were unable to examine details centrally and to simultaneously monitor their peripheral fields for stimuli that might be candidates for closer inspection (Mackworth and Bruner, 1970).

Children show an increase in systematic *scanning* of pictures between the ages of 3 and 11. Younger children are, in general, more affected by the contextual factors, as in symmetrical characteristics of a display that aid visual scanning or complex patterns that interfere with scanning. As might be expected, increasing age brings improved efficiency of scanning in terms of its systematic quality, its appropriate exhaustiveness and its focus upon the most informative aspects of the visual scene. In particular, the finding that context can affect the scanning behavior of younger children suggests that contextual manipulation could be effective in improving the scanning behavior of the intellectually handicapped (Ross and Ross, 1981).

The ability to *focus* on the most important parts of a visual display is another aspect of visual scanning that increases with age. Visual scanning must be sufficient to bring the relevant stimulus into view. In addition, the child's ability to maintain the fixation to permit evaluation of the information is essential (Ross and Ross, 1981).

Studies have shown that there is a marked tendency among children to *fixate* on a detail of a picture that is often of irrelevant significance (Travers and Alvarado, 1970). In a study by Alvarado, children were repeatedly, briefly presented with the same pictures. After each presentation, the children were asked what they had seen. There was a striking tendency for the young children to focus exclusively on one particular object in the picture and to fail to observe other items. On successive trials, the children repeatedly reported the same item.

Westling and Koorland (1979) described some of the problems associated with visual attention and discrimination among the *mentally retarded*. When learning attention and discrimination skills, *mentally retarded* individuals were not as competent as normal individuals of equivalent mental age. Mentally retarded individuals tended to focus on a number of stimulus characteristics. For example, they sometimes attended to the color of an object in a situation where it was more important to focus on its shape or configuration.

Many of the studies of picture perception have been conducted with children involved in spontaneous, unguided analysis of pictures. The evidence from these studies has shown that children frequently fail to notice critical features of pictures, focus on irrelevant details, dwell exclusively on one aspect of a picture and have difficulty interpreting the depiction of action. Picture perception may be enhanced through the use of various methods of *prompting* that modify and guide the types of observations children make. The topic of prompting is discussed in Chapter Ten.

A number of studies have revealed that children at various age levels prefer different types of pictures. Although pictures of different types may attract attention, provide extended study and stimulate thought, further study is required to determine the relationship, if any, between *picture preference* and memory. Myatt and Carter (1979) recorded the following observations after reviewing the literature.

(a) Most children, regardless of age, prefer a realistically colored picture to a black-and-white picture.

(b) Most children, when forced to choose between photographs and other illustrations, whether in color or black-and-white, prefer the photograph.

(c) Realism in form and color is preferred by children at all grade levels.

(d) Younger children prefer simple rather than complex pictures.

(e) Older children prefer complex rather than simple pictures.

Myatt and Carter (1979) conducted an extensive study of the *picture preference* of children in *grades K, 1, 2, 3, 5, 9* and *11*. Six styles of pictures were presented. Strong picture preference was not in evidence in grades k and 1; however, by grade 2 picture preference appeared and was consistent throughout the remaining grades. In order of preference, in grades 3, 5, 9 and 11, children preferred most photographs, full line-drawings, painterly pictures, collages, simple line-drawings and, least of all, cartoons.

References

Abikoff, H. (1979). Cognitive training interventions in children: Review of a new approach. *Journal of Learning Disabilities, 12,* 65-77.

Acredolo, L., Pick, H., & Olsen, M. (1975). Environmental differentiation and familiarity as determinants of children's memory for spatial location. *Developmental Psychology, 11,* 495-501.

Adams, J.A. (1980). *Learning and memory.* Homewood, Ill.: The Dorsey Press.

Aiken, E.G., Thomas, G.S., & Shennon, W.R. (1975). Memory for a lecture: Effect of notes, lecture rate and information density. *Journal of Educational Psychology, 67,* 439-444.

Allen, G., Chinsky, J., Larcen, S., Lochman, J., & Selinger, H. (1976). *Community psychology and the schools: A behaviorally oriented multi-level preventive approach.* Hillsdale, N.J.: Lawrence Erlbaum Associates.

Anderson, R.C. (1972). How to construct achievement tests to assess comprehension. *Review of Educational Research, 42,* 145-170.

Anderson, R.C., & Biddle, W.B. (1975). On asking people questions about what they are reading. In G. Bower (Ed.), *Psychology of learning and motivation* (Vol. 9). New York: Academic Press.

Anderson, R.C., & Myrow, D.L. (1971). Retroactive inhibition of meaningful discourse. *Journal of Educational Psychology, 62,* 81-94.

Anderson, T.H. (1978). Study strategies and adjunct aids. In R.J. Spiro, B.C. Bruce, & W.F. Brewer (Eds.), *Theoretical issues in reading comprehension.* Hillsdale. N.J.: Lawrence Erlbaum Associates.

Anderson, T.H., & Armbruster, B.B. (1982). Reader and text studying strategies. In W. Otto, & S. White (Eds.), *Reading expository materials.* New York: Academic Press.

Andre, M., & Anderson, T. (1978-1979). The development and evaluation of a self-questioning study technique. *Reading Research Quarterly, 14* 605-623.

Appel, L.F., Cooper, R.G., McCarrell, N., Sims-Knight, J., Yussen, S.R., & Flavell, J.H. (1972). The development of the distinction between perceiving and memorizing. *Child Development, 43*, 1365-1381.

Arnold, S., & Forchand, R. (1978). A comparison of cognitive training and response cost procedures in modifying cognitive styles of impulsive children. *Cognitive Therapy and Research, 2*, 183-187.

Asarnow, J., & Meichenbaum, D. (1979). Verbal rehearsal and serial recall: The mediational training of kindergarten children. *Child Development, 50*, 1173-1177.

Atkinson, R.C. (1975). Mnemotechnics in second-language learning. *American Psychologist, 30*, 821-828.

Atkinson, R., & Raugh, M. (1975). An application of the mnemonic keyword method to the acquisition of a Russian vocabulary. *Journal of Experimental Psychology: Human Learning and Memory, 104*, 126-133.

Atkinson, R.C., & Shiffrin, R.M. (1968). Human memory: A proposed system and its control processes. In K.W. Spence & J.T. Spence (Eds.), *The psychology of learning and motivation: Advances in research and theory* (Vol. 2). New York: Academic Press.

Atkinson, R.C., & Wickens, T.D. (1971). Human memory and the concept of reinforcement. In R. Glaser (Ed.), *The nature of reinforcement.* New York: Academic Press.

Atwood, G.E. (1969). *Experimental studies of mnemonic visualization.* Unpublished doctoral dissertation, University of Oregon.

Ausubel, D.P. (1963). *The psychology of meaningful verbal learning.* New York: Grune and Stratton.

Bacharach, V.R., Carr, T.H., & Mehner, D.S. (1976). Interactive and independent contributions of verbal descriptions to children's picture memory. *Journal of Experimental Child Psychology, 22*, 492-498.

Baer, D. (1981). *How to plan for generalization.* Lawrence, KS.: H and H Enterprises.

Bain, K. (1983). *Spelling acquisition: Comparison of direct and self-instruction with spelling delayed students.* Unpublished masters thesis, University of Alberta, Edmonton, Alberta, Canada.

Baine, D. (1982). *Instructional design for special education.* Englewood Cliffs, N.J.: Educational Technology Publications.

Baker, L., & Stein, N. (1981). The development of prose comprehension skills. In C.M. Santa & B.L. Hayes (Eds.), *Children's prose comprehension: Practice and research.* Newark, Delaware: International Reading Association.

Bandura, A. (1968). Social-learning theory of identification processes. In D.A. Goslin (Ed.), *Handbook of socialization theory and research.* Chicago: Rand McNally.

Bandura, A. (1977). *Social learning theory.* Englewood Cliffs, N.J.: Prentice-Hall.

Bandura, A., & Harris, M.B. (1966). Modification of syntactic style. *Journal of Experimental Child Psychology, 4,* 341-352.

Bandura, A., & Jeffrey, R. (1973). Role of symbolic coding and rehearsal processes in observational learning. *Journal of Personality and Social Psychology, 26,* 122-130.

Barnes, B.R., & Clawson, E.V. (1974). Do advance organizers facilitate learning? Recommendations for further research based on an analysis of 32 studies. *Review of Educational Research, 45,* 637-659.

Barrett, T. (1968). Taxonomy of cognitive and affective directions of reading comprehension. Included in the chapter by T. Clymer in *The Sixty-seventh yearbook of the National Society for the Study of Education* (Pt. 2). Chicago: University of Chicago Press.

Barry, N., & Overmann, P. (1977). Comparison of the effectiveness of adult and peer models with EMR children. *American Journal of Mental Deficiency, 82,* 33-36.

Bartlett, B.J. (1978). *Top-level structure as an organizational strategy for recall of classroom text.* Unpublished doctoral dissertation, Arizona State University.

Bartlett, F.C. (1932). *Remembering.* Cambridge, England: Cambridge University Press.

Becker, S., & Glidden, L.M. (1979). Imitation in EMR boys: Model competency and age. *American Journal of Mental Deficiency, 83,* 360-366.

Becker, W., & Engelmann, S. (1978). Systems for basic instruction: Theory and applications. In A. Catania & T. Brigham (Eds.), *Handbook of applied behavior analysis: Social and instructional processes.* New York: Irvington.

Becker, W.C., Engelmann, S., & Carnine, D. (1982). The direct instruction model. In R. Rhine (Ed.), *Encouraging change in America's schools: A decade of experimentation.* New York: Academic Press.

Becker, W.C., Engelmann, S., & Thomas, D. (1971). *Teaching: A course in applied psychology.* Toronto: Science Research Associates.

Bellezza, F.S. (1981). Mnemonic devices: Classification, characteristics, and criteria. *Review of Educational Research, 51,* 247-275.

Bellugi, U., Klima, E.S., & Siple, P. (1974-1975). Remembering in signs. *Cognition: International Journal of Cognitive Psychology, 3,* 93-125.

Belmont, J.M. (1978). Individual differences in memory: The cases of normal and retarded development. In M.M. Gruneberg & P. Morris (Eds.), *Aspects of Memory.* London: Methuen.

Belmont, J.M., & Butterfield, E.C. (1969). The relation of short-term memory to development and intelligence. In L.P. Lipsett & H.W. Reese (Eds.), *Advances in Child Development and Behavior* (Vol. 4). New York: Academic Press.

Belmont, J.M., & Butterfield, E.C. (1971). Learning strategies as determinants of memory deficiencies. *Cognitive Psychology, 2,* 411-420.

Belmont, J.M., Butterfield, E.C., & Borkowski, J. (1978). Training retarded people to generalize memorization methods across memory tasks. In M. Gruneberg, P. Morris, & R. Sykes (Eds.), *Practical aspects of memory.* New York: Academic Press.

Bender, B.G., & Levin, J.R. (1976a). Motor activity, anticipated motor activity, and young children's associative learning. *Child Development, 47,* 560-562.

Bender, B.G., & Levin, J.R. (1976b, April). *Why do pictures facilitate young children's learning of oral prose?* Paper presented at the annual meeting of the American Educational Research Association.

Bender, B.G., & Levin, J.R. (1978). Pictures, imagery and retarded children's prose imagery. *Journal of Educational Psychology, 20,* 583-588.

Bender, N. (1977). Verbal mediation as an instructional technique with young trainable mentally retarded children. *Journal of Special Education, 11,* 449-455.

Berkowitz, S., & Taylor, B. (1981). The effects of text type and familiarity on the nature of information recalled by readers. In M.L. Kamil (Ed.), *Direction in reading: Research and instruction.* Washington: National Reading Conference.

Berlyne, D.E. (1970). Attention as a problem in behavior. In D.I. Mostofsky (Ed.), *Attention: Contemporary theory and analysis.* New York: Appleton-Century-Crofts.

Bilsky, L., & Evans, R.A. (1970). Use of associative clustering techniques in the study of reading disability: Effects of list organization. *American Journal of Mental Deficiency, 74,* 771-776.

Bilsky, L., Evans, R.A., & Gilbert, L. (1972). Generalization of associative clustering tendencies of mentally retarded adolescents: Effects of novel stimuli. *American Journal of Mental Deficiency, 77,* 77-84.

Bird, J.E., & Bennett, A.F. (1974). A developmental study of recognition of pictures and nouns. *Journal of Experimental Child Psychology, 18,* 117-126.

Bjork, R.A. (1975). Short-term storage: The ordered output of a central processor. In F. Restle, R.M. Shiffrin, N.J. Castellan, H.R. Lindeman, & D.B. Pisoni (Eds.), *Cognitive Theory* (Vol. 1). Hillsdale, N.J.: Lawrence Erlbaum Associates.

Bjorklund, D.F., Ornstein, P.A., & Haig, J.R. (1977). Developmental differences in organization and recall: Training in the use of organizational techniques. *Developmental Psychology, 13,* 175-183.

Black, M.M., & Rollins, H.A. (1982). The effects of instructional variables on young children's organization and free recall. *Journal of Experimental Child Psychology, 33,* 1-19.

Blake, K. (1976). Massed and distributed practice and retarded and normal pupil's learning sight vocabulary. *Journal of Research and Development in Education, 9,* 13-14.

Bloom, K.C., & Shuell, T.J. (1981). Effects of massed and distributed practice on the learning and retention of second language vocabulary. *Journal of Educational Research, 74,* 245-248.

Bloom, L., & Lahey, M. (1978). *Language development and language disorders.* New York: Wiley.

Bobrow, S.A., & Bower, G.H. (1969). Comprehension and recall of sentences. *Journal of Experimental Psychology, 80,* 455-461.

Bommarito, J., & Meichenbaum, D. (1978). Enhancing reading comprehension by means of self-instructional training. Unpublished manuscript, University of Waterloo.

Borkowski, J.G., & Cavanaugh, J.C. (1979). Maintenance and generalization of skills and strategies by the retarded. In N.R. Ellis (Ed.), *Handbook of mental deficiency: Psychological theory and research* (2nd ed.) Hillsdale, N.J.: Lawrence Erlbaum Associates.

Borkowski, J., Cavanaugh, J., & Reichart, G. (1978). Maintenance of children's rehearsal strategies. Effects of amount of training and strategy form. *Journal of Experimental Child Psychology, 26,* 288-298.

Bormuth, J.R. (1968). *Readability in 1968.* Champaign, Ill.: National Council of Teachers of English.

Bormuth, J.R., Manning, J., Carr, J., & Pearson, D. (1970) Children's comprehension of between- and within-sentence syntactic structures. *Journal of Educational Psychology, 61,* 349-357.

Bornstein, M., Bellack, A., & Hersen, M. (1980). Social skills training for highly aggressive children. Treatments in an inpatient psychiatric setting. *Behavior Modification, 4,* 173-186.

Bornstein, P.H., & Quevillon, R.P. (1976). The effects of a self-instructional package on overactive preschool boys. *Journal of Applied Behavior Analysis, 9,* 179-188.

Botel, M., & Granowsky, A. (1972). A formula for measuring syntactic complexity: A directional effort. *Elementary English, 49,* 513-516.

Bower, G.H. (1972). Mental imagery and associative learning. In L.W. Gregg (Ed.), *Cognition in learning and memory.* New York: Wiley.

Bower, G.H. (1972). Mental imagery and associative learning. Fifth Annual Symposium on Cognition. Carnegie-Mellon University, Pittsburgh, Pennsylvania, 1969. In L. Gregg (Ed.), *Cognition in learning and memory.* New York: Wiley.

Bower, G.H. (1973). How to . . . uh . . . remember. *Psychology Today, 7,* 63-70.

Bower, G.H., & Clark, M.C. (1969). Narrative stories as mediators for serial learning. *Psychonomic Science, 14,* 181-182.

Bower, G.H., & Reitman, J.S. (1972). Mnemonic elaboration in multilist learning. *Journal of Verbal Learning and Verbal Behavior, 11,* 478-485.

Bower, G.H., & Winzenz, D. (1970). Comparison of associative learning strategies. *Psychonomic Science, 20,* 119-120.

Bransford, J.C., Franks, J.J., Morris, C.D., & Stein, B.S. (1979). Some general constraints on learning and memory research. In L.S. Cermak & F. Craik (Eds.), *Levels of processing in human memory.* Hillsdale, N.J.: Lawrence Erlbaum Associates.

Bransford, J.D. (1979). *Human cognition: Learning, understanding and remembering.* Belmont, Calif.: Wadsworth.

Brezin, M.J. (1980). Cognitive monitoring: From learning theory to instructional applications. *Educational Communication and Technology, 28,* 227-242.

Britton, B.K. (1978). Lexical ambiguity of words used in English text. *Behavior Research Methods and Instrumentation, 10,* 1-7.

Britton, B., Glynn, S., Meyer, B., & Penland, M. (1982). Effects of text structure on use of cognitive capacity during reading. *Journal of Educational Psychology, 74,* 51-61.

Brody, P.J. (1980). Do social studies texts utilize visual illustration effectively? *Educational Technology, 20,* 59-61.

Brooks, P.H., & Baumeister, A.A. (1977a). A plea for consideration of ecological validity in the experimental psychology of mental retardation: A guest editorial. *American Journal of Mental Deficiency, 81,* 407-416.

Brooks, P.H., & Baumeister, A.A. (1977b). Are we making a science of missing the point? *American Journal of Mental Deficiency, 81,* 543-546.

Brown, A.L. (1974). The role of strategic behavior in retardate memory. In N.R. Ellis (Ed.), *International review of research in mental retardation* (Vol. 7). New York: Academic Press.

Brown, A.L. (1975a). Recognition, reconstruction and recall of narrative sequences by preoperational children. *Child Development, 46,* 156-166.

Brown, A.L. (1975b). The development of memory: Knowing, knowing about knowing, and knowing how to know. In H.W. Reese (Ed.), *Advances in child development and behavior.* New York: Academic Press.

Brown, A.L. (1977). Development, schooling, and the acquisition of knowledge about knowledge: Comments on Chapter 7 by Nelson. In R.C. Anderson, R.J. Spiro, & W.E. Montague (Eds.), *Schooling and the acquisition of knowledge.* Hillsdale, N.J.: Lawrence Erlbaum Associates.

Brown, A.L. (1978). Knowing when, where, and how to remember: A problem of metacognition. In R. Glaser (Ed.), *Advances in instructional psychology* (Vol. 1). Hillsdale, N.J.: Lawrence Erlbaum Associates.

Brown, A.L. (1981). Metacognition: The development of selective attention strategies for learning from texts. In M.L. Kamil (Ed.), *Direction in reading: Research and instruction.* Washington: National Reading Conference.

Brown, A.L., & Barclay, C. (1976). The effects of training specific mnemonics on the metamnemonic efficiency of retarded children. *Child Development, 47,* 71-80.

Brown, A.L., & Campione, J.C. (1977). Training strategic study time apportionment in educable retarded children. *Intelligence, 1,* 97-107.

Brown, A.L., & Campione, J.C. (1978). The effects of knowledge and experience on the formation of retrieval plans for studying from texts. In M. Grunbgerg, P. Morris, & R. Sykes (Eds.), *Practical aspects of memory.* New York: Academic Press.

Brown, A.L., Campione, J.C., & Barclay, C. (1979). Training self-checking routines for estimating test readiness: Generalization from list learning to prose recall. *Child Development, 50,* 501-512.

Brown, A.L., Campione, J.C., Bray, N.W., & Wilcox, B.L. (1973). Keeping track of changing variables: Effects of rehearsal training and rehearsal prevention in normal and retarded adolescents. *Journal of Experimental Psychology, 101,* 123-131.

Brown, A.L., Campione, J.C., & Day, J. (1981). Learning to learn: On training students to learn from texts. *Educational Researcher, 10,* 14-21.

Brown, A.L., Campione, J.C., & Murphy, M.D. (1974). Keeping track of changing variables: Long-term retention of a trained rehearsal strategy by retarded adolescents. *American Journal of Mental Deficiency, 78,* 446-453.

Brown, A.L., Campione, J.C., & Murphy, M.D. (1977). Maintenance and generalization of trained metamnemonic awareness by educable retarded children. *Journal of Experimental Child Psychology, 24,* 191-211.

Brown, A.L., & Palincsar, A. (1982). Inducing strategic learning from texts by means of informed, self-control training. *Topics in Learning and Learning Disabilities, 1,* 1-17.

Brown, A.L., & Scott, M.S. (1971). Recognition memory for pictures in preschool children. *Journal of Experimental Child Psychology, 11,* 401-412.

Brown, A.L., & Smiley, S.S. (1977). Rating the importance of structural units of prose passages: A problem of metacognitive development. *Child Development, 48,* 1-8.

Brown, A.L., & Smiley, S.S. (1978). The development of strategies for studying texts. *Child Development, 49,* 1076-1088.

Brown, A.L., Smiley, S.S., Day, J., Townsend, M., & Lawton, S. (1977). Intrusion of a thematic idea in children's comprehension and retention of stories. *Child Development, 48,* 1454-1466.

Bruce, B. (1978). What makes a good story? *Language Arts, 55,* 460-466.

Bugelski, B.R. (1970). Words and things and images. *American Psychologist, 25,* 1002-1012.

Bugelski, B.R., Kidd, E., & Segmen, J. (1968). Image as a mediator in one-time paired-associate learning. *Journal of Experimental Psychology, 76,* 69-73.

Burgio, L., Whitman, T., & Johnson, M. (1980). A self-instructional package for increasing attending behavior in educable mentally retarded children. *Journal of Applied Behavior Analysis, 13,* 443-459.

Burron, D., & Bucher, B. (1978). Self-instructions as discriminative cues for rule-breaking or rule-following. *Journal of Experimental Child Psychology, 26,* 46-57.

Butterfield, E., & Belmont, J. (1972). The role of verbal process in short-term memory. In R.L. Schiefelbusch (Ed.), *Language research with the mentally retarded.* Baltimore: University Park Press.

Byrant, L., & Budd, K. (1982). Self-instructional training to increase independent work performance in preschoolers. *Journal of Applied Behavior Analysis, 15*, 259-271.

Camp, B., Blom, G., Hebert, F., & vanDoorinck (1977). "Think aloud." A program for developing self-control in young aggressive boys. *Journal of Abnormal Child Psychology, 5*, 157-168.

Campione, J.C., & Brown, A.L. (1977). Memory and metamemory development in educable retarded children. In R.V. Kail & J.W. Hagen (Eds.), *Perspectives on the development of memory and cognition.* Hillsdale, N.J.: Lawrence Erlbaum Associates.

Campione, J.C., & Brown, A.L. (1978). Training general metacognitive skills in retarded children. In M. Gruneberg, P. Morris, & R. Sykes (Eds.), *Practical aspects of memory.* New York: Academic Press.

Carnine, D.W. (1976). Effects of two teacher-presentation rates on off-task behavior, answering correctly, and participation. *Journal of Applied Behavior Analysis, 9*, 199-206.

Carnine, D.W. (1979). Direct instruction: A successful system for educationally high-risk children. *Journal of Curriculum Studies, 11*, 29-45.

Carnine, D.W. (1980). Two letter discrimination sequences: High-confusion alternatives first versus low-confusion alternatives first. *Journal of Reading Behavior, 12*, 41-48.

Carnine, D., & Silbert, J. (1979). *Direct instruction reading.* Columbus, OH.: Merrill.

Carroll, J.B., Davies, P., & Richman, B. (1971). *Word frequency book.* Boston: Houghton Mifflin.

Carroll, W., Rosenthal, T., & Brysh, C. (1972). Social transmission of grammatical parameters. *Journal of Educational Psychology, 63*, 589-596.

Cashen, V.M., & Leicht, K.L. (1970). Role of the isolation effect in a formal educational setting. *Journal of Educational Psychology, 61*, 484-486.

Cavanaugh, J., & Perlmutter, M. (1982). Metamemory: A critical examination. *Child Development, 53*, 11-28.

Cermak, L.S. (1975). *Improving your memory.* New York: Norton.

Childs, R. (1983). Teaching rehearsal strategies for spelling to mentally retarded children. *Education and Training of the Mentally Retarded, 17-18*, 318-320.

Christie, D.J., & Schumacher, G.M. (1975). Developmental trends in the abstraction and recall of relevant versus irrelevant thematic information from connected verbal material. *Child Development, 46*, 598-602.

Clark, H., Sherman, J., & Kelley, K. (1971, September). *Use of modeling and reinforcement to train generative sentence usage.* Paper presented at the meeting of the American Psychological Association, Washington, D.C.

Clements, P. (1975). *The effects of staging on recall from prose.* Unpublished dissertation, Cornell University.

Cole, M., Hood, L., & McDermott, R. (1982). Ecological niche picking. In U.

Neisser (Ed.), *Memory observed: Remembering in natural contexts.* San Francisco: W.H. Freeman.

Collins, A., Brown, J.S. & Larkin, K.M. (1980). Inference in text understanding. In R.J. Spiro, B.C. Bruce, & W.F. Brewer (Eds.), *Theoretical issues in reading comprehension.* Hillsdale, N.J.: Lawrence Erlbaum Associates.

Conconnon, S. (1975). Illustrations in books for children: Review of research. *Reading Teacher, 29,* 254-256.

Conway, J.B., & Bucher, B.D. (1974).Transfer and maintenance of behavior change in children: A review and suggestions. In E.J. Mash, L.A. Hamerlynck, & L.C. Handy (Eds.), *Behavior modification and families.* New York: Brunner/Mazel.

Corsini, D.A., Jacobus, K.A., & Leonard, D. (1969). Recognition memory of preschool children for pictures and words. *Psychonomic Science, 16,* 192-193.

Craighead, W., Wilcoxon-Craighead, L., & Meyers, A. (1978). New directions in behavior modification with children. In M. Hessen, R. Eisler, & P. Miller (Eds.), *Progress in behavior modification* (Vol. 6). New York: Academic Press.

Craik, F.I.M., & Lockhart, R. (1972). Levels of processing: A framework for memory research. *Journal of Verbal Learning and Verbal Behavior, 11,* 671-684.

Craik, F.I.M., & Tulving, E. (1975). Depth of processing and the retention of words in episodic memory. *Journal of Experimental Psychology, 104,* 268-294.

Craik, F.I.M., & Watkins, M.J. (1973). The role of rehearsal in short-term memory. *Journal of Verbal Learning and Verbal Behavior, 12,* 599-607.

Cromer, W. (1970). The difference model: A new explanation for some reading difficulties. *Journal of Educational Psychology, 61,* 471-483.

Crouse, J.H., & Idstein, P. (1972). Effects of encoding cues on prose learning. *Journal of Educational Psychology, 63,* 309-313.

Crovitz, H.F. (1970). *Galton's Walk.* New York: Harper & Row.

Crovitz, H.F., & Daves, W. (1962). Tendency to eye movement and perceptual accuracy. *Journal of Experimental Psychology, 63,* 495-498.

Cullinan, D. (1976). Verbalization in EMR children's observational learning. *American Journal of Mental Deficiency, 81,* 65-72.

Cullinan, D., Lloyd, J., & Epstein, M. (1980). Strategy training: A structured approach to arithmetic instruction. *Exceptional Education Quarterly, 1,* 41-49.

Dale, E., & Chall, J. (1948). A formula for predicting readability. *Educational Research Bulletin, 27,* 11-20.

Danner, F.W., & Taylor, A.M. (1973). Integrated pictures and relational imagery training in children's learning. *Journal of Experimental Child Psychology, 16,* 47-54.

Darley, C.F., & Glass, A.L. (1975). Effects of rehearsal and serial list position on recall. *Journal of Experimental Psychology: Human Learning and Memory, 104,* 453-458.

Davidson, R.E. (1976). The role of metaphor and analogy in learning. In J.R. Levin and V.L. Allen (Eds.), *Cognitive learning in children: Theories and strategies.* New York: Academic Press.

Davies, G.M., & Brown, L. (1978). Recall and organization in five year old children. *British Journal of Psychology, 69,* 343-349.

Davies, G., & Rushton, A. (1979). Presentation mode and organizational strategies in young children's free recall. In M.P. Friedman, J.P. Das, & N. O'Connor (Eds.), *Intelligence and Learning.* New York: Plenum Press.

Day, J.D. (1980). *Training summarization skill: A comparison of teaching methods.* Unpublished doctoral dissertation, University of Illinois.

Dearborn, W.F., Johnson, P.W., & Carmichael, L. (1951). Improving the readability of type-written manuscripts. *Proceedings of the National Academy of Sciences, 37,* 670-672.

DeGraaf, C.A. (1972). *Teaching action concept usage to institutionalized retardates with systematic instructions and still pictorial illustrations.* Unpublished doctoral dissertation, Southern Illinois University.

Delin, P. (1969). Learning and retention of English words with successive approximations to a complex mnemonic instruction. *Psychonomic Science, 17,* 87-88.

Denney, D. (1975). The effects of exemplary and cognitive models and self-rehearsal on children's interrogative strategies. *Journal of Experimental Child Psychology, 19,* 476-488.

Denney, N.W., & Turner, M.C. (1979). Facilitating cognitive performance in children: A comparison of strategy modeling and strategy modeling with overt self-verbalization. *Journal of Experimental Child Psychology, 28,* 119-131.

Denney, N.W., & Ziobrowski, M. (1972). Developmental changes in clustering criteria. *Journal of Experimental Child Psychology, 13,* 275-283.

Deshler, D., Alley, G., Warner, M., & Schumaker, V. (1981). Instructional practices for promoting skill acquisition and generalization in severely learning disabled adolescents. *Learning Disability Quarterly, 4,* 415-421.

Devore, G., & Stern, C. (1970). Real objects versus pictures in the instruction of young children. *Journal of School Psychology, 8,* 77-81.

Dixon, R., & Engelmann, S. (1976). *Morphographic spelling.* Chicago: Science Research Associates.

Dixon, R., Engelmann, S., & Olen, L. (1981). *Spelling mastery.* Chicago: Science Research Associates.

Doctorow, M., Wittrock, M.C., & Marks, C. (1978). Generative processes in reading comprehension. *Journal of Educational Psychology, 70,* 109-118.

Dore, L., & Hilgard, E. (1938). Spacing practice as a test of Snoddy's two processes in mental growth. *Journal of Experimental Psychology, 23,* 359-374.

Douglas, V., Parry, P., Marton, P., & Garcon, C. (1976). Assessment of a cognitive training program for hyperactive children. *Journal of Abnormal Child Psychology, 4,* 389-410.

Drabman, R.S., Hammer, D., & Rosenbaum, M.S. (1979). Assessing generalization in behavior modification with children: The generalization map. *Behavioral Assessment, 1*, 203-219.

Driskell, J.L. (1976). A study of the effectiveness of a guided note-taking and study skills system upon the level of academic success among entering University of Idaho freshmen (Doctoral dissertation, University of Idaho, 1976). *Dissertation Abstracts International, 37*, 1305A. (University Microfilms No. 76-21, 235)

Duchastel, P.C. (1980a). Research on illustrations in text: Issues and perspectives. *Educational Communication and Technology, 28*, 283-287.

Duchastel, P.C. (1980b). Test of the role in retention of illustrations in text. *Psychological Report, 47*, 204-206.

Duchastel, P., & Chen, Y.P. (1980). The use of marginal notes in text to assist learning. *Educational Technology, 20*, 41-43.

Dunham, T.C., & Levin, J.R. (1979). Imagery instructions and young children's prose learning: No evidence of support. *Contemporary Educational Psychology, 4*, 107-113.

Durkin, D. (1974). *Teaching them to read.* Boston: Allyn and Bacon.

Dwyer, F.M. (1971). An experimental evaluation of the instructional effectiveness of black and white and colored illustrations. *Didakta Medica, 3*, 96-101.

D'Zurilla, T., & Goldfried, M. (1971). Problem solving and behavior modification. *Journal of Abnormal Psychology, 78*, 107-126.

Ellis, D. (1976). The assessment of self-instructional training in developing self control of aggressive behavior in impulsive-aggressive boys. *Dissertation Abstracts International, 37*, 3070.

Ellis, H., Bennett, T., Daniel, T., & Rickert, E. (1979). *Psychology of learning and memory.* Monterey: Brooks/Cole.

Ellis, N.R. (1970). Memory processes in retardates and normals. In N.R. Ellis (Ed.), *International review of research in mental retardation* (Vol. 4). New York: Academic Press.

Emmerich, H., & Akerman, B. (1976). The effect of pictorial detail and elaboration on children's retention. *Journal of Experimental Child Psychology, 21*, 241-248.

Engle, R.W., & Nagle, R.J. (1979). Strategy training and semantic encoding in mildly retarded children. *Intelligence, 3*, 17-30.

Engelmann, S. *Direct instruction.* Englewood Cliffs, N.J.: Educational Technology Publications, 1980.

Engelmann, S., Becker, W., & Carnine, L. (1976). *Corrective reading program.* Chicago: Science Research Associates.

Engelmann, S., & Bruner, E. (1974). *DISTAR Reading, Level 1* (rev. ed.). Chicago: Science Research Associates.

Engelmann, S., & Bruner, E. (1983). *Reading mastery.* Chicago: Science Research Associates.

Engelmann, S., & Carnine, D. (1982a). *Corrective Mathematics.* Chicago: Science Research Associates.

Engelmann, S., & Carnine, D. (1982b). *Theory of instruction: Principles and applications.* New York: Irvington.

Engelmann, S., & Osborne, J. (1976). *Distar Language I* (2nd ed.). Chicago: Science Research Associates.

Ericksen, S. (1942). Variability of attack in massed and distributed practice. *Journal of Experimental Psychology, 31,* 339-385.

Ericsson, K.A., Chase, W.G., & Faloon, S. (1980). Acquisition of a memory skill. *Science, 208,* 1181-1182.

Ernest, C. (1977). Imagery ability and cognition: A critical review. *Journal of Mental Imagery, 2,* 181-216.

Evertson, M., & Wicker, F. (1974). Pictorial concreteness and mode of elaboration in children's learning. *Journal of Experimental Child Psychology, 17,* 264-270.

Fagan, J.F. (1969). Free recall learning in normal and retarded children. *Journal of Experimental Child Psychology, 8,* 9-19.

Ferguson, R.P., & Bray, N.W. (1976). Component processes of an overt rehearsal strategy in young children. *Journal of Experimental Child Psychology, 21,* 490-506.

Ferster, C. (1972). Clinical reinforcement. *Seminar in Psychiatry, 4,* 101-111.

Fischer, J.A. (1973). Effects of cue synthesis procedure and postquestions on the retention of prose material. *Dissertation Abstracts International, 34,* 615.

Fitzgerald, J., and Spiegel, D.L. (1983). Enhancing children's reading comprehension through instruction in narrative structure. *Journal of Reading Behavior, 15*(2), 1-17.

Flagg, B.N., Weaver, P.A., Fenton, T., Gelatt, R., & Pray, R. (1980). *Children's use of pictures in comprehending written text.* Paper presented at the annual meeting of the American Educational Research Association, Boston.

Flavell, J.H. (1970). Developmental studies of mediated memory. In H.W. Reese & L.P. Lipsitt (Eds.), *Advances in child development and behavior* (Vol. 5). New York: Academic Press.

Flavell, J.H., Beach, D.R., & Chinsky, J.M. (1966). Spontaneous verbal rehearsal in a memory task as a function of age. *Child Development, 37,* 283-299.

Flavell, J.H., Friedrichs, A.G., & Hoyt, J.D. (1970). Developmental changes in memorization processes. *Cognitive Psychology, 1,* 324-340.

Flavell, J.H., & Wellman, H.M. (1977). Metamemory. In R.V. Kail & J.W. Hagen (Eds.), *Perspectives on the development of memory and cognition.* Hillsdale, N.J.: Lawrence Erlbaum Associates.

Fleming, M.L. (1979). On pictures in educational research. *Instructional Science, 8,* 235-251.

Foster, J.J. (1979). The use of visual cues in text. In P.A. Kolers, M.E. Molstad, & H. Bouma (Eds.), *Processing of visible language.* New York: Plenum.

Fowler, R.L., & Barker, A.S. (1974). Effectiveness of highlighting for retention of text material. *Journal of Applied Psychology, 59,* 358-364.

Frase, L.T. (1967). Learning from prose material: Length of passage, knowledge of results, and position of questions. *Journal of Educational Psychology, 58*, 266-272.

Frase, L.T. (1968). Effect of question location, pacing, and mode upon retention of prose materials. *Journal of Educational Psychology, 59*, 244-249.

Frederiksen, C.H. (1975). Representing logical and semantic structure of knowledge acquired from discourse. *Cognitive Psychology, 7*, 371-458.

Friedman, M., Krupski, A., Dawson, G., & Rosenberg, P. (1977). Metamemory and mental retardation. Implications for research and practice. In P. Mittler (Ed.), *Research to practice in mental retardation.* Baltimore: University Park Press.

Fry, E. (1968). A readability formula that saves time. *Journal of Reading, 11*, pp. 513-516; 575-578.

Furukawa, J.M. (1970). The chunking method of determining size of step in programmed instruction. *Journal of Educational Psychology, 61*, 247-254.

Furukawa, J.M. (1972). Critical chunk, physical length, and number of words per chunk in programmed instruction. *Journal of Educational Research, 65*, 361-364.

Gagne, E.D. (1978). Long-term retention of information following learning from prose. *Review of Educational Research, 48*, 629-665.

Gallagher, J.R. (1969). A comparison of retardates and normals on subjective organization in short-term memory. *American Journal of Mental Deficiency, 73*, 661-665.

Gambrell, L., Koskinen, P.S., & Cole, J.N. (1981). The effects of induced mental imagery upon comprehension: A comparison of written versus oral presentation. In M.L. Kamil (Ed.), *Direction in reading: Research and instruction.* Washington: National Reading Conference.

Ganske, L. (1981). Note-taking: A significant and integral part of learning environments. *Educational Communication and Technology, 29*, 155-175.

Garcia, E. (1974). The training and generalization of conversational speech form in nonverbal retarded. *Journal of Applied Behavior Analysis, 7*, 137-149.

Gerjuoy, I.R., & Spitz, H.H. (1966). Associative clustering in free recall: Intellectual and developmental variables. *American Journal of Mental Deficiency, 70*, 918-927.

Ghatala, E.S., & Levin, J.R. (1976). Children's recognition memory processes. In J.R. Levin & V.L. Allen (Eds.), *Cognitive learning in children: Theories and strategies.* New York: Academic Press.

Gillis, J.S. (1971). Ecological relevance and the study of cognitive disorders. In J. Hellmuth (Ed.), *Cognitive studies: Deficits in cognition* (Vol. 2). New York: Brunner/Mazel.

Glidden, L.M. (1977). Developmental effects in free recall learning. *Child Development, 48*, 9-12.

Glynn, S.M. (1978). Capturing reader's attention by means of typographical cuing strategies. *Educational Technology, 18*, 7-12.

Goetz, E., & Baer, D. (1973). Social control of form diversity and the emergence of new focus in children's blockbuilding. *Journal of Applied Behavior Analysis, 6,* 105-113.

Gold, M., & Barclay, C. (1973). The effects of verbal labels on the acquisition and retention of a complex assembly task. *The Training School Bulletin, 70,* 38-42.

Goldschmid, M., & Bentler, P. (1968). *Manual: Concept-Assessment Kit-Conservation.* San Diego: Educational and Industrial Testing Service.

Goodman, G.S. (1980). Picture memory: How the action schema affects retention. *Cognitive Psychology, 12,* 473-495.

Goodman, K., & Goodman, Y. (1977). Learning about psycholinguistic processes by analyzing oral reading. *Harvard Educational Review, 47,* 317-333.

Gordon, C., Hansen, J., & Pearson, P.D. (1978). *Effects of background knowledge on silent reading comprehension.* Paper presented at the annual meeting of the American Educational Research Association, Toronto.

Gordon, C. & Braun, C. (1983). Using story schemata as an aid to reading and writing. *The Reading Teacher, 37,* 116-121.

Graham, E.C. (1966). *The Basic dictionary of science.* Cambridge, England: The Orthological Institute.

Greeno, G. (1964). Paired associate learning with massed and distributed repetitions of items. *Journal of Experimental Psychology, 67,* 286-295.

Gruneberg, M., Monks, J., Sykes, R., & Osborne, D. (1974). Some correlates of rated memorability of sentences. *British Journal of Psychology, 65,* 519-527.

Guttmann, J., Levin, J.R., & Pressley, G.M. (1977). Pictures, partial pictures and young children's oral prose learning. *Journal of Educational Psychology, 69,* 473-480.

Hagen, J.W., & Kingsley, P.R. (1968). Labelling effects in short-term memory. *Child Development, 39,* 113-121.

Hall, J. (1982). *An invitation to learning and memory.* Boston: Allyn and Bacon.

Hamre-Nietupski, S., Nietupski, J., Vincent, L., & Wambold, C. (1982). Effects of strategy training on free-recall performance of mildly and moderately mentally retarded adolescents. *American Journal of Mental Deficiency, 86,* 421-424.

Haring, M.J. (1982). Picture enrichment of delayed recall: Support from a unique source. *British Journal of Educational Psychology, 52,* 104-108.

Haring, M.J., & Frye, M.A. (1979). Effect of pictures on children's comprehension of written text. *Educational Communication and Technology Journal, 27,* 185-190.

Haring, N.G. (1977-1978). *Field initiated research study: An investigation of phases of learning and facilitating instructional events for the severely handicapped, annual progress report.* Seattle: College of Education, University of Washington.

Harris, G.J., & Burke, D. (1972). The effects of grouping on short-term serial recall of digits by children: Developmental trends. *Child Development, 43*, 710-716.

Harris, J.E. (1982). External memory aids. In U. Neisser (Ed.), *Memory observed: Remembering in natural contexts.* San Francisco: W.H. Freeman.

Harris, K. (1980). The sustained effects of cognitive modification and informed teachers on children's communication apprehension. *Communication Quarterly, 28*, 47-56.

Harris, K. (1981, May). *Self-speech, language, and cognitive training: A review of theory and practice.* Paper presented at the meeting of the International Communication Association, Minneapolis.

Harris, K. (1982). Cognitive-behavior modification: Applications with exceptional children. *Focus on Exceptional Children, 15*, 1-16.

Harris, M., & Hassemer, W. (1972). Some factors affecting the complexity of children's sentences: The effect of modeling, age, sex and bilingualism. *Journal of Experimental Child Psychology, 13*, 447-455.

Hartley, J., & Burnhill, P. (1976). Explorations in space: A critique of the typography of BPS publications. *Bulletin of the British Psychological Society, 29*, 97-107.

Hauck, P., Walsh, C., & Kroll, N. (1976). Visual imagery mnemonics: Common versus bizarre mental images. *Bulletin of the Psychonomic Society, 7*, 160-162.

Hershberger, W.A., & Terry, D.F. (1965). Typographical cuing in conventional and programmed texts. *Journal of Applied Psychology, 49*, 55-60.

Hiew, C. (1977) Sequence effects in rule learning and conceptual generalization. *American Journal of Psychology, 90*, 207-218.

Higa, W., Tharp, R., & Calkins, R. (1978). Developmental verbal control of behavior: Implications for self-instruction training. *Journal of Experimental Child Psychology, 26*, 489-497.

Higbee, K.L. (1977). *Your memory: How it works and how to improve it.* Englewood Cliffs, N.J.: Prentice-Hall.

Higbee, K.L. (1979). Recent research on visual mnemonics: Historical roots and educational traits. *Review of Educational Research, 49*, 611-629.

Higgins, L.C. (1980). Literalism in the young child's interpretation of pictures. *Educational Communication and Technology, 28*, 99-119.

Hittleman, D.R. (1978). *Developmental reading: A psycholinguistic perspective.* Chicago, Rand McNally.

Holmes, P., & Murray, D. (1974). Free recall of sentences as a function of imagery and predictability. *Journal of Experimental Psychology, 102*, 748-750.

Holt, M., Richard, H., & Ellis, N. (1972). A note on word modeling in retarded adolescents. *American Journal of Mental Deficiency, 77*, 237-239.

Holyoak, K., Hogeterp, H., & Yuille, C. (1972). The developmental comparison of verbal and pictorial mnemonics in paired associate learning. *Journal of Experimental Child Psychology, 14,* 53-65.

Horner, R., Bellamy, G., & Colvin, G. (1982). *Responding in the presence of non-trained stimuli: Implications of generalization error patterns.* Centre on Human Development, University of Oregon, Eugene.

Horner, R., & McDonald, R. (1982). Comparison of single instance and general case instruction in teaching a generalized vocational skill. *TASH Journal, 8,* 7-20.

Horner, R., Sprague, J., & Wilcox, B. (1982). General case programming for community activities. In B. Wilcox & G. Bellamy (Eds.), *Design of high school programs for severely handicapped students.* Baltimore: Paul Brookes.

Horowitz, A.B. (1969). Effect of stimulus presentation modes on children's recall and clustering. *Psychonomic Science, 14,* 297-298.

Hortin, J., & Bailey, G. (1983). Visualization: Theory and applications for teachers. *Reading Improvement, 20,* 70-74.

Hull, M., Barry, O., & Clark, D. (1976). *Procedures for teaching vocational concepts to special needs students: Final report.* Austin, Texas: Texas A and M University, College Station. (ERIC Document Reproduction Service No. ED 133 599)

Hunter, I.M. (1964). *Memory.* Baltimore: Penguin Books.

Hunter, I.M., (1979). Memory in everyday life. In M.M. Gruneberg & P.E. Morris (Eds.), *Applied problems in memory.* New York: Academic Press.

Idstein, P., & Jenkins, J.R. (1972). Underlining versus repetitive reading. *The Journal of Educational Research, 65,* 321-323.

Istomina, Z.M. (1975). The development of voluntary memory in preschool-age children. *Soviet Psychology, 13,* 5-64.

Istomina, Z.M. (1982). The development of voluntary memory in children of preschool age. In U. Neisser (Ed.), *Memory observed: Remembering in natural contexts.* San Francisco: W.H. Freeman.

James W. (1950). *The principles of psychology.* New York: Dover. (Originally published in 1890.)

Jensen, A.R., & Rohwer, W.D. (1963). Verbal mediation in paired-associate and serial learning. *Journal of Verbal Learning and Verbal Behavior, 1,* 346-352.

Johnson, D.D., & Barrett, T.C. (1981). Prose comprehension: A descriptive analysis of instructional practices. In C.M. Santa & B.L. Hayes (Eds.), *Children's prose comprehension: Practice and research.* Newark, Delaware: International Reading Association.

Johnson, M.J. (1981). Research and the reality of reading. In C.M. Santa & B.L. Hayes (Eds.), *Children's prose comprehension: Research and practice.* Newark, Delaware: International Reading Association.

Johnson, N., & Mandler, J. (1980). A tale of two structures: Underlying and surface forms in stories. *Poetics, 9,* 51-86.

Johnson, R. (1970). Recall of prose as a function of the structural importance of the linguistic units. *Journal of Verbal Learning and Verbal Behavior, 9,* 12-20.

Johnson, R.E. (1974). Abstractive processes in the remembering of prose. *Journal of Educational Psychology, 66,* 772-779.

Johnson, S., Bolstad, O., & Lobitz, G. (1976). Generalization and contrast phenomena in behavior modification with children. In E.J. Mash, L.A. Hamerlynck, & L.C. Hardy (Eds.), *Behavior modification and families.* New York: Bruner/Mazel.

Jonassen, D.H. *et al.* (1982, 1985). *The technology of text: Techniques for structuring, designing and displaying text* (Volumes One and Two). Englewood Cliffs, N.J.: Educational Technology Publications.

Kail, R. (1979). *The development of memory in children.* San Francisco: W.H. Freeman.

Kazdin, A. (1975). *Behavior modification in applied settings.* Homewood, Ill.: The Dorsey Press.

Kazdin, A., & Esveldt-Dawson, K. (1981). *How to maintain behavior.* Lawrence, KS: H and H Enterprises.

Keeney, T.J., Cannizzo, S.R., & Flavell, J.H. (1967). Spontaneous and induced verbal rehearsal in a recall task. *Child Development, 38,* 953-966.

Kendall, C.R., Borkowski, J., & Cavanaugh, J. (1978). *Maintenance and generalization of an interrogative strategy by EMR children.* Paper presented at the 10th Annual Gatlinberg Conference on Research in Mental Retardation, Gatlinberg, Tenn.

Kendall, C.R., Borkowski, J.G., & Cavanaugh, J.C. (1980). Metamemory and the transfer of an interrogative strategy by EMR children. *Intelligence, 4,* 255-270.

Kendall, P.C. (1977). On the efficacious use of verbal instructional procedures with children. *Cognitive Therapy and Research, 4,* 331-341.

Kendall, P.C., & Braswell, L. (1982). Cognitive-behavioral self-control therapy for children: A components analysis. *Journal of Consulting and Clinical Psychology, 50,* 672-689.

Kendall, P.C., & Finch, A. (1979). Developing nonimpulsive behavior in children: Cognitive-behavioral strategies for self-control. In P.C. Kendall & S.D. Hollon (Eds.), *Cognitive-behavioral interventions: Theories, research and procedures.* New York: Academic Press.

Kendall, P.C., & Wilcox, L. (1980). A cognitive-behavioral treatment for impulsivity: Concrete versus conceptual training in non-self-controlled problem children. *Journal of Consulting and Clinical Psychology, 48,* 80-91.

Kendler, T., Kendler, H., & Carrick, M. (1966). Verbal labels and inferential problem solution of children. *Child Development, 37,* 749-763.

Kennedy, B.A., & Miller, D.J. (1976). Persistent use of verbal rehearsal as a function of information about its value. *Child Development, 47,* 566-569.

Keogh, B., & Glover, A. (1980). The generality and durability of cognitive training effects. *Exceptional Education Quarterly, 1,* 75-82.

Keogh, B., & Margolis, J. (1976). A component analysis of attentional problems of educationally handicapped boys. *Journal of Abnormal Child Psychology, 4*, 349-359.

Kestner, J., & Borkowski, J.G. (1979). Children's maintenance and generalization of an interrogative learning strategy. *Child Development, 50*, 485-494.

Kimble, G. (1949). Performance and reminiscence in motor learning as a function of the degrees of distribution of practice. *Journal of Experimental Psychology, 39*, 500-510.

Kintsch, W. (1974). *The representation of meaning in memory.* Hillsdale, N.J.: Lawrence Erlbaum Associates.

Kintsch, W. (1977). On comprehending stories. In M. Just & P. Carpenter (Eds.), *Cognitive processes in comprehension.* Hillsdale, N.J.: Lawrence Erlbaum Associates.

Kintsch, W., Kosminsky, E., Streby, W.J., McKoon, G., & Keenan, J.M. (1975). Comprehension and recall as a function of content variables. *Journal of Verbal Learning and Verbal Behavior, 14*, 196-214.

Kintsch, W., & Van Dijk, T. (1978). Toward a model of text comprehension and production. *Psychological Review, 85*, 363-394.

Kintsch, W., & Vipond, D. (1978). Reading comprehension and readability in educational practice and psychological theory. In L.G. Nilsson (Ed.), *Memory processes and problems.* Hillsdale, N.J.: Lawrence Erlbaum Associates.

Kintsch, W. (1982). Text representations. In W. Otto, & S. White (Eds.), *Reading expository materials.* New York: Academic Press.

Klapp, S., Marshburn, E., & Lester, P. (1983). Short-term memory does not involve the "working memory" of information processing: The demise of a common assumption. *Journal of Experimental Psychology: General, 112*, 240-264.

Klare, G., Mabry, J.E., & Gustafson, L.M. (1955). Relationship of patterning (underlining) to immediate retention and to acceptability of technical material. *Journal of Applied Psychology, 39*, 40-42.

Klare, G., Nichols, W., & Shuford, E. (1957). The relationships of typographic arrangement to the learning of technical training material. *Journal of Applied Psychology, 41*, 41-45.

Kobasigawa, A. (1974). Utilization of retrieval cues by children in recall. *Child Development, 45*, 127-134.

Kobasigawa, A., & Middleton, D. (1972). Free recall of categorized items by children at three grade levels. *Child Development, 43*, 1067-1072.

Koenke, K., & Otto, W. (1969). Contribution of pictures to children's comprehension of the main idea in reading. *Psychology in the Schools, 6*, 298-302.

Kolers, P. (1975). Memorial consequences of automatized encoding. *Journal of Experimental Psychology: Human Learning and Memory, 1*, 689-701.

Kolers, P., & Ostry, D.J. (1974). Time course of loss of information regarding pattern analyzing operations. *Journal of Verbal Learning and Verbal Behavior, 13*, 599-612.

Kosiewicz, M., Hallahan, D., Lloyd, J., & Graves, A. (1982). Effects of self-instruction and self-correction procedures on handwriting performance. *Learning Disabilities Quarterly, 5,* 71-78.

Kosoff, T.O. (1981). The effects of three types of written introductions on children's processing of text. In M.L. Kamil (Ed.), *Direction in reading: Research and instruction.* Washington: National Reading Conference.

Kramer, J.L., Nagle, R.J., & Engle, R.W. (1980). Recent advances in mnemonic strategy training with mentally retarded persons: Implications for educational practice. *American Journal of Mental Deficiency, 85,* 306-314.

Kreutzer, M., Leonard, C., & Flavell, J. (1975). An interview study of children's knowledge about memory. *Monographs of the Society for Research in Child Development, 40* (1, Serial No. 159).

Kryzanowski, J., & Carnine, D. (1980). The effects of massed versus spaced formats in teaching sound-symbol correspondences to young children. *Journal of Reading Behavior, 12,* 225-229.

Kucera, H., & Francis, W.N. (1967). *Computational analysis of present-day American English.* Providence, R.I.: Brown University Press.

Kulhavy, R.W. (1972). Effects of embedded orienting stimuli in a prose passage. *Psychonomic Science, 28,* 213-214.

Kuypers, D., Becker, W., & O'Leary, K. (1968). How to make a token system fail. *Exceptional Children, 35,* 101-109.

Langone, J., & Westling, D. (1979). Generalization of prevocational and vocational skills: Some practical tactics. *Education and Training of the Mentally Retarded, 14,* 216-221.

Laycock, S.R., & Russell, D.H. (1941). An analysis of thirty-eight how to study manuals. *School Review, 49,* 370-379.

Ledwidge, B. (1978). Cognitive behavior modification: A step in the wrong direction? *Psychological Bulletin, 85,* 353-375.

Lefevre, C. (1964). *Linguistics and the teaching of reading.* New York: McGraw-Hill.

Lesgold, A.M., DeGood, H., & Levin, J.R. (1977). Pictures and young children's prose learning: A supplementary report. *Journal of Reading Behavior, 9,* 353-360.

Lesgold, A.M., McCormick, C., & Golinkoff, R.M. (1975). Imagery training and children's prose learning. *Journal of Educational Psychology, 67,* 663-667.

Levin, J.R. (1976). What we have learned about maximizing what children learn? In J.R. Levin & V.L. Allen (Eds.), *Cognitive learning in children: Theories and strategies.* New York: Academic Press.

Levin, J.R. (1981). The mnemonic '80's: Keywords in the classroom. *Educational Psychologist, 16,* 65-82.

Levin, J.R., Bender, B.G., & Pressley, M. (1979) Pictures, imagery and children's recall of central versus peripheral sentence information. *Educational Communication and Technology, 27,* 89-95.

Levin, J.R., & Berry, J.K. (1980). Children's learning of all the news that's fit to picture. *Educational Communication and Technology Journal, 28,* 177-185.

Levin, J.R., & Divine-Hawkins, P. (1974). Visual imagery as a prose-learning process. *Journal of Reading Behavior, 6,* 23-30.

Levin, J.R., Divine-Hawkins, P., Kerst, S.M., & Guttmann, J. (1974). Individual differences in learning from pictures and words: The development and application of an instrument. *Journal of Educational Psychology, 66,* 296-303.

Levin, J.R., & Lesgold, A.M. (1978). On pictures in prose. *Educational Communication and Technology Journal, 26,* 233-243.

Levin, J.R., McCabe, R.E., & Bender, G.B. (1975). A note on imagery inducing motor activity in young children. *Child Development, 46,* 263-266.

Levin, J.R., McCormick, C.B., & Dretzke, B. (1981). A combined pictorial mnemonic strategy for ordered information. *Educational Communication and Technology Journal, 29,* 219-225.

Levin, J.R., McCormick, C.B., Miller, G.E. Berry, J.K., & Pressley, M. (1982). Mnemonic versus nonmnemonic vocabulary-learning strategies for children. *American Educational Research Journal, 19,* 121-136.

Levin, J.R., & Pressley, M. (1978). A test of the developmental imagery hypothesis in children's associative learning. *Journal of Educational Psychology, 70,* 691-694.

Levin, J.R., & Pressley, M. (1981). Improving children's prose comprehension: Selecting strategies that seem to succeed. In C.M. Santa & B.L. Hayes (Eds.), *Children's prose comprehension: Practice and research.* Newark, Delaware: International Reading Association.

Levin, J.R., & Rohwer, W.D. (1968). Verbal organization and the facilitation of serial learning. *Journal of Educational Psychology, 59,* 186-190.

Levin, J.R., Shriberg, L.K., Miller, G.E., McCormack, C.B., & Levin, B.B. (1980). The keyword method in the classroom: How to remember the states and their capitals. *The Elementary School Journal, 82,* 185-191.

Lewisohn, P., Danaher, B., & Kikel, S. (1977). Visual imagery as a mnemonic aid for brain-injured persons. *Journal of Consulting and Clinical Psychology, 45,* 717-723.

Litrownik, A.J. (1972). Observational learning in retarded and normal children as a function of delay between observation and opportunity to perform. *Journal of Experimental Child Psychology, 48,* 117-125.

Litrownik, A., Franzini, L., & Turner, G. (1976). Acquisition of concepts by TMR children as a function of type of modeling, role verbalization, and observer gender. *American Journal of Mental Deficiency, 80,* 620-628.

Lloyd, J. (1980). Academic instruction and cognitive behavior modification: The need for attack strategy training. *Exceptional Education Quarterly, 1,* 53-63.

Lorayne, H., & Lucas, J. (1974). *The memory book.* New York: Stein and Day.

Lovitt, T., & Curtis, K. (1968). Effects of manipulating antecedent event on mathematic response rate. *Journal of Applied Behavior Analysis, 1*, 329-333.

Lovaas, O.I., Schreibman, L., Koegel, R., & Rehm, R. (1971). Selective responding by autistic children to multiple sensory input. *Journal of Abnormal Psychology, 77*, 211-222.

Luria, A.R. (1968). *The mind of a mnemonist* (L. Solotaroff, Trans.). New York: Basic Books.

Macht, M., & Scheirer, C. (1975). The effects of imagery on accessibility and availability in a short-term memory paradigm. *Journal of Verbal Learning and Verbal Behavior, 14*, 523-533.

Mackworth, N.H., & Bruner, J.S. (1970). How adults and children search and recognize pictures. *Human Development, 13*, 149-177.

MacMillian, D.L. (1970). Facilitative effects of verbal mediation on paired-associate learning by EMR children. *American Journal of Mental Deficiency, 74*, 611-615.

Mahoney, M. (1977). Reflections on the cognitive learning trend in psychotherapy. *American Psychologist, 32*, 5-13.

Malamuth, Z. (1979). Self-management training for children with reading problems: Effects on reading performance and sustained attention. *Cognitive Therapy and Research, 3*, 279-289.

Mandler, J.M., & Johnson, N.S. (1977). Remembrance of things parsed: Story structure and recall. *Cognitive Psychology, 9*, 111-151.

Marks, C.B., Doctorow, M.J., & Wittrock, M.C. (1974). Word frequency and reading comprehension. *Journal of Educational Research, 67*, 259-262.

Marshall, N. (1976). *The structure of semantic memory for text.* Doctoral dissertation, Cornell University.

Marshall, N., & Glock, M. (1978-1979). Comprehension of connected discourse: A study into the relationship between the structure of text and information recalled. *Reading Research Quarterly, 14*, 10-56.

Martin, A.S. (1970). *The effect of the novelty-familiarity dimension on discrimination learning by mental retardates.* Unpublished doctoral dissertation. University of Connecticut.

Mastropieri, M., Scruggs, T., Levin, L., & Levin, J. (1984). Mnemonic strategies for handicapped and gifted learners. *Exceptional Children, 50*, 559.

Masur, F.E., McIntyre, C.W., & Flavell, J.H. (1973). Developmental changes in apportionment of study time among items in a multitrial free recall test. *Journal of Experimental Child Psychology, 15*, 237-247.

McCarty, D.L. (1980). Investigation of a visual imagery mnemonic device for acquiring face-name associations. *Journal of Experimental Psychology: Human Learning and Memory, 6*, 145-155.

McGivern, J. (1981). *An investigation of the interaction between children's vocabulary knowledge and variations of the keyword method.* Unpublished master's thesis, University of Wisconsin, Madison.

McKinney, J., & Haskins, R. (1980). Cognitive training and the development of problem-solving strategies. *Exceptional Education Quarterly, 1*, 41-51.

McKoon, G. (1977). Organization of information in text memory. *Journal of Verbal Learning and Verbal Behavior, 16*, 247-260.

Means, B.M., & Rohwer, W.D. (1974). *A developmental study of adding verbal analogues to pictured paired associates.* Unpublished manuscript, University of California-Berkeley.

Meichenbaum, D. (1977). *Cognitive-behavior modification: An integrative approach.* New York: Plenum.

Meichenbaum, D. (1979). Cognitive-behavior modification: The need for a fairer assessment. *Cognitive Therapy and Research, 3*, 127-132.

Meichenbaum, D. (1980). A cognitive-behavioral perspective on intelligence. *Intelligence, 4*, 271-283.

Meichenbaum, D., & Asarnow, J. (1979). Cognitive-behavioral modification and metacognitive development: Implications for the classroom. In P. Kendall & S. Hollon (Eds.), *Cognitive behavioral interventions.* New York: Academic Press.

Meichenbaum, D., & Burland, S. (1979). Cognitive-behavior modification with children. *School Psychology Digest, 8*, 426-433.

Meichenbaum, D., & Goodman, J. (1971). Training impulsive children to talk to themselves: A means of developing self-control. *Journal of Abnormal Psychology, 77*, 115-126.

Mercer, C.D., & Algozzine, B. (1977). Observational learning and the retarded: Teaching implications. *Education and Training of the Mentally Retarded, 12*, 345-353.

Meyer, B.J.F. (1975a). Identification of the structure of prose and its implications for the study of reading and memory. *Journal of Reading Behavior, 7*, 7-47.

Meyer, B.J.F. (1975b). *The organization of prose and its effect on memory.* Amsterdam: North Holland.

Meyer, B.J.F. (1977). The structure of prose: Effects on learning and memory and implication for educational practice. In R.C. Anderson, R. Spiro, & W.E. Montague (Eds.), *Schooling and the acquisition of knowledge.* Hillsdale, N.J.: Lawrence Erlbaum Associates.

Meyer, B.J., Brandt, D., & Bluth, G. (1980). Use of top-level structure in text: Key for reading comprehension of ninth-grade students. *Reading Research Quarterly, 16*, 72-103.

Meyer, B.J., & McConkie, G.W. (1973). What is recalled after hearing a passage? *Journal of Educational Psychology, 64*, 72-75.

Michael, D., & Maccoby, N. (1961). Factors influencing the effects of student participation on verbal learning from films: Motivating versus practice efforts, feedback, and overt versus covert responding. In A.A. Lumsdaine (Ed.), *Student response in programmed instruction.* Washington, D.C.: National Academy of Science-National Research Council.

Milgram, N.A. (1967). Verbal context versus visual compound in paired-associate learning by children. *Journal of Experimental Child Psychology, 5*, 597-603.

Milgram, N.A. (1968a). Retention of mediation set in paired-associate learning of normal children and retardates. *Journal of Experimental Child Psychology, 5*, 341-349.

Milgram, N.A. (1968b). The effects of MA and IQ on verbal mediation in paired associate learning. *Journal of Genetic Psychology, 113*, 129-243.

Milgram, N.A., & Riedel, W. (1969). Verbal context and visual compound in paired associate learning of mental retardates. *American Journal of Mental Deficiency, 73*, 755-761.

Miller, E.J. (1973). Cross-cultural research in the perception of pictorial materials. *Psychological Bulletin, 80*, 135-150.

Miller, G.A. (1956). The magical number seven, plus or minus two: Some limits on our capacity for processing information. *Psychological Review, 63*, 81-97.

Moely, B.E. (1968). *Children's retention of conceptually related items under varying presentation and recall conditions.* Unpublished doctoral dissertation, University of Minnesota.

Moely, B.E. (1977). Organizational factors in the development of memory. In R. Kail & J. Hagen (Eds.), *Perspectives on the development of memory and cognition.* Hillsdale, N.J.: Lawrence Erlbaum Associates.

Moely, B.E., & Jeffrey, W.E. (1974). The effects of organization training on children's free recall of category items. *Child Development, 45*, 135-143.

Moely, B.E., Olsen, F.A., Halwes, T., & Flavell, J. (1969). Production deficiency in young children's clustered recall. *Developmental Psychology, 1*, 26-34.

Moynahan, E.D. (1973). The development of knowledge concerning the effect of categorization upon free recall. *Child Development, 44*, 238-246.

Mulligan, M., Guess D., Holvoet, J., & Brown, F. (1980). The individualized curriculum sequencing model (1): Implications from research on massed, distributed, or spaced trial training. *JASH, 5*, 325-336.

Mulligan, M., Lacy, L., & Guess, D. (1982). Effects of massed, distributed, and spaced trial sequencing on severely handicapped students' performance. *JASH, 7*, 48-61.

Myatt, B., & Carter, J.M. (1979). Picture preference of children and young adults. *Educational Communication and Technology Journal, 27*, 45-53.

Myers, N., & Perlmutter, M. (1978). Memory in the years from two to five. In P. Ornstein (Ed.), *Memory development in children.* Hillsdale, N.J.: Lawrence Erlbaum Associates.

Nappe, G., & Wollen K. (1973). Effects of instructions to form common and bizarre mental images on retention. *Journal of Experimental Psychology, 100*, 6-8.

Nash, W., & Torrance, E. (1974). Creative reading and the questioning abilities of young children. *Journal of Creative Behavior, 8*, 15-19.

Neff, N.A., Iwata, B.A., & Page, T.J. (1980). The effects of interspersal training versus high density reinforcement on spelling acquisition and retention. *Journal of Applied Behavior Analysis, 13*, 153-158.

Negin, G.A. (1978). Mnemonics and demonic words. *Reading improvement, 15*, 180-182.

Neisser, U. (1982). Memory: What are the important questions? In U. Neisser (Ed.), *Memory observed: Remembering in natural contexts.* San Francisco: W.H. Freeman.

Nelson, K. (1969). The organization of free recall by young children. *Journal of Experimental Child Psychology, 8*, 284-295.

Nelson, K. (1971). Memory development in children: Evidence from nonverbal tasks. *Psychonomic Science, 25*, 346-348.

Nelson, K., Fivush, R., Hudson, J., & Lucariello, J. (1983). Scripts and development of memory. In M. Chi (Ed.), *Contributions to human development: Vol. 9. Trends in memory development research.* New York: Karger.

Nelson, K.E., & Kosslyn, S.M. (1976). Recognition of previously labeled or unlabeled pictures by 5-year-olds and adults. *Journal of Experimental Child Psychology, 21*, 40-45.

Nelson, W.J., & Birkimer, J. (1978). Role of self-instruction and self-reinforcement in the modification of impulsivity. *Journal of Consulting and Clinical Psychology, 46*, 183.

Newell, A. (1979). One final word. In D.T. Tuma & F. Reif (Eds.), *Problem solving and education: Issues in teaching and research.* Hillsdale, N.J.: Lawrence Erlbaum Associates.

Nezworski, T., Stein, N.L., & Trabasso, T. (1982). Story structure versus content in children's recall. *Journal of Verbal Learning and Verbal Behavior, 21*, 196-206.

Norman, D.A. (1976). *Memory and attention: An introduction to human information processing* (2nd ed.). New York: John Wiley and Sons.

Norman, D.A. (1982). *Learning and memory.* San Francisco: W.H. Freeman.

Nye, W.C., McManis, D.L., & Haugen, D.M. (1972). Training and transfer of categorization by retarded adults. *American Journal of Mental Deficiency, 77*, 199-207.

O'Connor, N., & Hermelin, B. (1961). Recognition of stages by normal and subnormal children. *British Journal of Psychology, 52*, 281-284.

Odom, R., Liebert, R., & Hill, J. (1968). The effects of modeling, cues, reward, and attentional set on the production of grammatical and ungrammatical syntactic construction. *Journal of Experimental Child Psychology, 6*, 131-140.

Ogden, C.K. (1943). *Basic for science.* London: Kegan Paul.

Ogden, C.K. (1968). *Basic English: International second language.* New York: Harcourt, Brace & World.

Ogden, C.K. (Ed.). (1970). *General basic English dictionary.* Totowa, N.J.: Rowman.

O'Leary, S., & O'Leary, K. (1976). Behavior modification in the school. In H.

Leitenberg (Ed.), *Handbook of behavior modification and behavior therapy.* Englewood Cliffs, N.J.: Prentice Hall.

O'Leary, S. (1980). A response to cognitive training. *Exceptional Education Quarterly, 1,* 89-94.

O'Shea, L., & Sindelar, P. (1983). The effects of segmenting written discourse on the reading comprehension of low- and high-performance readers. *Reading Research Quarterly, 18,* 458-465.

Paivio, A. (1968). Effects of imagery instructions and concreteness of memory pegs in a mnemonic system. *Proceedings of the 76th Annual Convention of the American Psychological Association,* 77-78.

Paivio, A. (1971). *Imagery and verbal processes.* New York: Holt, Rinehart and Winston.

Paivio, A. (1980). Imagery as a private audio visual aid. *Instructional Science, 9,* 295-309.

Paivio, A., & Desrochers, A. (1979). Effects of an imagery mnemonic on second language recall and comprehension. *Canadian Journal of Psychology, 33,* 17-28.

Paivio, A., Smythe, P., & Yuille, J. (1968). Imagery versus meaningfuless of nouns in paired-associate learning. *Canadian Journal of Psychology, 22,* 427-441.

Paivio, A., Yuille, J., & Madigan, S. (1968). Concreteness, imagery and meaningfulness values of 925 nouns. *Journal of Experimental Psychology, 76* (1, Pt.2), 1-25.

Paivio, A., Yuille, J.C., & Rogers, T.B. (1969). Noun imagery and meaningfulness in free and serial recall. *Journal of Experimental Psychology, 79,* 509-514.

Palkes, H., Stewart, M., & Freedman, J. (1972). Improvement in maze performance on hyperactive boys as a function of verbal training procedures. *Journal of Special Education, 5,* 237-342.

Palmatier, R.A. (1968). Acquisition and utility of three note-taking procedures (Doctoral dissertation, Syracuse University, 1968). *Dissertation Abstracts International, 37,* 219A. University Microfilms No. 69-08640.

Panyan, M., & Hall, R. (1978). Effects of serial versus concurrent task sequencing on acquisition, maintenance and generalization. *Journal of Applied Behavior Analysis, 11,* 67-74.

Paris, S., & Lindauer, B. (1976). The role of inference in children's comprehension and memory for sentences. *Cognitive Psychology, 8,* 217-227.

Paris, S., Newman, R., & McVey, K. (1981). *From tricks to strategies: Learning the functional significance of mnemonic actions.* Unpublished manuscript, University of Michigan.

Pearson, P.D. (1974). The effects of grammatical complexity on children's comprehension, recall, and conception of certain semantic relations. *Reading Research Quarterly, 10,* 155-192.

Pearson, P.D., & Johnson, D.D. (1978). *Teaching reading comprehension.* New York: Holt, Rinehart & Winston.

Pelton, L.H. (1969). Mediational construction vs. mediational perception in paired-associate learning. *Psychonomic Science, 17,* 199-200.

Peng, C.Y., & Levin, J.R. (1979). Pictures and children's story recall: Some questions of durability. *Educational Communication and Technology, 27,* 39-44.

Perlmutter, M., & Myers, N.A. (1976). Recognition memory in preschool children. *Developmental Psychology, 12,* 271-272.

Peters, D.L. (1972). Effects of notetaking and rate of presentation on short-term objective test performance. *Journal of Educational Psychology, 63,* 276-280.

Peterson, L., Wampler, R., Kirkpatrick, M., & Saltzman, D. (1964). Effect of spacing presentations on retention of a paired associate over short intervals. *Journal of Experimental Psychology, 67,* 286-295.

Petros, T., & Hoving, K. (1980). The effects of review on young children's memory for prose. *Journal of Experimental Child Psychology, 30,* 33-43.

Piaget, J. (1948). *The moral judgment of the child.* Glencoe, Ill.: Free Press.

Pressley, M. (1976). Mental imagery helps eight-year-olds remember what they read. *Journal of Educational Psychology, 68,* 355-359.

Pressley, M. (1977). Imagery and children's learning: Putting the picture in developmental perspective. *Review of Educational Research, 47,* 585-622.

Pressley, M. (1979). Increasing children's self-control through cognitive interventions. *Review of Educational Research, 49,* 319-370.

Pressley, M. (1982). Elaboration and memory development. *Child Development, 53,* 296-309.

Pressley, M., & Levin, J.R. (1978). Developmental constraints associated with children's use of the keyword method of foreign language vocabulary learning. *Journal of Experimental Child Psychology, 26,* 359-372.

Pressley, M., Levin, J.R., & Delaney, H.D. (1982). The mnemonic keyword method. *Review of Educational Research, 52,* 61-91.

Pressley, M., Levin, J.R., & McCormick, C.B. (1980). Young children's learning of foreign language vocabulary: A sentence variation of the keyword method. *Contemporary Educational Psychology, 5,* 22-29.

Pressley, M., Levin, J.R., & Miller, G.E. (1981). How does the keyword method affect vocabulary comprehension and usage? *Reading Research Quarterly, 16,* 213-226.

Pressley, M., Levin, J., & Miller, G. (1982). The keyword method compared to alternative vocabulary-learning strategies. *Contemporary Educational Psychology, 7,* 50-60.

Rankin, E.F., & Culhane, J. (1970). One picture worth 1000 words? *Reading Improvement, 7,* 37-40.

Reese, H.W. (1977). Imagery and associative memory. In R. Kail & J. Hagen (Eds.), *Perspectives on the development of memory and cognition.* Hillsdale, N.J.: Lawrence Erlbaum Associates.

Reynolds, B., & Adams, J. (1953). Effects of distribution and shift in distribution within a single training session. *Journal of Experimental Psychology, 46,* 137-145.

Rhode, G., Morgan, D., & Young, K. (1983). Generalization and maintenance of treatment gains of behaviorally handicapped students from resource rooms to regular classrooms using self-evaluation procedures. *Journal of Applied Behavior Analysis, 16,* 171-188.

Richards, I.A. (1943). *Basic English and its uses.* New York: Norton.

Richards, I.A., & Gibson, C. (1974). *Techniques in language control.* Rowley, Mass.: Newbury House.

Richardson, J. (1974). Imagery and free recall. *Journal of Verbal Learning and Verbal Behavior, 13,* 709-713.

Richardson, J. (1976). Imageability and concreteness. *Bulletin of the Psychonomic Society, 7,* 429-431.

Richardson, J. (1978a). Mental imagery and the distinction between primary and secondary memory. *Quarterly Journal of Experimental Psychology, 30,* 471-485.

Richardson, J. (1978b). Reported mediators and individual differences in mental imagery. *Memory and Cognition, 6,* 376-378.

Richardson, J. (1979). Mental imagery, human memory and the effects of closed head injury. *British Journal of Social and Clinical Psychology, 18,* 319-327.

Richardson, J.T. (1980). Mental Imagery and stimulus concreteness, *Journal of Mental Imagery, 4,* 87-97.

Richmond, M.G. (1976). The relationship of the uniqueness of prose passages to the effect of question placement and question relevance on the acquisition and retention of information. In W.D. Miller & G.H. McNinch (Eds.), *Reflections and investigations on reading.* 25th National Reading Conference Yearbook. Clemson, S.C.: National Reading Conference.

Rickards, J.P. (1979). Adjunct postquestions in text: A critical review of methods and processes. *Review of Educational Research, 49,* 181-196.

Rickards, J.P. (1980). Notetaking, underlining, inserted questions, and organizers in text: Research conclusions and educational implications. *Educational Technology, 20,* 5-11.

Rickards, J.P., & August, G.J. (1975). Generative underlining strategies in prose recall. *Journal of Educational Psychology, 67,* 860-865.

Rickards, J.P., & Denner, P.R. (1979). Depressive effects of underlining and adjunct questions on children's recall of text. *Instructional Science, 8,* 81-90.

Rickards, J.P., & Friedman, F. (1978). The encoding versus the external storage hypothesis in notetaking. *Contemporary Educational Psychology, 3,* 136-143.

Ridberg, E., Parke, R., & Heatherington, E. (1971). Modification of impulsive and reflective cognitive styles through observation of film mediated models. *Developmental Psychology, 5,* 369-377.

Rigney, J., & Lutz, K. (1976). Effects of graphic analogies of concepts in chemistry on learning and attitude. *Journal of Educational Psychology, 68,* 305-311.

Robinson, F.P. (1961). *Effective study* (rev. ed.). New York: Harper and Row.

Roediger, H.L. (1980). The effectiveness of four mnemonics in ordinary recall. *Journal of Experimental Psychology: Human Learning and Memory, 6,* 558-567.

Rohwer, W.D. (1966). Constraint, syntax, and meaning in paired-associate learning. *Journal of Verbal Learning and Verbal Behavior, 5,* 541-547.

Rohwer, W.D. (1970). Images and pictures in children's learning: Research results and educational implications. *Psychological Bulletin, 73,* 393-403.

Rohwer, W.D. (1973). Elaboration and learning in childhood and adolescence. In H.W. Reese (Ed.), *Advances in child development and behavior* (Vol. 8). New York: Academic Press.

Rohwer, W.D., Ammon, M.S., & Levin, J.R. (1971). *Learning efficiency and elaboration training among four- and five-year-old children* (Final Report, OEO Contract No. B99-4776).

Rohwer, W., & Bean, J. (1973). Sentence effects and noun-pair learning: A developmental interaction during adolescence. *Journal of Experimental Child Psychology, 15,* 521-533.

Rohwer, W., Kee, D., & Guy, K. (1975). Developmental changes in the effects of presentation media on noun-pair learning. *Journal of Experimental Child Psychology, 19,* 137-152.

Rohwer, W.D., Lynch, S., Levin, J.R., & Suzuki, N. (1967). Pictorial and verbal factors in the efficient learning of paired associates. *Journal of Educational Psychology, 58,* 278-284.

Rosenbaum, M., & Drabman, R. (1979). Self-control training in the classroom: A review and critique. *Journal of Applied Behavior Analysis, 12,* 467-485.

Rosenthal, J. (1979). Vicarious tactics to promote children's conceptual skills. *Journal of Research and Development in Education, 13,* 90-99.

Rosenthal, T., Alford, G., & Rasp, L. (1972). Concept attainment, generalization and retention through observation and verbal coding. *Journal of Experimental Child Psychology, 13,* 183-194.

Rosenthal, T., & White, G. (1972). Initial probability, rehearsal, and constraint in associative class selection. *Journal of Experimental Child Psychology, 13,* 261-274.

Rosenthal, T., & Zimmerman, B. (1972). Instructional specificity and outcome expectation in observationally-induced question formulation. *Journal of Educational Psychology, 63,* 500-504.

Ross, A.O. (1975). *Psychological aspects of learning disabilities and reading disorders.* New York: McGraw-Hill.

Ross, D.M. (1970). Effects on learning of psychological attachment to a film model. *American Journal of Mental Deficiency, 74,* 701-707.

Ross, D.M. (1974). *The ability of young EMR children to use multiple associates in sentences.* Unpublished manuscript, University of California, San Francisco.

Ross, D.M., & Ross, S.A. (1978). Facilitative effect of mnemonic strategies on multiple-associate learning in EMR children. *American Journal of Mental Deficiency, 82,* 460-466.

Ross, D.M., Ross, S.A., & Downing, M.L. (1973). Intentional training versus observational learning of mediational strategies in EMR children. *American Journal of Mental Deficiency, 78,* 292-299.

Ross, L., & Ross, S. (1981). The visual scanning and fixation behavior of the retarded. *International Review of Research in Mental Retardation, 10,* 1-30.

Rothkopf, E.Z. (1966). Learning from written materials: An exploration of the control of inspection behavior by test-like events. *American Educational Research Journal, 3,* 241-249.

Rothkopf, E.Z. (1972). Variable adjunct question schedules, interpersonal interaction and incidental learning from written material. *Journal of Educational Psychology, 63,* 87-92.

Rothkopf, E.Z., & Bisbicos, E.E. (1967). Selective facilitative effects of interspersed questions on learning language from written material. *Journal of Educational Psychology, 58,* 56-61.

Rothkopf, E.Z., & Bloom, R.D. (1970). Effects of interpersonal interaction on the instructional value of adjunct questions in learning from written material. *Journal of Educational Psychology, 61,* 417-422.

Rowls, M.D. (1976). The facilitative and interactive effects of adjunct questions on retention of eighth graders across three prose passages: Dissertation in prose learning. *Journal of Educational Psychology, 68,* 205-209.

Ruch, M.D., & Levin, J.R. (1977). Pictorial organization versus verbal repetition of children's prose: Evidence for processing differences. *AV Communication Review, 25,* 269-280.

Rumelhart, D. (1976). *Toward an interactive model of reading* (Technical report No. 56). San Diego, California: University of California, Center for Human Information Processing.

Ryan, E., Ledger, G., Short, E., & Weed, K. (1982). Promoting the use of active comprehension strategies by poor readers. *Topics in Learning and Learning Disabilities, 1,* 53-60.

Ryan, J. (1969). Grouping and short-term memory: Different means and patterns of grouping. *Quarterly Journal of Experimental Psychology, 21,* 137-147.

Salatas, H., & Flavell, J.H. (1976). Retrieval of recently learned information: Development of strategies and control skills. *Child Development, 47,* 941-948.

Samuels, S.J. (1970). Effects of pictures on learning to read, comprehension and attitudes. *Review of Educational Research, 40,* 397-407.

Samuels, S.J., Biesbrock, E., & Terry, P. (1974). The effect of pictures on children's attitudes toward presented stories. *Journal of Educational Research, 67,* 243-246.

Santogrossi, D., O'Leary, K., Romanczyk, R., & Kaufman, K. (1973). Self-evaluation by adolescents in a psychiatric hospital school token program. *Journal of Applied Behavior Analysis, 6*, 277-287.

Saski, J., Swicegood, P., & Carter, J. (1983). Notetaking formats for learning disabled adolescents. *Learning Disability Quarterly, 6*, 265-272.

Schroeder, G., & Baer, D. (1972). Effects of concurrent and serial training on generalized vocal imitation in retarded children. *Developmental Psychology, 6*, 293-301.

Schulman, A.I. (1971). Recognition memory for targets from a scanned word list. *British Journal of Psychology, 62*, 335-346.

Schworm, R., & Abelseth, J. (1978). Teaching the individual with severe learning problems: Strategies which point to success. *Education and Training of the Mentally Retarded, 13*, 146-153.

Scribner, S., & Cole, M. (1972). Effects of constrained recall training on children's performance in a verbal memory task. *Child Development, 43*, 845-857.

Seamon, J.G. (1980). *Memory and cognition: An introduction.* New York: Oxford University Press.

Senter, R.J., & Hoffman, R.R. (1976). Bizareness as a nonessential variable in mnemonic imagery: A confirmation. *Bulletin of the Psychonomic Society, 7*, 163-164.

Serpell, R. (1976). *Culture's influence on behavior.* London: Methuen.

Shallice, T., & Warrington, E.K. (1970). Independent functioning of verbal memory stores: A neuropsychological study. *Quarterly Journal of Experimental Psychology, 22*, 261-273.

Shaughnessy, J., Zimmerman, J., & Underwood, B. (1974). The spacing effect in the learning of word pairs and the components of word pairs. *Memory and Cognition, 2*, 742-748.

Shaw, H. (1965). *Spell it right.* New York: Barnes and Noble.

Shea, J.B., & Morgan, R.L. (1979). Contextual interference effects on the acquisition, retention and transfer of a motor skill. *Journal of Experimental Psychology: Human Learning and Memory, 5*, 179-187.

Shiffrin, R.M. (1975). Short-term store: The basis for a memory system. In F. Restle, R.M. Shiffrin, N.J. Castellan, H.R. Lindman, & D.B. Pisoni (Eds.), *Cognitive Theory* (Vol. 1). Hillsdale, N.J.: Lawrence Erlbaum Associates.

Short, E. (1981). *A self-instructional approach to remediating the use of schematic knowledge, causal attributions and task persistence of less skilled readers.* Unpublished doctoral dissertation, University of Notre Dame.

Sigel, I.E. (1978). The development of pictorial comprehension. In R.S. Randhawa & W.E. Coffman (Eds.), *Visual learning, thinking and communication.* New York: Academic Press.

Silbert, J., Carnine, D., & Stein, M. (1981). *Direct instruction mathematics.* Columbus, Ohio: Charles E. Merrill.

Singer, H. (1978). Active comprehension: From answering to asking questions. *Reading Teacher, 31*, 901-908.

Singer, R.N. (1978). Motor skills and learning strategies. In H.F. O'Neil (Ed.), *Learning strategies.* New York: Academic Press.

Smirnov, A.A., & Zinchenko, P.I. (1969). Problems in the psychology of memory. In M. Cole & I. Maltzman (Eds.), *A handbook of contemporary soviet psychology* (pp. 452-502). New York: Basic Books.

Smith, F. (1975). *Comprehension of learning: A conceptual framework for teachers.* New York: Holt, Rinehart and Winston.

Spache, G. (1953). A new readability formula for primary-grade reading materials. *Elementary School Journal, 53,* 410-413.

Spates, C., & Kanfer, F. (1977). Self-monitoring, self-evaluation and self-reinforcement in children's learning: A test of a multistage self-regulation model. *Behavior Therapy, 8,* 9-16.

Standing, L., Conezio, J., & Haber, R. (1970). Perception and memory for pictures: Single-trial learning of 2500 visual stimuli. *Psychonomic Science, 19,* 73-74.

Stauffer, R.G. (1975). *Directing the reading-thinking process.* New York: Harper and Row.

Stein, N., & Nezworski, T. (1978). The effects of organization and instructional set on story memory. (ERIC Document Reproduction Service No. 149 327).

Stein, N.L., & Glenn, C.G. (1977). *The role of structural variation in children's recall of simple stories.* Paper presented at the meeting of the Society for Research in Child Development, New Orleans.

Stein, N.L., & Glenn, C.G. (1978). An analysis of story comprehension in elementary school children. In R. Freedle (Ed.), *Discourse processing: Multidisciplinary perspectives.* Hillsdale, N.J.: Ablex.

Stein, N.L., & Glenn, C.G. (1979). An analysis of story comprehension in elementary school children. In R. Freedle (Ed.), *New directions in discourse processing* (Vol. 2). Hillsdale, N.J.: Ablex.

Stephens, W.A., & Ludy, I. (1975). Action-concept learning in retarded children using photographic slides, motion picture sequences and live demonstration. *American Journal of Mental Deficiency, 80,* 227-280.

Stokes, T., & Baer, D. (1977). An implicit technology of generalization. *Journal of Applied Behavior Analysis, 10,* 349-367.

Stokes, T., Baer, D., & Jackson, R. (1974). Programming the generalization of a greeting response in four retarded children. *Journal of Applied Behavior Analysis, 7,* 599-610.

Strichart, S. (1974). Effects of competence and nurturance on imitation of nonretarded peers by retarded adolescents. *American Journal of Mental Deficiency, 78,* 665-673.

Swanson, H.L. (1977). Response strategies and stimulus salience with learning disabled and mentally retarded children on a short-term memory task. *Journal of Learning Disabilities, 10,* 635-642.

Talkington, L., & Hall, S. (1975). Relative effects of response cost and reward on model on subsequent performance of EMRs. *The Journal of Developmental Disabilities, 1,* 23-27.

Taylor, A.M., Josberger, M., & Knowlton, J.Q. (1972). Mental elaboration and learning in EMR children. *American Journal of Mental Deficiency, 77,* 69-76.

Taylor, A.M., Josberger, M., & Prentice, J.L. (1970). *Imagery organization and children's recall.* Paper presented at the meeting of the American Educational Research Association, Minneapolis.

Taylor, B.M. (1980). Children's memory for expository text after reading. *Reading Research Quarterly, 15,* 399-411.

Thorndyke, P. (1977). Cognitive structures in comprehension and memory of narrative discourse. *Cognitive Psychology, 9,* 77-110.

Thorndyke, P.W., & Hayes-Roth, B. (1979). The use of schemata in the acquisition and transfer of knowledge. *Cognitive Psychology, 11,* 82-106.

Tierney, R.J., Bridge, C., & Cera, M.J. (1978-79). The discourse processing operations of children. *Reading Research Quarterly, 14,* 539-573.

Travers, R.M.W., & Alvarado, V. (1970). The design of pictures for children in elementary school. *AV Communication Review, 18,* 47-64.

Triplett, D.G. (1980). *A test of two prose learning strategies: Imagery and paraphrase.* Unpublished doctoral dissertation, University of Wisconsin, Madison.

Tulving, E. (1972). Episodic and semantic memory. In E. Tulving & W.A. Donaldson (Eds.), *Organization of memory.* New York: Academic Press.

Turnure, J.E., & Thurlow, M.L. (1973). Verbal elaboration and the promotion of transfer of training in educable mentally retarded children. *Journal of Experimental Child Psychology, 15,* 137-148.

Turnure, J.E., & Walsh, M.K. (1971). Extended verbal mediation in the learning and reversal of paired associates by EMR children. *American Journal of Mental Deficiency, 76,* 60-67.

Valentine, E.P., & Francks, O.R. (1979). To teach a social studies concept—chunk it! *Reading Horizons, 20,* 47-54.

Van Wagenen, R., & Travers, R. (1963). Learning under conditions of direct and vicarious reinforcement. *Journal of Educational Psychology, 54,* 356-362.

Varley, W.H., Levin, J.R., Severson, R.A., & Wolff, P. (1974). Training imagery production in young children through motor involvement. *Journal of Educational Psychology, 66,* 262-266.

Vurpillot, E. (1968). The development of scanning strategies and their relation to visual differentiation. *Journal of Experimental Child Psychology, 6,* 632-650.

Wallace, W.P. (1965). Review of the historical, empirical and theoretical status of the von Restorff Phenomenon. *Psychological Bulletin, 63,* 410-424.

Wanschura, P.B., & Borkowski, J.G. (1974). Development and transfer of mediational strategies by retarded children in paired-associate learning. *American Journal of Mental Deficiency, 78,* 631-639.

Wanschura, P., & Borkowski, J. (1975). Long-term transfer of a mediational strategy by moderately retarded children. *American Journal of Mental Deficiency, 80,* 323-333.

Ward, W.C., Legant, P. (1971). Naming and memory in nursery school children in the absence of rehearsal. *Developmental Psychology, 5,* 174-175.

Waters, H. (1982). Memory development in adolescence: Relationship between metamemory strategy use and performance. *Journal of Experimental Child Psychology, 33,* 183-195.

Watts, G.H. (1973). The arousal effect of adjunct questions on recall from prose materials. *Australian Journal of Psychology, 25,* 81-87.

Watts, G.H., & Anderson, R.C. (1971). Effects of three types of inserted questions on learning from prose. *Journal of Educational Psychology, 62,* 387-394.

Waugh, N.C., & Norman, D.A. (1965). Primary memory. *Psychological Review, 72,* 89-104.

Websters New Collegiate Dictionary. (1980). Springfield, Mass.: G. and C. Merriam.

Weener, P. (1974). Notetaking and student verbalization as instrumental learning activities. *Instrumental Science, 3,* 51-74.

Wehman, P., Abramson, M., & Norman, C. (1977). Transfer of training in behavior modification programs: An evaluative review. *The Journal of Special Education, 11,* 217-229.

Weiss, M. (1982). Developmental modeling: Enhancing children's motor skill acquisition. *Journal of Physical Education, Recreation and Dance, 53,* 49-50.

Wellman, H.M., Ritter, K., & Flavell, J.H. (1975). Deliberate memory behavior in the delayed reactions of very young children. *Developmental Psychology, 11,* 780-787.

Wellman, H.M., Rysberg, J., & Sattler, H. (1979). The development of accurate assessments of comprehension readiness: A study of cognitive monitoring in young readers. In press.

Westling, D.L., & Koorland, M.K. (1979). Some considerations and tactics for improving discrimination learning. *Teaching Exceptional Children, 11,* 97-100.

White, R., & Haring, N. (1980). *Exceptional teaching.* Columbus: Charles E. Merrill.

Wickelgren, W.A. (1981). Human learning and memory. *Annual Review of Psychology, 32,* 21-52.

Wilhelm, H., & Lovaas, O.I. (1976). Stimulus overselectivity: A common feature in autism and mental retardation. *American Journal of Mental Deficiency, 81,* 26-31.

Williams, K.G., & Goulet, L.R. (1975). The effects of cueing and constraint instructions on children's free recall performance. *Journal of Experimental Child Psychology, 19,* 464-475.

Williams, W., Coyne, P., DeSpain, C., Johnson, F., Scheverman, N., Stengert,

J., Swetlik, B., & York, B. (1978). Teaching math skills using longitudinal sequences. In M.E. Snell (Ed.), *Systematic instruction of the moderately and severely handicapped.* Columbus: Charles E. Merrill.

Williams, W., & York, R. (1978). Developing instructional programs for severely handicapped students. In E. Haring & D. Bricker (Eds.), *Teaching the severely handicapped* (Vol. 3). Seattle: American Association for the Education of the Severely/Profoundly Handicapped.

Wimmer, H., & Tornquist, K. (1980). The role of metamemory and metamemory activation in the development of mnemonic performance. *International Journal of Behavioral Development, 3,* 71-81.

Winschel, J.F., & Lawrence, E.A. (1975). Short-term memory: Curricular implications for the mentally retarded. *Journal of Special Education, 9,* 395-408.

Wittrock, M.C. (1974). Learning as a generative process. *Educational Psychologist, 11,* 87-95.

Wolfe, P., Levin, J., & Longobardi, E. (1974). Activity and children's learning. *Child Development, 45,* 221-223.

Wolfe, V.F., & Cuvo, A.J. (1978). Effects of within-stimulus and extra-stimulus prompting on letter discriminations by mentally retarded persons. *American Journal of Mental Deficiency, 83,* 297-303.

Wollen, K.A. (1969, November). *Variables that determine the effectiveness of picture mediators in paired-associate learning.* Paper presented at the meeting of Psychonomic Society, St. Louis.

Wollen, K.A., Weber, A., & Lowry, D. (1972). Bizareness versus interaction of mental images as determinants of learning. *Cognitive Psychology, 3,* 518-522.

Woodrow, H. (1927). The effect of type of training upon transference. *Journal of Educational Psychology, 18,* 159-172.

Yando, R., Sertz, V., & Zigler, E. (1978). *Imitation: A developmental perspective.* Hillsdale, N.J.: Lawrence Erlbaum Associates.

Yendovitskaya, T.V. (1971). Development of memory. In A.V. Zaporozhets & D.B. Elkonin, (Eds.), *The psychology of preschool children.* Cambridge, Mass.: MIT Press.

Yost, M., Avila, L., & Vexler, E.B. (1977). Effects on learning of postinstructional responses to questions of differing degrees of complexity. *Journal of Educational Psychology, 69,* 399-408.

Yuille, J.C., & Catchpole, M.J. (1973). Associative learning and imagery training in young children. *Journal of Experimental Child Psychology, 16,* 403-412.

Yussen, S.R. (1974). Determinants of visual attention and recall in observational learning by preschoolers and second graders. *Developmental Psychology, 10,* 93-100.

Yussen, S.R., Kunen, S., & Buss, R. (1975). The distinction between perceiving and memorizing in the presence of category cues. *Child Development, 46,* 763-768.

Zeaman, D., & House, B.J. (1963). An attention theory of retardate discrimination learning. In N.R. Ellis (Ed.), *Handbook of mental deficiency*. New York: McGraw-Hill.

Zimmerman, B.J., & Jaffe, A. (1977). Teaching through demonstration: The effects of structuring, imitation, and age. *Journal of Educational Psychology, 69*, 773-778.

Zimmerman, B., & Rosenthal, T.L. (1974). Observational learning of rule-governed behavior by children. *Psychological Bulletin, 81*, 29-42.

Zinober, J.W., Cermak, L.S., Cermak, S.A., & Dickerson, D.J. (1975). A developmental study of categorical organization in short-term memory. *Developmental Psychology, 11*, 398-399.

Index